Susie and Me Days beautifully recounts a story of love and pathos, one that reverberates in the deepest centers of human emotion as the reader vicariously lives this gripping saga of a journey through the ever-darkening forest of Alzheimer's disease, a journey relevant to the life of every American as the world faces the reality of the demographics of aging. Ms. Garbett has the knack of leading the reader to experience the feelings engendered by "reading between the lines", unlocking a far-too-often unrecognized personal identification with love and loss experienced by others. This combination of fact and humanity creates a superb text, one that will not leave the reader untouched.

Alva S. Baker, MD
Former Director
The Copper Ridge Institute

Susie and Me Days is an authentic, honest, moving portrayal of the journey the author took with her father as he lived with dementia. The book provides facts and practical information, along with heartfelt reactions and responses to what was happening with the family throughout the ordeal. It offers hope for continued connections and engagement with the person with dementia by using what remains, by going to where the person is, and by sharing time, attention, and love. *Susie and Me Days* is truly a great read, but it's also an impressive guide to others dealing with the illness.

Teepa Snow MS, ORT/L, FAOTA
Dementia Care Training Specialist

In *Susie and Me Days*, Susan Garbett has captured the joy and satisfaction of providing care to a loved one with dementia. Her book distills what I have heard from hundreds of caregivers in my thirty years as a geriatrician and gives a loving and accurate portrait of her father. She provides insight into the vagaries of caring for a person with dementia from the perspective of someone who has experienced the full range of human emotions 'in the trenches'. This book is an invaluable addition to the literature chronicling the progress of memory loss and there is no doubt that many caregivers will gain strength and comfort from the author's hard-won wisdom.

Nancy Jane C. Friedley, MD, CMD
Former Chief of Geriatrics
Good Samaritan Hospital/MedStar Health

Susan Garbett's new book, *Susie and Me Days*, is a loving, captivating account of her relationship with her father, and of their journey with his advancing Alzheimer's disease. Susan so clearly and concisely captures what so many families experience when dealing with a loved one's diagnosis – the questions, the losses and grief, the obstacles faced in navigating the medical community, the internal familial challenges, and finally, creating new special memories. Her book is written with such an extraordinary amount of passion and detail that the reader will feel as if they are living the moments personally. *Susie and Me Days* is a wonderful, inspirational tribute to the love between and a father and daughter, amidst the struggles of a distressing and overwhelming illness.

Marcie Koenig
Director of Copper Ridge

Susan Garbett captures the heart of dementia care in her poignant and loving chronicle of a family's struggle with the challenges of Alzheimer's disease. Being a witness to her dad's decline, and realizing the disease has the upper hand, Susan reinvents special moments in *Susie and Me Days* to create new memories for herself and re-infuse joy and happiness for her dad. Susan gives a snapshot of the broken medical community, a facility that restores her faith in a fragmented system, and the legacy she creates while joining her dad's journey.

Pam Polowski, Program Specialist,
Alzheimer's Association, Florida Gulf Coast Chapter

Susie and Me Days

Joy in the Shadow of Dementia

Each person's journey is different. Hope you enjoy reading about mine.

Best;
Susan L. Garbett

Susie and Me Days

Joy in the Shadow of Dementia

Susan L. Garbett

PARQUETRY PRESS · SARASOTA, FL

Published in the United States by Parquetry Press, an imprint of:

S.I.S. Publishing
P.O. Box 1360
Osprey, FL 34229-1360

This is a true story. Some names have been changed to respect individual privacy.

The views in this book are solely those of the author and were not intended to present medical, legal or financial advice. If such assistance or advice is required, a competent professional should be consulted.

Cover design by Janet B. Mishner
Printed in the United States of America
Interior design by Serbin Printing, Inc. · Sarasota, Florida

ISBN 978-0-9824611-6-7
Library of Congress Control Number: 2010911165

1. Health & Fitness/Disease/Alzheimer's & Dementia
2. Family & Relationships/Aging/Eldercare 3. Medical/Caregiving

10 9 8 7 6 5 4 3 2 1

First Edition

In memory of my father,
Leslie "Bim" Miller

CONTENTS

ACKNOWLEDGEMENTS

To the entire Copper Ridge staff for their dedication to enriching the quality of life of persons with Alzheimer's disease and other memory-impairing illnesses.

To the Copper Ridge Institute and the Johns Hopkins Neuropsychiatry and Memory Group for their commitment to improving dementia care through research and education.

To the Copper Ridge residents and their families, who touched my life and enriched it in so many ways.

To Elizabeth Fanto, my writing workshop instructor at the Renaissance Institute at the College of Notre Dame of Maryland, for editing the first draft of this book; and to my RI writing class for their encouragement and constructive criticism.

To Janet B. Mishner, an incredible artist, for designing the book cover.

To Kevin Kremer, my editor, for his insight, support, and assistance with publishing this book.

To Robin Clark, for her patience, guidance, and vision with printing this book.

To Chuck, my husband, for his love, for believing in me, and for being my rock as we shared this journey.

To my sons, Craig and Scott, who light up my life each day.

TO THE READER

Dementia, with Alzheimer's disease being the most common form, is an illness that is ravaging the senior population and places an enormous burden on our present and future generations. It exacts a devastating toll on everyone involved. While many people are aware of the negative physical, emotional, and psychological ramifications that dementia brings, there is another dimension to this disease—a positive one.

This disease can bring unexpected gifts if we as caregivers have the capacity and the knowledge to enter their world and accept the person for who they are, no matter what their mental state is at any given moment. If caregivers are equipped to let go of any negative thinking about what once was, or what could have been, in order to embrace what is happening right now, they have the opportunity to create rewarding experiences for and with their loved ones.

The possibilities are endless and the rewards can be incredible. It was those special shared moments with my dad, which I share with the reader. In capturing the essence of my father before the dementia and after the diagnosis, this book presents the paradox between sadness and joy, pain and tenderness, heartbreak and hope. It is about the approaches I personally used to preserve my father's dignity and enhance his quality of life.

My goal in writing *Susie and Me Days; Joy in the Shadow of Dementia* is to empower caregivers and families with practical ideas and solutions that will help them journey through the uncomfortable realities and consequences of this disease. Woven within this story are suggested communication strategies, behavior and stress management techniques, and interventions that worked well for me. This book is not a clinical document, but rather a guide for caregivers and families as they try to cope from day-to-day.

PROLOGUE

Among my most cherished childhood memories are my Saturday walks with Dad. I always looked forward to Saturday and my own special ritual with my father. For me, nothing seemed as special as our leisurely strolls down Liberty Heights Avenue to the playground at Howard Park School #218. We always took the same route. We passed the Gywnn and Ambassador Theaters, the Ben Franklin 5 & 10, Read's Drugstore, and Toots Barger's Duckpin Bowling Alley. We passed Betty Lou's Dance Studio where I took ballet and the Union Trust Bank where I had my Hopalong Cassidy savings account. How I loved pausing to look in the shop windows and watching people as they got on and off the streetcars. I can almost hear the clang of the bell, see the sparks on the wires above, and feel the "payment" (Baltimore slang for pavement) vibrating under my feet as the streetcars passed by.

We would walk hand in hand, my tiny, pink-nailed fingers wrapped around his long, hairy ones. My little legs tried to keep up with his quick, long energetic strides. My neck strained to look up at his handsome face and his thick, black pompadour as he told me tales from his childhood on North Oliver Street and Belle Avenue, and of his growing up with my grandparents, aunts and uncles. He told of boyhood antics and adolescent dreams, of working at Hutzler's Department Store, of hard times during the Depression, and tragic ones from World War II. He was the master storyteller with a seemingly limitless memory for anecdotes, stories, and jokes. He talked to me. He made me laugh. He listened to me. He made me feel special. He swung me higher than my mother would have ever approved. What wonderful times they were! I hated for the day to end. Yet, I knew we would end our outing by stopping by Silber's Bakery for a free chocolate-top cookie. Life was good. Life was sweet.

* * *

Fifty years have passed. We don't leave from the same house anymore. I pick him up now. He no longer drives. Our special day has also changed; it's no longer a Saturday. I call several times to remind him of our next "Susie and Me Day." I have to talk much louder. A great deal has changed, but we still enjoy our walks, my dad and I.

Warm weather takes us to parks, to the Inner Harbor, to Fells Point, and to Canton. The cold weather limits our excursions to shopping malls. Dad loves to visit the play area at the malls, content to just sit and watch the children, delighting in their endless energy and uninhibited behavior. I often take his hand to give added support. I wrap my hand around his swollen, arthritic-bent fingers, between his permanently crippled, L-shaped thumb. Our pace is slower; he walks slightly bent over. He seems more fragile. We stop more often to rest. I look down to talk to him now. His snow white hair is brittle and thinning. His sweet, gentle face is aged and wrinkled. He still tells me stories about his childhood, about my childhood, and the times with his fraternity and war buddies. He recalls and retraces past moments with astonishing clarity. I listen to his stories over and over, as if they are new. His repetition challenges my patience. He gets a little agitated when his short-term memory fails and the reality of aging surfaces. Sometimes I fill in the blanks. He still listens intently, wanting to know about me and his grandsons. He has a joke for everything. He still makes me laugh, and I'm still Daddy's little girl. Our walks are still wonderful, just very different. Now it's Dad who wants the cookie.

PART ONE

The New Reality

ONE

Several more years passed. I gave Dad the date of our next "Susie and Me Day" on large day-glow yellow paper. He put it on top of his huge calendar on his untidy desk as a reminder. I knew he would still call, often several times a day, to find out when our next day together was scheduled. That was all right, but sometimes I cringed when I saw his number come up on our caller ID.

I took the elevator up to Dad and Shirley's condo. Dad no longer met me downstairs. It was better that way, because some days his balance wasn't good, and his sense of time was somewhat diminished. One time Shirley, my stepmom, received a call from the night doorman telling her that Dad was downstairs in the lobby. It was 4:00 A.M. He was waiting for me to pick him up for "Susie and Me Day." He didn't want to be late.

Before we left, he asked me to pay some bills for him.

I kept his checkbooks with me because he continuously misplaced them and got things confused. He was ready for me that day, with his red folder we made together marked "Bills to Pay." I wrote the checks for him and he signed them hesitatingly. His signature was often shaky, unevenly formed, and spaced. We went over each check several times. He continuously asked about the check that was just completed. He asked me repeatedly if we had included his account number on the check. I tried to reassure him. I heard my voice getting louder. I took a deep breath and softened my tone. I looked away for a moment and noticed he had taken the check out of the envelope. I took another deep breath. An hour and a half had passed, since I came over. We had written three checks and they were ready for mailing. Finally, we could begin our day.

At least that was what I was hoping. I needed to wait while Dad finished his bathroom routine. It had become an obsession with him, and he got agitated if he was not successful. I tried to wait patiently.

He was finally ready, and now we needed to have a discussion on why it was necessary to wear a jacket or a heavier coat. I was concerned because he seemed frail and his skin was thin. I knew I had to choose my battles and I didn't want to argue with him. If I made no headway, I would just let it go.

While we were in the elevator, we decided where we wanted to go for lunch. We walked to my car and I unlocked the door. Dad stood there and I reminded him to get in the car. At the restaurant, he glanced at the menu and chose what he wanted to eat. The waitress had to ask him his choice again because he didn't hear what she'd asked. He refused to wear his hearing aids, but paid insurance on them to sit in his dresser drawer. We no longer argued about that. The waitress waited patiently while he told her he wanted a sandwich and a Coke. He was embarrassed when she asked what kind. He looked at me and I told him to think about it.

"A grilled cheese, please," he replied and jokingly said, "I'm getting to be a piece of work!"

The waitress smiled reassuringly and said, "A grilled cheese it will be."

While waiting for our meal, I tried to bring up things that would challenge his memory in open-ended sentences, so he could easily get involved. Dad liked to talk about the weather. He rarely mentioned sports anymore unless I initiated the conversation. He used to tell me all about the Orioles and what place they were in the standings. He didn't follow the Ravens because he thought it was just terrible that Art Modell brought the team here to Baltimore from Cleveland. That just reminded Dad of the heartache everyone in Baltimore felt when Colts owner, Bob Irsay, moved our team to Indianapolis in the middle of the night. But just mention legendary quarterback Johnny Unitas or his beloved Baltimore Colts, and we could talk about them all day. It was the same with stories about his childhood, working at Hutzler's Department Store, World War II, and his Delta Kappa Pi high school fraternity boys—all links to his past. I had heard them a thousand times, but I tried to listen intently as if it was the first. I noticed that familiar names now often eluded him, and he looked to me to fill in the gaps. I often tried to bring him back to the present with stories about the news, his grandsons, or me. We did not talk politics, but that had never been a good subject between us. Previously, Dad would have told several jokes during our meal. He was always great with dialects and delivery. Now it was the same couple of jokes over and over. I bit my tongue, trying not to give the punch line away, and I laughed with feigned fervor after he delivered it.

After lunch, we went for a short walk down the block. I nonchalantly put my arm around his, hoping he wouldn't notice. He looked up at me and smiled. No words were spoken. We had a silent understanding, and he was grateful for the help. His gait was a bit unsteady, and that day he was barely picking up his feet as we walked. Our pace was slower now. I had to shorten my stride, take small steps to stay even with him so I wouldn't get ahead. I saw that he was getting very tired and realized this was as much as he could handle for that day. He seemed relieved when I suggested we head for home.

Kissing him good–bye, I silently wondered how many more "Susie and Me Days" we would have with each other.

TWO

The light on the kitchen phone was flashing red. I dialed the number to retrieve my messages. The first one was a reminder about my dentist appointment on Monday. The second was to call my cousin Carole back. The third began with incoherent meanderings. I strained to hear and understand. I realized it was my dad. He was upset and crying.

In a desperate voice he pleaded, "Susie, please call me as soon as you get in! I think something has happened to Shirley! I can't find her anywhere! I've looked all over! She's not here!"

Sobbing, he cried, "I'm really worried! I don't know what to do! Please, please call me!"

The next message was Dad again, rambling, panic-stricken, repeating the same scenario that he'd left before.

I took a deep breath, and dialed his number. The line was busy. I waited a few minutes and tried again—another busy signal. Dad probably hadn't hung up the phone properly.

This happened often lately. Despite my efforts to help him by putting red and blue circles on both the handset and the base so he could place the phone back on its cradle by matching the colors, he still had difficulty. He usually didn't hear the loud, annoying, raucous signal that the telephone company puts on the line to indicate the phone was left off the hook.

I waited ten minutes and called back. To my relief, it rang. Eight rings. Fifteen rings. Still no answer. Now I had two missing people to look for!

I grabbed my keys and then decided to call the desk at their condo building. Identifying myself, I asked Lynn if anyone had seen my father or Shirley. She replied, "Your father was in the lobby earlier, very distraught, looking for Shirley. He wanted to go outside to look for her, but the doorman and I convinced him to go back to his condo in case she calls."

"Thanks so much, Lynn, for your help and understanding," I said. "Please thank Lenny for me also."

Praying that Dad would find his way back to their unit, I tried his number once again. Dad usually remembered he lived on the seventh floor and the fact that when the elevator opened, the hall carpeting should be blue. I was so glad that this was an older building and the hallway carpeting on each floor was a different color. Seven rings.

I was getting a bit nervous. Finally, Dad answered.

"Dad, it's Susie."

"I'm very worried. I can't find Shirley," he said.

"Daddy," (I found myself using this endearment more often. It seemed to calm him.) "I'm sure she's OK. Did you just get up from a nap?"

Dad was often confused when he first woke up, not knowing if it was day or night, morning or evening.

I asked, "Did you check to see if Shirley left you a note on the kitchen table like she always does?"

Before I could say anything else, I realized he must have been heading to the kitchen to check. He didn't answer as I kept shouting his name. I hoped he remembered to return to the phone. On many occasions, when Dad went to get something or look for something, he left me hanging and forgot to come back to the phone. We had thought about getting him a portable phone but decided against it since he was constantly misplacing or hiding his things, especially the television remote. This would have been just another thing Shirley would need to search for, and she had enough to cope with already.

When Dad returned, he told me, "There is a big note on the kitchen table." I asked him to read it to me. I was grateful he could still read and comprehend what he read. "Darling—I didn't want to wake you. I went to the grocery store, the bank, and to get gas. I might do a few other errands. I will be back around 4:00 P.M. Love, Your Shirley."

I knew my stepmom always allowed an extra hour on her note, just in case she was running late. She knew he worried about so many things. I told Dad, "It's only three o'clock," and I reassured him she was all right and would be home soon.

I heard him sobbing. "I don't know what to do. I just don't know what to do!"

"Daddy, tell me about the time when you met Johnny Unitas at the airport while you were waiting for me to come home from Europe." (Sometimes when I changed the subject it worked, and other times it didn't.)

"It was so great, Susie," he told me. "Johnny U was waiting for his daughter to come back. I can't remember from where. We just got to talking, just two fathers shooting the breeze. He's such a plain guy. We... Wait! I hear something!"

I heard him drop the phone. In a few seconds I heard, "Hi darling, I'm so glad you're home. I thought something terrible happened to you."

"I'm fine, honey," I heard Shirley say. "Can you help me with my packages?"

The next thing I knew there was a dead phone! Fifteen minutes passed. I called Shirley back and shared everything that had happened with her. She thanked me. We both knew this was nothing new, just a different day and another repeat performance. Dad had called my son, husband, and nephew before, asking them to go look for Shirley at the mall. He had even called the police. I made a mental note to call some agencies to see if I could find someone to stay with Dad for a few hours, a couple days a week. This would give everyone some peace of mind.

September 22

Dear Dr. Holt:

Our family has seen a decline in my father
Leslie Miller's mental capacity since he saw
you last. He was not receptive to his internist's
suggestion about having an evaluation at
Levindale geriatric facility, and was suspicious
about his internist's motives during his yearly
check-up. He was adamant about not going.

We are trying to get him evaluated by a
neurologist to get a more definitive diagnosis. It
is in this area that we are asking for your help.
Since my father has followed through on all
your recommendations in the past years, we are
hoping you could suggest going to a neurologist
on the pretext of checking out his balance
and/or helping with his memory. He has an
appointment with you on September 30th.

Dad has fallen a few times, and admits to
being unsteady on awakening. He seems to be
listing to the left much more lately. I hope we
are not asking you to do anything unethical, just
confidential, but you are the last link to getting
him evaluated by a neurologist. I feel Dad is
depressed at times.

We both know that lately Dad is not very open
or receptive to suggestions. If he accepts your
suggestion, I hope you could send a cover letter
to the neurologist you recommend, explaining

his condition and pretext for the appointment
before he gets there. I will do the same.

Please let me know your feelings and thoughts
about this request either by phone or by e-mail.
Looking forward to hearing from you. Many
thanks for your cooperation and understanding.

Sincerely,

Susan

THREE

Dad always looked forward to our "Susie and Me Days." He rarely cancelled unless the weather was bad or he wasn't feeling well. He seemed to push himself more to get ready, whereas for other outings he seemed to become more overwhelmed.

There were days when I honestly had to admit I wasn't always up for our day. Sometimes I had many things to do that week, and sometimes I was tired and didn't feel like gearing myself up and coping with the effects of Dad's aging. I knew how important our day was to Dad, and I was aware of how important it was for Shirley's health. She needed a break once in awhile from her 24/7 caregiving. I really loved being with Dad, but lately it took much longer to get from point A to point B, more patience, and more self-control on my part. Did I feel guilty about thinking like this? Of course, it was part of being a Jewish mother. Yet, I came to terms with those thoughts and realized that it was unrealistic to expect myself to be all things to all people all of the time. Some days I even said a silent prayer in the car while on the way over to pick Dad up, asking God to give me the patience and stamina to get through the next few hours with him. I never regretted our time together, since Dad was usually more animated, more alert, and more eager to do things on "Susie and Me Days." Most times, it was Dad who lifted *my* spirits.

Naturally, Shirley was seeing more of a decline in Dad since she was with him more. Every day was a challenge for her, trying to anticipate his reactions to what had been routine daily tasks that had become severe struggles. Dad often went back to bed after breakfast, an escape from the reality he couldn't handle. His bed was a secure place, his personal space, where no thinking was required.

Shirley was careful how she approached him and how she chose her words. She tried not to sound like a nag or his "mother" when she reminded him of things or made suggestions, particularly when it came to his safety. Oftentimes Dad resented her telling him what to do and felt he was being treated like a child. He made his feelings very clear, and many times conveyed them in a nasty tone.

At other times, Dad looked to Shirley for direction and help. He was aware that his abilities were diminishing. He told Shirley more than once, "something is happening to me, but I don't know what it is." She tried her best to reassure him, to appease him, to be his loving spouse, and not take his outbursts personally. She was taking things one day at a time, treasuring the good days and hoping there would be more of them. She, too, was aware that this was not the same man she'd married over thirty years ago.

Shirley's e-mails to me repeatedly reflected her frustrations. Those e-mails provided a safe, private place for her to vent. Dad frequently hovered over her like a child does when he wanted his independence, but he also wanted to keep his parent nearby and in sight. She wasn't able to talk as freely on the phone anymore, so being able to e-mail to stay in touch with family and friends was her salvation. Dad resented her being on the computer. *Was the computer just a reminder of something else he wasn't able to do, or did he not like the time Shirley was spending away from him? I thought it was the latter.*

I was very proud when Shirley acquired her computer skills in her late seventies, after my brother, Dave, convinced her that she would love it if she would just try it. Oftentimes I noticed that she wrote her e-mails to me in the middle of the night, when she knew Dad would be asleep. This meant she wasn't getting the proper rest she needed. It was difficult enough to cope with things when you were sleep deprived, but it was much harder when your spouse was draining you more and more each day. Many times her e-mails drained *me*, and some days I dreaded opening them. I didn't want to read "your father said this, your father did that." I understood her frustration because I knew dealing with Dad's decline wasn't easy, but at times I wished she realized

Dad frequently was reacting to her approach, responses, reactions, and personality. I could acknowledge her feelings and circumstances, sympathize with her, and give her some suggestions. I could try to talk to Dad for her, but I was not a professional. I couldn't provide the answers.

I confronted Shirley about the situation with Dad many times. Some days she was in denial, not wanting to admit Dad's decline was progressing. At other times she was very clear about what was happening, having gone through it with her mother and aunt. *Maybe her memories of their Alzheimer's disease were too painful. The possibility of facing the disease again with her husband was too much for her to bear. At times, I thought being in denial was her only way of coping.*

Shirley had discussed Dad's problems with their internist, Dr. Rudman. He prescribed Aricept for Dad, but Dad developed terrible stomach pains and discontinued it on his own by flushing the pills down the toilet after only a few days. Dr. Rudman listened and returned Shirley's calls but was of little help with any concrete solutions. *I felt that many doctors who work with the elderly are well intentioned, but are not as knowledgeable as they should be about the resources available in their geographic area to guide both the patient and their family, when acute memory decline is evident. It's not that they are not caring. Many are so focused on micro-managing their office; they don't spend the time needed to satisfy all your concerns. The family and/or the caregiver are actually the experts in this situation, since they are living with the person 24/7. They know what*

they see and they want answers. They know that things are
not right.

We constantly sought ways to help Dad become more
involved with the larger world beyond his home, but he
continued to withdraw within himself. Sometimes I took
Dad to "News and Shmooze" and "Lunch and Learn" at
our synagogue. Rabbi Adler facilitated both events and
led the small group discussions. Dad seemed to enjoy
them and often contributed, but it became more and
more difficult to get him to attend with any regularity.
As hard as we tried, we were never successful in getting
him to try the Senior Center. "That's for old people," he
would say.

Dave was taking him out for dinner more after work
or for breakfast on Sundays. Although he admitted Dad
was slowing down, I didn't feel he was facing the reality
of Dad's decline. He would call me and tell me, "I had
Dad out tonight and we had a great time. I didn't think
he was so bad."

Dad's four grandsons were all working, but they
still tried to visit more often and include him in their
activities. They even organized a *Boys' Day* which was
something their grandfather had done with them before,
when they were younger. How they loved Boys' Day,
when all four of them spent the entire day with their
Zaide (grandfather) doing all sorts of fun things together.
I was so proud of them. I cried when my youngest son
Scott called to tell me they were working on making this
happen.

Shirley continued to try to make things as normal

as possible for Dad. She knew keeping his routine was important. Dad was sleeping much more during the day. This had a profound effect on the way they lived. Everything had changed. Before, they went out to eat, took walks together, occasionally went to the movies, went for long rides in the car, and took vacations. Dad liked to go with Shirley when she ran errands; I believed it was more out of fear of being alone than any great desire to go shopping. The errands took much longer, required much more patience, and Shirley forfeited her *break* when Dad went with her.

I thought Shirley needed some relief from the constant strain of caring for Dad. On a number of occasions, I told her it might be time to get someone to stay with Dad for a few hours a couple days a week. She knew that with Dad's personality, this would be difficult, and continually told me she would let me know when she was ready. *Did Shirley feel people would think she had failed as a wife, or was it more a statement that she was not ready to relinquish her role as primary caregiver?*

Shirley was from that generation of women where the responsibilities of homemaking and child rearing were not divided equally between spouses—where the wife, in most cases, constantly waited on her husband. I tried to reassure her that Dave and I knew she was doing the best she possibly could, and no one could expect more from her than what she was already doing. She repeated to me again, "When I am ready."

I gave Shirley the telephone number for Jewish Family Services. I hoped she would call to begin some type of counseling or support group. I knew how physically and emotionally demanding caring for Dad was—and the strain she was under. I told her, "While you spend your days reassuring and nurturing Dad, who is reassuring and nurturing *you*?"

She called me after her first appointment and thanked me for pushing her to make the call. She told me, "I already feel like a new person."

January 19

Dear Dr. Aaron,

My father, Leslie Miller, has an appointment with you on January 26th. He is 84, and is willing to see you in the hopes that you will be able to help him with his memory loss. He is not aware of other things that we have seen over the last few years. Attached is a list of behaviors that we have noticed. Some behaviors have always been there, but have been magnified with age. Hopefully this list will be helpful with your evaluation.

Because of his unpredictable behavior of late, Dr. Rudman put him on the medication, Depakote. My father thinks he's taking it for memory loss, not as an anti-depressant. He doesn't feel he needs an anti-depressant. Although he was not taking it as prescribed because he often forgets, we have observed some positive effects in the last month. We feel it seems to be a step in the right direction for him, because he seems calmer and appears to be less worried about everyday happenings. His wife has said that although Dad has had his moments, he's been more "on" than "off" lately. She can't figure out why he goes off without warning. She tries to disregard his behavior until it passes.

About two weeks ago, Dad stopped taking Depakote on his own. He told me he recently read the printout from the pharmacy and it mentioned possible hair loss, and "I can't afford to lose anymore hair." He is adamant about not taking it.

My father's nature is to worry. Because of this, I fear and am convinced that any negative diagnosis that he is made aware of, could trigger a deeper depression and cause him to give up completely. I trust that you will keep this correspondence confidential.

I am looking forward to meeting you Monday. Thank you.

Sincerely,

Susan Garbett

FOUR

We waited four months to get an appointment with Dr. Aaron, the neurologist who was recommended. Three days before Dad's appointment, Dr. Aaron's secretary called to reschedule because he had to be out of town. After waiting five months for this late afternoon appointment, I understood why Dad wanted to leave after sitting more than an hour and a half waiting for Dr. Aaron.

I remembered Dad saying, "I'm supposed to be the one with the memory problem, but this guy forgot what time it is." The entire waiting room broke out in laughter. My husband, Chuck, took Dad for a walk in the hallway to ease the monotony from waiting so long.

When we finally did see the doctor, there were no introductions. Dr. Aaron sat down behind his desk and proceeded to read the packet of information I had faxed him that his office had requested. He ignored both of us. Dad kept glancing over at me looking perturbed. After ten minutes, Dr. Aaron asked Dad why he was there. Dad told him that he could remember things from years ago but couldn't remember what he had for breakfast. He was hoping to get some help with his memory.

Dr. Aaron then directed most of the other questions to me. I could see Dad's annoyance, so I nicely reminded the doctor to speak directly to my father. The doctor ignored my request and continued to talk only to me, as if Dad wasn't even there. Dad's facial expression showed his agitation. I felt Dad was justified when he banged his hand on the doctor's desk and told him that he wasn't deaf or dumb. Furthermore, Dad told the doctor that he would appreciate it if he asked *him* the questions. After all, he was the patient. I was proud of Dad. He said, "Most doctors treat old people this same way, and one day you will be on the other side of the desk, and I'm sure you won't like it one bit either."

Dr. Aaron finally took notice and things went much better. He talked with Dad for awhile and then examined him. While Dad was getting dressed, Dr. Aaron spoke to me. He felt Dad's long-term memory was relatively good, but his short-term was very poor. This was no huge revelation, since our family had been aware of his decline. Dr. Aaron suspected this was probably early Alzheimer's, but said he wouldn't make a definitive diagnosis until he could review the results of Dad's MRI. I had prepared myself for this diagnosis, and asked Dr. Aaron what to expect from this disease. He could not predict how severe the decline would be or give any timetable for its progression. "It's different in every person, but one thing we do know is that it only gets worse, never better."

Dr. Aaron spoke to Dad about having an MRI, and about a new medication approved that year that had shown some success in improving memory. He told Dad that he wanted him to start Namenda and gave him a starter-pack. "I want you to begin taking Namenda a little bit at a time for a week, and then increase the dosage as directed on the package," said Dr. Aaron. "The dosage can be a little confusing in the beginning, so it's good to have someone check it each time you take a pill. Do you have someone that will be able to help you with that, Mr. Miller?"

Dad answered, "My wife takes very good care of me, so she can help."

Dr. Aaron went over the medication schedule with both of us. He reminded us that to be effective, you must take Namenda correctly.

Dad seemed pleased to be getting free pills and something to help him remember better. I was pleased that Dr. Aaron was astute enough to withhold the medication description booklet from the pack. He gave it to me when Dad wasn't looking. I stuck the booklet in the notepad I brought with me.

Neither of us liked being deceptive, but we also understood that if Dad knew Namenda was for the treatment of Alzheimer's disease, it may cause him to become upset. This was something we wanted to avoid. Dad had been distressed ever since his best friend and high school fraternity brother was diagnosed with Alzheimer's disease. He knew his friend didn't recognize his family anymore, and this disturbed Dad greatly. Dr. Aaron told us that the Depakote Dad's internist prescribed for him was an appropriate medication and that it could work in conjunction with the Namenda. This was yet another ploy, but we would do anything to get Dad to comply.

Dad told Dr. Aaron, "Under no circumstances am I going to take Depakote. I read the printout from the pharmacy, and it says this medication may cause hair loss."

You wouldn't think someone eighty-four years old would worry about such things, but Dad was resolute about not taking that particular medication. After referring to his huge pharmaceutical reference book, Dr. Aaron had a very clever retort for my father. "Mr. Miller, studies have shown that Depakote may cause hair loss, but only in young females, of which you are neither."

I had to look the other way to control my laughter. Dad would not budge on this one, so Dr. Aaron recommended that he try ten milligrams of Lexapro to treat his depression for a month. To my surprise, Dad agreed.

Dad fell asleep in the car as soon as we left the parking lot. He didn't even stir when I opened the car door after stopping at the drugstore to have his prescription filled. I was grateful Chuck was with me so I wouldn't have to leave Dad alone in the car.

As soon as the pharmacist handed me the prescription, I removed the medication printout and asked the clerk to staple the bag again for me. I put the printout in my pocketbook and prayed Dad would be too tired to ask about it.

At home, we added Lexapro to his medication bag. Dad had his own system for taking his meds, and refused to sort his daily pills into one of the large labeled pill holders we bought for him. He read somewhere that you should not mix medications together, and for some reason he never forgot that. He had an insulated lunch bag marked *morning* and one marked *evening*. As he took each pill, he turned the plastic bottle over to remind him that he had taken that particular medication. When all the bottles were upside down, Dad knew he had taken all his pills for the day. He would then turn all of them right side up in preparation for the next day. He repeated the same routine each evening. It was the "Miller method" and it usually worked well for Dad, unless he napped too often and lost track of day or night.

No matter how tactfully or lovingly Shirley was when she reminded him about taking his medications, Dad often became annoyed with her. "I'm not a child, and you're not my mother!" he would say.

Before Chuck and I left Dad's condo, I made a revised medication list for him. I taped it to the cabinet where he kept his medication bags.

When we got in our car, I was delighted when Chuck suggested we go out for dinner. He asked me, "What do you feel like eating?" I answered, "Surprise me." I was too exhausted to make any more decisions that day. The next thing I knew, I heard Chuck calling my name. Now it was me who had fallen asleep.

Ever since I could remember, Dad's best friend and high school fraternity brother was part of my life. He was a quiet, gentle man, always smiling, and a friend to just about everyone. I was so incensed when Alzheimer's disease robbed him and his family of the man he once was that I expressed my anger in the following poem:

Memories

Memories—
like illustrations in a book,
chapter after chapter,
full page photographs
of vivid images
that complement the autobiographical
text.

Memories—
like illustrations in a book,
g r a d u a l l y begin to fade—
once sharp photographs
becoming muted,
dis tort ed,
hazy gray images
often frag mented,
non-sequential
words, names,
faces, places
lifted off the page
until
systematically
the page is—blank.
Alzheimer's.

May 8

Re: Leslie Miller

Dear Dr. Aaron:

   This past Thursday my Dad, Leslie Miller, became so agitated and verbally abusive to his wife, repeatedly berating her about the same few things, that she wasn't able to deal with his behavior. She was unable to figure out what triggered these latest outbursts.

   My brother and I talked with Dad Friday and convinced him that he needs to take his medication to help retain the memory that he presently has. As you know, if my father knew he was taking an antidepressant, he would stop taking it. He is adamant about not taking Lexapro because it makes him constipated and very uncomfortable. He stopped taking it about a week ago. We think we have convinced him to go back on the Depakote previously prescribed by Dr. Rudman. He seemed calmer, less agitated while taking it. We went back and forth with him about the hair loss side effect he is so concerned about and reiterated what you said about it only affecting young females. He started Depakote again on Friday. I made a calendar for him on how to take the medication.

   I wanted to make you aware of this change in his medication and hope that it meets with your approval. All of us are aware that this cooperation may be temporary due to his short-term memory loss, but we feel calming him is our first priority. His wife will be contacting Jewish Family Eldercare Services to find out what our options may be in the future.

My questions to you are:
1. Does this change in medication meet with your approval?
2. Can he take Depakote and Namenda at the same time?

Please contact me with your thoughts at your earliest convenience.
Thank you very much for your help and understanding.

Sincerely,

Susan Garbett

FIVE

I had just stepped out of the shower, when Chuck told me that Shirley called. She said my father wasn't feeling well, so they wouldn't be going with us to the baby naming in Pennsylvania. I hadn't even heard the phone ring.

Here we go again, another cancellation. Was Dad truly sick or was he using illness as an excuse not to go because he was overwhelmed by the thought of going out of town for the day? I really thought he was excited about going with us, especially since this was such a special celebration for my cousins who had adopted a child. I knew Shirley must be very disappointed. She was really looking forward to going, being with family, and having a change of scenery.

I called her back, hoping Dad wouldn't answer the phone. Of course, he picked up right away, as did Shirley.

"Hi Dad, I heard you weren't feeling well this morning. What's bothering you?"

He answered, "My stomach is upset and I've been in the bathroom a lot."

"We're not leaving for the baby naming for a couple of hours. Do you think you should try to lie down for an hour and see if you feel better and this passes?" I asked.

"No, I've already tried that, and I still don't feel good," he replied.

"I'll call you later, to see how you feel," I told him.

I knew Shirley was still on the line and listening to our conversation. When I called to talk to Dad, Shirley and I had an understanding and a signal if I didn't want her to hang up. Before I began talking, I waited for the click of the phone, signaling Dad had hung up. (This plan didn't always work, since he had difficulty placing the receiver back on the base.)

"Do you think he's really sick?" I asked.

Shirley answered, "It's hard to tell these days."

I heard the frustration in her voice when she told me she would be staying home. "I know how disappointed you are, but don't give up just yet. I want you to get ready, but don't put on your outfit. I want to see what I can do to get someone to stay with him today. No promises, but I'm going to try. Call me back in half an hour."

Think fast, Susan. We don't have a whole lot of time before we have leave to be there by one o'clock.

Chuck offered to stay with Dad so Shirley and I could go. I told him that I would call Dave, even though I knew I'd probably wake him up.

I could tell when Dave answered that he was still asleep. After I explained the situation and how important this was for Shirley, he told me that he could come over and probably stay with Dad until three or four o'clock. He already had another commitment later that day. I told him to be at their home by ten, and I would see if Dad's grandsons could cover the rest of the time we were gone.

Luckily, both Craig and Scott, my sons, said they could change their plans and would go over later in the afternoon.

This is another example of something your children do that makes you so proud. I know how blessed I am. I must have done something right while raising them.

Dad was surprised to see Chuck and me when we came into his bedroom. I told Dad how sorry I was that he wasn't able to go along with us and about the arrangements I had made with Dave, Craig, and Scott. I handed him the schedule. He wasn't too happy when he realized that Shirley was still going, especially since he didn't think a baby naming was important enough for her to leave him alone.

I assured him again that he was not going to be alone, and it probably would be fun spending some time with his son and grandsons. He seemed satisfied when I said, "They are all looking forward to being with you."

Dad was a bit distant to Shirley when she said good-bye. She told him she would see him later.

Any hesitation or guilt we had about leaving Dad

behind faded when we saw my cousins' joy in holding their baby daughter in front of family and friends. What a difference Gail had made in their lives! It seemed that all the memories of those difficult years of trying to conceive had disappeared, replaced by happiness, love, and fulfillment. Everyone was so elated and excited for both of them. By the time their Rabbi spoke and the new parents talked about the wonderful people Gail was named after, there wasn't a dry eye in the congregation. It was truly a double blessing to be there and to share in their happiness.

The celebration continued at my cousin's beautiful home, where we all gathered for a wonderful luncheon in their backyard. Even the weather cooperated, as it was a warm, picture-perfect June afternoon.

When the Miller family got together, it was never dull or quiet. There was always lots of schmoozing, laughter, and catching up to do. It had been that way for as long as I could remember, but I thought we appreciated it even more as we grew older— lots older!

Not everyone lived in Baltimore anymore, so Chuck and I tried to make the rounds to talk to everybody. We joined the circle of chairs with Shirley and my aunts and uncles.

When one of my uncles asked how my Dad was doing, I decided to seize the moment with Dad's sister and brother and their spouses, and to let them know what really had been going on with Dad. I had been struggling with telling them for awhile because I felt, to some extent, it would be an invasion of Dad's privacy.

This might not be the best time to bring it up, but who knew when I would have the opportunity again to chat with all of them face to face.

They listened intently. I didn't think anyone was really that surprised, since they knew Dad had relinquished his position as leader of the Miller family Passover Seder (an annual religious service and traditional meal with special Passover food) to someone else. Dad had been conducting our family Seder for more than fifty years, and recently had been trying to pass his role to his brother, who really didn't want it. Dad was so relieved and pleased when my cousin Jill offered to take over. *Did he know his memory was failing him much sooner than we did? Did he have a real fear that he might make a mistake and embarrass himself? Or was he afraid he couldn't properly fulfill the religious obligation of leading our annual Seder service?*

Shirley remained silent while I tried to explain things. I gave my aunts and uncles examples of some of the things we had noticed, letting them know that this was more than just natural aging and forgetfulness. I wanted them to be aware of what Shirley had been dealing with, in hopes they would be able to give her more support. They asked questions. They wanted to know what the doctors had said, if Dad was on any special medication, and what the next step was. No one realized that Dad's memory was declining at the pace that it was, or the impact his memory loss was having on both him and Shirley.

I was happy when other family members joined our circle, and we started talking about other things. I didn't want to dwell on the subject and spoil that special day, but I was happy things were now out in the open.

On the way home, Shirley repeatedly thanked us for bringing her. She was relaxed and we could tell how much she enjoyed the day. She became less and less talkative the closer we got to Baltimore. I was sure she was silently thinking about what things were going to be like when she got home.

I had called Dad earlier to check on him. All was well. He seemed happy telling me what he was doing with Craig and Scott, and what he had done with Dave earlier. Chuck and I didn't press Shirley to talk. She was relieved when we told her we would be going up to see Dad for awhile when we got back, and she wouldn't be alone.

Dad was in good humor, eating pizza with his grandsons and one of their girlfriends. It seemed like he'd made a miraculous recovery and all was forgiven for the moment. We talked about the baby naming and told him that everyone asked about him. As we were leaving, we told Shirley to call if she needed us.

Several more weeks passed. Dad suddenly seemed a little better; less agitated, more alert, more cooperative, and not as forgetful. Nothing had changed medically. His medications were the same. We didn't question it or try to analyze why this sudden change had occurred. All of us were just enjoying it for what it was, knowing this transformation could be short-lived.

No one was more delighted with this change than Shirley. It was a welcomed reprieve, even though things were still far from perfect. Dad was happier and so was Shirley. Their days were calmer and they were both getting out a little more.

Things had improved to the point that Shirley thought that getting away for a few days would be good for both of them. She had made plans to stay at the same hotels in Wildwood and Cape May, New Jersey, where they had always vacationed every summer and celebrated their anniversary. Shirley thought that familiarity was the key for the success of the trip. Dad was all for it, which was really a welcomed surprise.

Shirley tried to make things easier for Dad by keeping tasks simple, helping him pack, finding his toiletries, and getting things in order. Dad told me how excited he was that they were going away.

I really thought that this might be too much for Shirley to handle alone, but she was optimistic about making the trip. Maybe it was just a pipedream for her, a way of clinging to the life and the special times they once shared. I could honestly admit that I was also looking forward to their trip, since having both of them away would give me a much-needed breather.

Little did I know that the night before their trip, Shirley was forced to have the locks changed in their condo because Dad was paranoid about someone breaking in and stealing everything. (They did have a break-in not long after they first moved to their new condo, but not much was taken.) It seemed that Dad became more suspicious when he was overwhelmed or couldn't find some things. It was just easier for him to blame someone else (his neighbor came in and stole his two umbrellas), than admit he could be at fault. Shirley didn't want a confrontation and tried to calmly reason with him, but he was adamant. She finally called a locksmith just to appease him so they both could get some rest.

Shirley was encouraged when they reached the motel, because Dad recognized Kate, the owner. "He was all smiles when she greeted him," Shirley told me later on the phone. Dad's enthusiasm didn't last long once he was in their room. He became a bit disoriented and frustrated when he was unable to find his things. He repeatedly asked Shirley where his things were. He became agitated when they weren't where he thought he had put them.

Shirley and Dad enjoyed their days. They went out to eat, took strolls on the beach, and people watched on the boardwalk. It was the nights, though, that really confused and upset Dad. He was worried that someone was going to break in and hurt Shirley, so he put a chair in front of the door and slept there standing guard.

Shirley said, "After awhile I didn't have the strength or the patience to convince him otherwise, so I just let him sleep there and prayed he wouldn't wander if I dozed off." She had alerted Kate, who already recognized that Dad had declined a lot since she had seen him the year before. Kate was such a comfort for Shirley during this trying trip. *Was Dad's illness progressing or was it his fear that he would be left alone and unable to cope if something happened to Shirley? Whatever the reason or rationale, the fear was very real for him at that moment.*

Shirley told me, "By the morning, your father had

forgotten all about the incident, and our day went relatively smoothly." The same scenario took place each remaining night and again when they moved from Wildwood to Cape May. By then Shirley was exhausted. She recognized that she probably should shorten their trip and return to Baltimore. On the other hand, she knew there probably wouldn't be another opportunity to use the bed and breakfast gift certificate that her children, Bob and Jan, had given them. Shirley ended our conversation by telling me, "It was the trip from hell!"

How things had changed in just a few months. We invited Dad to spend a week with us earlier in May so Shirley could visit her sister-in-law in Pennsylvania before she moved to Colorado. Chuck and I felt that maybe we could help Dad and, at the same time, give Shirley a much-needed respite. At first Dad didn't like the idea that Shirley was going away without him, but Chuck convinced him that the ladies wanted to do "girly" things and he would probably be bored stiff if he went with her. The challenge was to get him to agree to stay with us, since he thought he could handle things at home by himself. I persuaded Dad it would be fun having him over, and we could have a "Susie and Me" day every day he stayed with us. He liked that idea.

We visited the Fire Museum in Timonium, where we watched a film about the 1904 fire that nearly destroyed Baltimore. We picnicked at Fort McHenry National Park and toured the Public Works Building downtown. We reminisced and we laughed. Dad had so much to say about all the places we went. We took walks together and went to the playground across from where we lived so Dad could watch the children playing. Every night we went across the street to the mall for ice cream. Chuck helped by engaging Dad in conversations about a variety of topics he thought would interest Dad. Dad adored Chuck.

Dad seemed like his old self, except for his constant repetition and frequent word loss. Of course, he had been the center of attention for six days, and that was when I realized how hard it would be to keep up this pace and engagement 24/7. What a challenge this must be for Shirley day in and day out. No errands, no social contacts, no time for herself. I was there for Dad's every need that week, but I also had Chuck there for support. Shirley was alone, and she must become exhausted at times. No one should expect a caregiver to give that much attention to a loved one every single hour of every single day.

September 13

Dear Dr. Aaron:

My Dad, Leslie Miller, has an appointment with you on September 20 and I wanted to give you an update. My father refused to take Depakote again because he read there is a possible side effect of hair loss, so Dr. Rudman put him on Zyprexa. Dad stopped the Lexapro that you prescribed because he said that it made him constipated.

When speaking to you to make an appointment for a follow-up, you thought that Zyprexa was not an appropriate medication for older adults. It made my father extremely fatigued; where he was really only awake at meals. At my "diplomatic suggestion," Dr. Rudman agreed to stop the Zyprexa to see if it helped with the fatigue. It has made a difference, and so has taking Atenolol at bedtime rather than in the morning. My father had a cardiolite stress test about a month ago which was fine for his age.

My father has had a terrible week. He cancelled his Rosh Hashanah synagogue honor ahead of time. I feel he is afraid that someone will ask him to do something in synagogue and he will be embarrassed because he can't remember. He always went to synagogue on the Sabbath and holidays. He gave up blessing the congregation on holidays because he was afraid of "messing up." His normal practice of praying daily is now hit or miss. He did not attend Rosh Hashanah services either day, but did join the family for lunch both days, although he appeared bewildered at times.

Dad has verbally lashed out more at his wife lately. He told her, "He doesn't know what is happening to him and he doesn't know what prayers to say or what to do." He cries occasionally and is upset about his situation. He has said, "It would be better to just go and not have to deal with all this." He often says, "No one tells me anything."

I believe Dad will deny he is depressed, although he has admitted to his family that not remembering things makes him sad at times. He is content to go back to bed after breakfast and shows very little initiative. He says, "Lying in bed makes my arthritic shoulder feel better." Routine daily tasks seem to overwhelm him.

Dad continues to take Namenda. At times, we feel his short-term memory is a little better, because sometimes he can remember a series of words or numbers. At other times, he doesn't know if it is day or night, or that he just had lunch an hour ago. We are aware of his short-term memory loss, repetition, and confusion with time and date. Lately, we are seeing what we would consider long-term memory loss of things that ordinarily would be second nature to him. He still relates his "down-pat" childhood and war stories triggered after he hears a word or event he knows, but is having difficulty with sequencing and remembering names.

I am helping him with his checkbook. He forgets to enter things and forgets whether he paid a bill or not. He is still capable of adding a small column of figures, paying the correct amount at a restaurant, and making out a check with much help; although it is very difficult for him to stay focused, write legibly, or enter the correct information on the appropriate line.

In closing, we have seen some deterioration since we last saw you in February.

May the New Year bring you and your family the blessings of peace, joy, and good health. Thank you.

Sincerely,

Susan Garbett

SIX

Dad's MRI (magnetic resonance imaging of the brain without contrast) report concluded:

1. Age-related microvascular ischemic changes are seen within the periventricular and subcortical white matter of the subcerebral hemispheres.
2. No evidence of intracranial hemorrhage or mass effect.
3. Flair images are degraded due to patient motion. The patient refused additional scanning.

I called Dr. Aaron concerning the results of the MRI, but he had an emergency medical crisis himself, and his secretary didn't know when he would return. Dad's internist didn't want to comment on the test results from another physician, especially since the scan was incomplete.

Dad was not thrilled about going to see Dr. Aaron for his

six month follow-up appointment. I was able to convince him to go by telling him how important it was to have his medications periodically reviewed by his doctor. In talking with Dad, I was silently wondering if he remembered his first visit with Dr. Aaron. That visit didn't start very well because the doctor talked only to me, leaving Dad out of the conversation. *It was ironic that I was taking him to a neurologist for help with his memory, but I was hoping he didn't remember certain things.*

Dr. Aaron extended his hand to Dad when we entered his office.

"Good to see you again, Les," he said.

Dad shook hands with Dr. Aaron and said, "Good to see you too, Doctor." I was delighted with Dr. Aaron's approach and Dad's smile also showed his pleasure. He questioned Dad about how he was taking his medications, if they were causing any problems for him, and whether he had noticed any memory improvement since beginning the Namenda.

Dad responded saying, "My long-term memory is good. I can remember things that happened a long time ago, but I can't remember things that happened yesterday."

Listening to Dad talk about his difficulties with his memory made me believe that he had limited insight into his cognitive decline. He knew his memory wasn't the best, but never verbalized any association with any type of dementia or Alzheimer's disease. Maybe he was in denial. Our family thought it would be counterproductive to use those terms in front of Dad, and his doctors agreed.

Dad wasn't sure if the Namenda was helping him or not. None of us had seen much improvement, but maybe it was too soon to tell. He told Dr. Aaron that he had two bags for his medicines, one for morning and one for night, and explained his own method for taking his pills. Dad was thrilled when Dr Aaron applauded his "system" for taking his meds. Dad didn't tell the doctor that he needed constant reminders about taking his meds, since he slept a lot and frequently became confused about the time of day.

Dr. Aaron asked Dad, "Les, how are things at home?" *I knew he was asking this because he had read my recent faxes.*

Dad stiffened. His expression changed, showing his agitation. He became angry and defensive. "That's really none of your business, Doctor!" Dad retorted. "What does that have to do with my memory?"

Dad's reaction startled both Dr. Aaron and me. Before Dr. Aaron could say anything else, Dad asked him, "How are things at your house, Doctor?" I had to look away, so I wouldn't start laughing.

Dr. Aaron replied, smiling, "Very well, thank you." He did not press the issue any further.

After Dad's examination, Dr. Aaron told me that Dad was pleasant and cooperative. Any agitation towards Dr. Aaron's earlier questioning seemed forgotten. Like before, I asked Dr. Aaron to send me a copy of his report when it was ready. I had a notebook at home for all of Dad's doctor reports, tests, and lab work. Dad returned to Dr. Aaron's office before I had a chance to discuss his MRI in detail. *I had the feeling that Dr. Aaron was being cautious about concluding that Dad definitely had Alzheimer's disease, since its symptoms can mimic other diseases, making it difficult to diagnose with absolute certainty. Instead, I believed Dr. Aaron felt that in Dad's case revealing a diagnosis of Alzheimer's would only further upset him. I felt he chose to treat only those symptoms and behaviors that he specifically saw in Dad at that time. For other patients, it may be preferable to hear the actual diagnosis rather than not knowing what's causing the problem, allowing people to plan for the future. I assume a physician has to make that call for each individual based on how familiar he is with the patient and the family.*

Dr. Aaron suggested adding another medication, Seroquel, under the guise that, along with the Namenda, it would help Dad with his memory. I had no idea what Seroquel treated, but Dr. Aaron was aware of Dad's history of excessive worrying, and he was more than willing to be a bit deceptive in order to get Dad to comply. He told Dad that he was to take 25 milligrams of Seroquel at bedtime. He wanted to see how Dad tolerated this new medication, before giving him a higher dosage.

Dad handed me his new prescription when we left Dr. Aaron's office. He told me he was tired, and I suggested I take him home first, before I had his prescription filled. He agreed and said, "There's no rush to get it filled tonight. It can wait until tomorrow. You can go home and make dinner for Chuck. I don't think my memory is going to improve in just one day."

I stopped to have his prescription filled before I went home. I was eager to read the printout on Seroquel to learn about the medication and its side effects. I took time to read it at the counter. It stated that Seroquel was "used in the treatment of manic episodes associated with bipolar disorder and schizophrenia."

That was just great! I knew if Dad read that, he would never take that medication. I hated to admit it, but sometimes I thought it would be easier and less upsetting for everyone if Dad couldn't understand everything he read, especially during times when he twisted things a bit and became upset.

I asked to speak to the pharmacist. He had seen me in the store with Dad before. I tried to give him a synopsis of Dad's history and to make him aware of how upset Dad could get after reviewing a printout. The pharmacist was very sympathetic and willing to honor my request. He gave me two blank prescription printout sheets that just had the store's pharmacy logo and information at the top. *I don't know how I got up the nerve to even ask him for the sheets, but I figured I had nothing to lose.*

While driving home, I made an urgent call to my brother. I told him about my day with Dad and our dilemma concerning the Seroquel. Being in the photo finishing business and adept at using Photoshop, Dave told me he'd be able to scan in the printout and make the necessary changes to adapt the printout for Dad's needs. He also told me to bring it to the store early the next morning with the appropriate changes.

Dave and one of his employees spent about four hours, in between customers, trying to change the wording and some of the side effects on the Seroquel printout to make it look as professional as the original. Dave told me that he needed to go through several layers in order to make the changes. I took his word for it, since his technological explanation was beyond my comprehension. I hated that we were doing this, but neither of us could think of another solution.

The revised printout read, "Seroquel is used in the treatment of mild to moderate memory loss." Under side effects, we eliminated those we thought would cause Dad anxiety and left in those we thought were standard. That section now read, "Use caution when driving, operating machinery, or performing other hazardous activities. Seroquel may cause dizziness or drowsiness. If you experience dizziness or drowsiness, avoid these activities. Dizziness may be more likely to occur when you rise from a sitting or lying position. Rise slowly to prevent dizziness and a possible fall. Avoid alcohol during treatment with Seroquel. Alcohol may increase drowsiness and dizziness caused by Seroquel." We left in the part that said, "Do not use Seroquel during pregnancy."

Dad thanked me for bringing him his new medication. He opened up the bag and read the label. He immediately took the new bottle and added it to his "night" medicine bag. Shirley added Seroquel to his medicine list on the cabinet door. I slipped her the original printout and told her to read it and hide it somewhere. I knew she needed to be aware of the actual side effects, so she could monitor and observe Dad.

Shirley asked me to stay for lunch and I took her up on it since I was starving. While Shirley made tuna salad, Dad helped her by getting out the placemats, napkins, and silverware. Then he proudly set the table.

I showed him the new printout on the table. He laid it by his placemat, never even glancing at it. While cleaning up after lunch, I discretely pushed the printout in front of him. He picked it up and asked, "What is this?" Shirley told him, and he said, "I will read it later." I couldn't believe it. Exasperated, I left their condo to go home. I didn't have the heart to call my brother and tell him that Dad never even looked at the new printout.

It was hard for me to see Dad declining more and more each time I was with him. Sometimes it was subtle and at other times, it was so obvious. For example, if he forgot the name of an object, he would cleverly conceal it by describing how to use the object or where you might find it, and continue with his conversation. At other times, he repeated the same exact conversation or story within minutes of just telling it, without being aware that he had just said the same thing.

He was well aware that his memory was decreasing. He still had wonderful verbal skills, although his ability to recall a specific word or name often eluded him. His thinking capacity wasn't what it once was but neither was mine. Mentally I knew that this was more than the "normal" aging process, but emotionally it was very difficult to accept the fact that the Dad I once knew was slowly becoming more childlike and egocentric. Unlike a child, however, who is learning and most likely to grow out of *this* stage, I knew that Dad's losses were permanent. He would not grow out of this.

In a very real way, our roles were reversing, but only in the sense that I needed to be more involved with his care and the monitoring of his needs. He would always be my dad, my parent, and I would always be his daughter.

I found the following prayer from *Talking to God* by Naomi Levy, written for a child who is caring for an aging parent. It really spoke to what I was feeling. I substituted *father* for *mother* from the original prayer.

It's so painful, God, to watch my father begin to falter. I have always counted on him, and now he needs to count on me. I love my father; I don't like the way our roles have reversed. I don't want to see him in his weakness. I know this reversal is humiliating for him at times. He doesn't want to feel helpless or dependent. But he needs me now, to love him even more. Help me, God, to rise to this critical occasion. Show me how to care for my father with respect, tenderness, and love. Fill me with compassion and patience. Shield me from anger and resentment. Calm my fears, give me strength, God. Help me to seek out relief and support when the burden is great. Give him strength, God. Bless him with dignity, grace, and health. Amen.

I kept this prayer on my night table, and I read it often.

SEVEN

With a good deal of persuasion, Shirley joined the Renaissance Institute at the College of Notre Dame of Maryland, a program for seniors over fifty years of age, where I had been taking non-credit classes. Originally both she and Dad were on a waiting list to be accepted, but when an opening finally became available, Dad didn't want to join. He was aware of his short-term memory decline and I believe he didn't want to put himself in a situation that he knew he couldn't handle.

Shirley was hesitant about enrolling. She was worried about leaving Dad alone, even for a few hours. I told her, "If you do not take advantage of this opportunity now, you may never get a chance to join since your name will go to the bottom of their waiting list. We're all concerned about Dad, but it's important not to neglect yourself while caring for him. This may be a test to see if he can handle things alone, or do we need to have someone with him when you're gone. You will never know unless you try."

To Dad's dismay, Shirley started classes in September. He soon became used to the idea that on Thursday's Shirley went to school for a few hours. His lunch was in the refrigerator, and she would call him during the day to check in and reassure him that she would be home soon. The receptionist in the lobby had her cell phone number just in case anyone saw Dad leaving the building.

Shirley blossomed at Renaissance. She had a new outlet. She started writing wonderful poetry and clever Haiku in class and at home. She met interesting people her own age. She talked with another woman who was going through a similar situation with her husband. Thursdays became her relief valve, but she was never totally relaxed for fear of something happening with Dad.

Shirley's other outlet was Jessica, an eldercare specialist at Jewish Family Services. She had been seeing Jessica since April. I believe Jessica helped Shirley feel better about herself and made it easier for her to understand and cope with Dad's decline. Jessica was reassuring, and it was comforting for Shirley to know that Jessica was available if she needed her.

I was also seeing a different social worker at Jewish Family Services once a month. It was great to be able to vent, express my fears and concerns, and get advice on the best ways to approach and deal with Dad, as well as Shirley and Dave. Each of us interpreted Dad's situation from our own perspective, so we didn't always agree or see things in the same light. I was grateful that I had Debbie to lean on and guide me through this difficult process.

It was now October and we were meeting with Jessica as a family to become familiar with community resources that could aid us with Dad's care. Dave had to work and couldn't make the meeting. *I had really hoped that he would be there. It would have made things a little easier on me.*

Shirley seemed very relaxed. Jessica gave each of us time to share the problems we were seeing with Dad. I told her Dad seemed paradoxical, fluctuating between confusion and paranoia, between irrational and rational behavior. We talked about what we already knew about Dad, about what we had observed, about what his doctors were telling us, and what medications he was taking.

After listening to both of us, Jessica enlightened us about our new reality. She told us, "Your husband and your dad may not be able to control his behavior, and his paranoia only magnifies the problem." Jessica categorized paranoia as a bit of the truth with a twist. She thought things would probably continue to be very unpredictable. Furthermore, she felt it was important to know where Dad was in regards to his memory loss. She thought it would be wise for us to investigate and consider some intermediate options and she was more than willing to help us with this.

Jessica recommended that we consider having Dad evaluated for his memory impairment at the Outpatient Assessment Clinic at Copper Ridge, an assisted-living facility whose sole specialty was dementia and Alzheimer's care. She told us that Copper Ridge was in partnership with the Johns Hopkins Neuropsychiatry and Memory Group. "Having an accurate diagnosis is critical in helping people who are experiencing memory loss," she said. "It would also help me better guide your family."

I told Jessica that none of us was very pleased with the neurologist Dad had been seeing. I had made an appointment for Dad to see Dr. Friedley, Chief of Gerontology at Good Samaritan Hospital, where three of my own doctors practiced. I'd picked up a flyer about senior care services at Good Samaritan during one of my appointments. What I read impressed me so much that I called as soon as I got home. I told Jessica about my lengthy conversation with Gina, Good Samaritan's geriatric nurse practitioner. She had informed me that I could expect this appointment to last two hours, and it would include taking a complete history, a neurological exam, a mental/memory test, and a review of Dad's prescriptions. She promised me that Dr. Friedley would definitely be talking directly to my dad at this appointment and she would be sharing her assessment with his other doctors and our family. I told Jessica how relieved I was when I hung up the phone after talking with Good Samaritan and how pleased I was that Dad seemed so receptive to the idea. Of course, I knew his enthusiasm could change, since we weren't sitting in Dr. Friedley's office yet.

Jessica had two questions for us to ask Dr. Friedley when Dad's evaluation was completed. First, did Dr. Friedley think it was safe to leave Dad at home alone?

Second, did she feel Dad was competent enough to make his own decisions? Jessica felt that the answers to these questions would make a difference in how she would direct us and what the next step might be for Dad.

I asked Jessica if she thought getting Dad evaluated at Copper Ridge would be a duplication of what he was going to have done in a few weeks at Good Samaritan Hospital. Since Dad was willing to see Dr. Friedley, she thought I shouldn't cancel that appointment. Jessica knew it would take at least a few months to get an appointment at Copper Ridge, and we needed some answers now to make more informed decisions. She gave us Copper Ridge's telephone number and I said I would call that day.

Jessica also suggested taking Dad to adult day care. In addition, she suggested hiring a geriatric assistant to get him ready for adult day care. That arrangement might avoid morning confrontations between Shirley and Dad. Another option she recommended was having a part-time home care geriatric companion for Dad for a few hours a day a couple of times a week. Shirley and I both looked at each other. Our mutual silence meant we both knew how difficult it would be getting Dad to be receptive to those changes, especially given the fact that we couldn't even get him to consider going to a senior center. At the same time, I knew things couldn't continue as they were. My brother and I were aware that Shirley, out of her love and devotion for him, often covered for Dad when he couldn't remember. I had often said to Shirley, "We don't want to have two people sick, and you need to take better care of yourself." *Was Dad or Shirley ready for this?*

It was so easy to discuss things with Jessica. She was a good listener. She talked about a few simple things that we could do right away. She stressed that everyone should let Dad do as much for himself as he was able. She thought it was important for Shirley to keep her cell phone turned on so she could make or receive calls if there was a crisis or an emergency. Jessica agreed that Shirley should not give Dad her cell phone number because he would probably call her constantly while she was out. She recommended that Shirley purchase a large wipe-off reminder board for the kitchen and place it where Dad could easily see it. Jessica felt that maybe labeling his dresser drawers would help make it easier for him to find his things.

Jessica suggested that when Dad was upset or disappointed, we might softly say to him, "I'm sorry you're upset," or "I'm sorry, I misunderstood," or "I'm sorry you didn't have a good time," or "I'm sorry things didn't work out for you today."

Those types of statements would affirm Dad's conversation, acknowledge his feelings, and help him recognize that we understood his dilemma and were there for him, whether we agreed with him or not. Jessica told us that, if possible, we should try not to argue with Dad because he might only become more agitated or combative. She recognized that it took a great deal of patience to listen without judgment or to distract his attention without reacting to his negative behavior or repetitive comments. She reminded us again that people with dementia couldn't always control their outbursts or their behavior.

Jessica recommended that Shirley have a plan in place just in case Dad became aggressive and lashed out at her, making it impossible for her to handle things on her own. We discussed several options together, trying to decide which one was best and most feasible. Shirley should go to a neighbor's or the front desk to get help if she ever felt threatened or in danger. If for some reason Dad blocked the front door, Shirley should get their portable phone and lock herself in the bathroom, and call 911 for emergency help.

Shirley didn't say a word, but her body language signaled her discomfort with contemplating having to leave her home and her husband. Jessica reminded her that this plan was precautionary in case there was a *worse case scenario* in the future. She just wanted Shirley to be prepared and not panic if Dad continued to decline and became violent, which Jessica said often happens in people with dementia. Jessica recommended that Shirley keep a small suitcase in her car with some extra clothing, toiletries, and her medications. I had already given Shirley keys to our home in case she needed a safe place to go.

Listening to Jessica was hard for me. Even though intellectually I knew everything she was saying could become a reality, emotionally it saddened me to think that one day this disease could control my dad, and none of us would have the skills necessary to handle him. I tried hard to hold back my tears and to put up a good front for Jessica and Shirley, but this was my father we were discussing.

Jessica strongly recommended that we read *The 36-Hour Day,* by Nancy L. Mace, M.A. and Peter V. Rabins, M.D. Shirley had read the book many years ago when both her mother and aunt were suffering with Alzheimer's disease. She expressed the willingness to read it again when Jessica mentioned the book had been updated. Jessica also asked Shirley to check Dad's long-term care policy to see if it covered dementia and Alzheimer's.

At Jessica's suggestion, we set up a combined appointment for Shirley, Dave, and me on a date after Dad's evaluation at Good Samaritan Hospital. Jessica told us we could call or e-mail her anytime if we had any questions or if any problems arose. Leaving Jewish Family Services, Shirley and I collectively breathed a sigh of relief.

Later that evening, I called Dave to let him know what transpired at the meeting with Jessica. It appeared to me that he was preoccupied and only half listening. I knew I had a lot to tell him and that I was very detail-oriented, but before I finished he said, "Sue, I got to go."

The next day I called the number Jessica had given me for Copper Ridge. I asked Naomi, the Assessment Clinic director, to tell me a little bit about their Outpatient Assessment Clinic. She told me their team of neuropsychiatrists, social workers, and nurses would evaluate my father using the latest advances for diagnosing memory-related illnesses. Then they would discuss their diagnosis with our family and recommend treatment. With this information we could decide whether Dad would be able to remain at home or need more care that only an assisted-living facility could provide.

Naomi asked me to tell her a little bit about my dad—if his wife was living, where Dad was residing, and how I came to make the phone call to Copper Ridge. I tried to make my explanation brief, only highlighting a few major points. I expressed my fear that I wouldn't be able to get Dad to show up for the evaluation. She said, "You get him here, and we will handle the rest."

After listening to me, Naomi told me she thought Dad would do well with a particular doctor on their staff. I asked her if I could visit Copper Ridge before I made an appointment. She suggested that I make the appointment now, since they were scheduling three months out and the earliest opening she had was in January. *Oh great, that's when Chuck and I were supposed to be away. I couldn't worry about that now. I had almost three months to figure something out.*

Naomi said she would let me know if there was a cancellation, but not to count on it since they evaluate people from all over the country. I made the appointment and set up a day to visit Copper Ridge the next week. Naomi told me what documentation they would need. She said she would send me a packet with information and forms to complete. She asked me if I wanted the packet sent to my father or to me. She was only too happy to send it to my address but asked me to fax a copy of Dad's power of attorney. She gave me directions to Copper Ridge before we hung up.

The leaves were in full bloom driving out to Copper Ridge in Sykesville, Maryland, and particularly beautiful along the two bridges that passed over Liberty Reservoir. Naomi's directions were easy to follow and I had no problem finding it. My main reason for visiting Copper Ridge was to see the layout of their facility—to see where the Assessment Clinic was located in relation to the residential part of the building. I didn't want Dad thinking I was deceiving him by bringing him to a nursing home, nor did I want him to see any signs or logos that said "dementia" or "Alzheimer's." I knew both would be counter-productive.

I was happy to see that the entrance sign only said "Copper Ridge" along with their address. Another sign in the parking lot said "Johns Hopkins Assessment Clinic" with an arrow pointing to the entrance to the building. Their lobby was impressive, and the receptionist directed me to the clinic.

Naomi greeted me and led me to her office. We went over the forms that I had completed plus other information that I'd brought. She told me she would send all of Dad's physicians the *Authorization to Release Medical Information* form. She said it often took over a month or two to get back the required medical records.

Naomi was most helpful with my questions and was delightful to talk with. I was more relaxed than I was when I first arrived. She said this was always a difficult time for family and caregivers, but the Assessment Clinic staff was there to help us through the process. She handed me her card and told me not to hesitate to call her. I felt confident with our decision to have Dad evaluated there, but I was not as confident about how I was going to convince Dad to buy into the plan.

Dad seemed in good spirits when he greeted me at the door. He told me he was sitting in the kitchen watching TV, so he would be sure he heard the doorbell when I came for our "Susie and Me Day." *Thank goodness, I had a key for the times he didn't hear the doorbell. Maybe if he'd kept his hearing aids in his ears instead of in his drawer, this wouldn't have been a problem. Enough sarcasm. It was a wonderful Indian summer day, so let's enjoy it.*

Dad was excited about something and took me over to the dining room window. The view of the fall foliage was spectacular from their seventh floor condo, and we spent a few minutes talking about it. I hugged Dad and thanked him for showing it to me. "The colors look more beautiful up here than from the ground," I told him. He agreed.

Helping him with his jacket, I suggested we take a ride and pick up some sandwiches for a picnic. Dad's smile let me know that he liked the idea. He stopped to pick up the mail on the kitchen table to put in the mailbox downstairs. I was delighted that he remembered. I knew Shirley was trying to give him responsibilities that she knew he could handle, at least for right now.

In the car, we decided to head north towards Aberdeen or Havre de Grace. Since we had been there before, I knew there was a picnic area in a park by the water. Dad commented how much he loved this time of year and how beautiful the trees were. He told me how much he used to enjoy driving his truck through the country roads in Pennsylvania in autumn. I asked him many questions about his old customers to keep him engaged. As we drove north, I pointed out Cal Ripken's Stadium on our left, which sparked a wonderful conversation about Cal Sr., Cal Jr., Billy, and the "O-re-os" (Dad's version of Orioles).

I was driving and talking away when I glanced over and saw that Dad was sound asleep. His silence gave me a chance to rehearse how I was going to lead into a conversation about him having an evaluation at Copper Ridge.

Dad was surprised that we were already in Havre de Grace when he woke up. As I parked the car, he didn't mention a thing about being there before. We picked a table in the sun with a great view of the yacht basin. As always, Dad commented about how good the sun felt on his arthritic shoulders as he helped me spread out the tablecloth I had in the trunk of my car.

Children's voices caught our attention, and it didn't take long for Dad to start talking to them and their mother. He told her how beautiful her children were. When she thanked him, he replied with his standard, "Don't thank me, thank the Lord."

Dad loved children and got a big kick out of watching them. We reminisced about what it was like when his grandsons were that little, and how they used the red Radio Flyer wagon in our basement as an ambulance. Craig played the injured patient and Scott was the eminent doctor. I could almost picture myself in our old kitchen, enjoying the squeals and laughter coming from downstairs.

Dad and I took a walk after lunch along the boardwalk promenade overlooking the Susquehanna River. I commented on the great job Havre de Grace did repairing the promenade after it was damaged by Hurricane Isabel. We paused to watch the ducks splashing in the water. How wonderful it was to feel the gentle warm breeze against our skin as we walked. We stopped and sat on a bench, silently enjoying the solace of this picture postcard moment. I put my hand over his. He looked up at me and smiled.

"I've wanted to talk to you about something, Dad." I quickly assured him that nothing was wrong and continued, "If I were to ask you what bothers you the most about getting older, what would you say?"

Without hesitation he answered, "My memory. Some days it's not too bad, but sometimes it makes me sad when I can't remember stuff or can't find things."

"You've told me that before, Dad, and I think I may have found a place that can help you with your memory. It's called Copper Ridge, and it's connected with Johns Hopkins. What they do is find out where you are concerning your memory. Then their doctors try to find ways to help you keep the memory you still have so it doesn't get any worse." I spoke slowly, hoping Dad would comprehend what I was telling him.

Dad remained silent. I told him we only wanted the best for him, and that I'd already gone out to Copper

Ridge to talk to the director. "I was really impressed with what they do. Because its part of Hopkins, they are doing a lot of research and have found out so many new things. Helping people with their memory is their specialty. That's all they do. I think you will like the people there, and I think it would be good for you to try it. I didn't want to make an appointment without talking to you first."

I waited for a response. "What do you think, Dad?" I asked.

I heard the hesitation in his voice when he asked me, "What would they ask me to do?"

I told him, "I think the doctor will probably ask you some questions, like how you feel when you can't remember a word or someone's name. I don't think there will be anything too difficult. You could think about it for a while. You don't have to make a decision right now." *I always tried to make Dad feel like he was in control, and that we weren't making all the decisions for him or trying to take over his life.*

I asked Dad if he felt tired or if he wanted to continue walking.

"Let's walk," he said. "Walking is the best thing for you!"

We walked together following the promenade to the Concord Point Lighthouse, one of the oldest lighthouses in continual use on the East Coast. Again we stopped to rest on a nearby bench. The lighthouse was only open to the public on the weekends. I was actually glad because I would have been very leery about taking Dad up that narrow, winding staircase. Sitting there, Dad recalled the time when he and Shirley climbed to the top of the lighthouse.

Dad's eyes lit up when I took out some chocolate chip cookies and a juice box from my purse. I knew I didn't even have to ask him if he would like one since he had always been the original Cookie Monster.

We started our walk back to the car. Our pace was slow but Dad didn't seem tired at all. I guess there's nothing like sugar to keep you going. There was not much conversation between us. I assumed we were both enjoying the beautiful day, and the impressive trees adorned in red, gold, and sienna.

Out of nowhere Dad said, "I guess I have nothing to lose by going to this new doctor, do I?"

Surprised that he even remembered, I replied, "No Dad, I think it would be a good thing."

"Let's do it then," he said.

EIGHT

The telephone rang as I was getting dressed to go to *shul* (synagogue). I thought it was probably Dad calling to let me know he wasn't going to synagogue that morning for the *Simchas Torah* holiday, a day of celebration on completing the year's cycle of Torah readings.

At eighty-five, struggling with short-term memory loss, Dad frequently cancelled our outings. Most days he had very little initiative. Even the simplest of tasks like getting dressed overwhelmed him. I was relieved when I noticed it wasn't his name on my Caller ID. I finished dressing and drove over to pick up Dad.

Dad greeted me with a hesitant look on his face. "*Chag Semeach* (Happy Holiday), Dad," as I bent over to give him a hug and a kiss. He said he was not sure about going. I reassured him that things would be fine. I helped him with his sport coat, holding it low so he could easily slip both arms in simultaneously without increasing his pain. Gently I eased the jacket over his shoulders, noticing how it hiked up in the back from his permanent spinal curvature. He checked his pocket for his yarmulke (skullcap).

Later, on the way down in the elevator, Dad told me he had forgotten his yarmulke. I showed him the one in his right pocket. As I buckled his seat belt, he again asked about the yarmulke. My answer was the same.

We didn't get far before he told me going to shul wasn't a good idea, and slapped his forehead as he shook his head in despair. This scenario repeated itself several more times. I ignored his words each time and quickly changed the subject. I drove a little faster. I knew things would be all right if I could just get him inside the synagogue.

Dad's mood was somber as we continued, but he commented about the weather and again asked about his yarmulke. With my eyes fixed on the road, I steadied the steering wheel with my left hand. I reached into his left pocket with my right hand and pulled out his yarmulke to show him. To my surprise, I noticed this one was white, meaning he now had two; the other one was black.

Getting out of the car, Dad told me he could get a yarmulke inside. Trying not to show my frustration, I agreed with him. He eagerly walked down the hall and took a *tallis* (prayer shawl) from the rack. Holding it outstretched, he said the prayer. I noticed he only said a few words as he tossed it over his shoulders. I smoothed his tallis so it lay evenly. We entered the sanctuary,

Dad's old second home. I began my reading, frequently glancing across at the men's section to see how much my father participated in the service. I wanted to see if he could remember the familiar prayers.

The Rabbi asked all *Kohens* (descendants of Aaron chosen by God to perform sacred rituals) and *Levites* (descendants of Levi who perform secondary duties of the sanctuary service) to prepare for the *Duchaning* (priestly blessing). My father, a Kohen, sat, not responding. He no longer blessed the congregation, fearing he wouldn't remember the words and would make a mistake. Not even the encouragement of the rabbi and cantor could change his mind. We all understood his reluctance.

The congregation stood as the curtains on the *Aron Kodesh* (Holy Ark) opened to reveal the Torah scrolls. On Simchas Torah, all of the scrolls are removed from the ark. The first *hakafah* (procession around the synagogue) began. My dad was not among the Kohens carrying the Torahs around the synagogue. He had told me many times lately that the scrolls were too heavy for him and I agreed. There was singing, clapping, and dancing for each hakafah. The sanctuary vibrated with jubilance. On the sixth hakafah, I had the honor of carrying a Torah, and I waited patiently for a male congregant to place the set of scrolls in my arms. As I carried the Torah next to my heart, I experienced an instantaneous connection with my faith. I held the same law given by God to Moses so many thousands of years ago.

The song changed as the procession proceeded through the men's section. I saw Dad just standing there. I approached him and engaged him with a smile. I encouraged him to walk around the synagogue with me.

At first, he hesitated. I asked, "Will you honor me by walking by my side?" I suggested he hold the bottom of the scrolls. He touched the wood and we moved forward together singing. We were both beaming. People responded as we continued. Many gave special recognition to my father, who was a past president of the congregation and chairman of our Hebrew School. The pace was slow but wonderful. My Torah was getting heavy but I didn't mind.

As we passed the rabbi on the *bimah* (alter), I glanced up at him. He knew what this Kodak moment meant to both my father and me, and he smiled warmly. I had to look away so I wouldn't burst out crying. I glanced at Dad. He was wearing a big grin.

Together we walked outside the synagogue for the seventh hakafah, where everyone circled around all the Torahs, singing and dancing. I finally relinquished my Torah to someone because it was really too heavy for me to continue. I joined my father as we clapped to traditional songs. He knew the words and sang with confidence. I was so emotional that I felt weak.

The rejoicing ended, and we reentered the synagogue as the service continued. I saw the cantor try to convince Dad to join all the Kohens on the bimah for the first *aliyah* (the honor of reciting a blessing over the Torah). My father refused and the cantor glanced at me with that "I tried" look. I appreciated his efforts. The reading of the Torah was complete and Dad was visibly tiring. We left synagogue before the service had ended.

During *Shabbat* (Sabbath) dinner at our house later that evening, my father and I discussed what a wonderful experience we had carrying the Torah together. I told him how proud I was to walk with him. He kissed me and said he was so very proud of me. We agreed to make this an annual Simchas Torah tradition. *I hoped God answered my silent prayer.*

DATE: November 5
TO: Peter Holt, M.D.
FAX #:
RE: Leslie Miller (confidential)
OF PAGES, INCLUDING COVER PAGE: 1

MESSAGE:

My Dad has an appointment with you on Nov. 8th. I am unable to take him, since I have a doctor's appointment. FYI:

1. Dr. Aaron put my father on Seroquel 25 mg twice a day. He told my dad it was for memory, so he would take it. He's been on it since Sept. 28th, and we have not really seen much improvement in his mood. He sleeps a lot and gets easily overwhelmed.
2. My father had a short appointment with Dr. Rudman on Monday, and he suggested

cutting his prednisone in half, but said he would defer to you since your specialty is rheumatology.

I am making you aware of these things as his health care agent because it is difficult for Dad to remember to tell you. He's aware of his short-term memory loss, but we are noticing some problems with long-term memory.

Shirley has a lot on her mind and is showing signs of caregiver's stress. I can't always rely on her to remember either.

Thanks,

Susan

November 9

Dear Dr. Friedley,

My father, Leslie Miller, has an appointment with you on November 11th. I am faxing the information your office requested in hopes that my father will not ask any questions that day about the information I am giving you. He has episodes of paranoia and has not seen these reports. I also thought it may be helpful for you to have them before we meet.

My father, who is eighty-five, is aware of his short-term memory loss. We have been noticing more long-term memory loss within the past six months. At no time do we mention dementia or Alzheimer's in front of him. We all feel this would be counterproductive. I hope you will honor our wishes when you speak to him. He is concerned about his memory and told me, "It makes me sad sometimes." I told him your specialty was working with older adults not only for memory, but also for their general health as well as seeing if the patient's medications are appropriate. He seemed satisfied with my explanation and is willing to see you.

I wanted to make you aware that his doctors have been telling him that the Seroquel he is taking is for memory also, in order to get him to take it. If he thought it was for emotional or mood disorders, he would not take it. He knows that Namenda is for memory, but he doesn't know that it is used to treat Alzheimer's.

I am looking forward to meeting you Thursday.

Sincerely,

Susan Garbett

Enclosures:
Doctor reports   Current medications
MRI summary   Unsuccessful medications
Recent blood work   Family observations

LESLIE MILLER - CONFIDENTIAL

Observations of his family

Physical:
- Difficulty with balance
  Needs to hold on to things particularly after awakening
  Leans to the left
  Has fallen several times
- Poor nutrition—(diet is mostly high glycemic carbohydrates, very little fruits and vegetables although they are offered to him)

Current Behaviors:
- Constant repetition
- Short-term memory loss causes agitation and frustration which sometimes results in angry outbursts, usually directed at his wife if she makes a suggestion or tries to help
- Constantly misplaces personal items
- Lack of initiative
  Frequently wants to go back to bed on the premise that it helps his arthritis
  Sleeps a lot during the day/wonders why he doesn't sleep at night
  Doesn't shower, shave, or dress unless he has somewhere to go
  Often cancels activity the night before or on the same day
- Fixation on small things

- Simple tasks tend to overwhelm him at times—is frustrated that it's taking him longer to do things (is unable to balance his checkbook)
- Often confused with the concept of time, dates, night, and day

Understandable behaviors:
- Retells stories from the past over and over, because that is what he can remember
- Often hears a word in a conversation which triggers an immediate response because it is about something he knows
- Mild hallucinating—makes up things when he can't remember to fill in the gaps, and then insists they happened that way
- Has a fear of dying

Personality traits:
Constant exaggerated worrying (magnified with age)
Examples:
- While he is still writing checks, closes blinds so people won't look in the window as he does paperwork. He lives on the 7th floor.
- Heard the news that it was going to be cooler one weekend and was worried about the roads being icy in May.
- Thinks the woman across the hall came in and stole his two umbrellas.
- Panics when his wife isn't home at a scheduled

time in the afternoon. Obsessed that something is going to happen to her.
• Excitable at times.

Long-term memory:
• Difficulty remembering things that were once second nature to him ex. He is an observant Jew who is very familiar with daily and holiday prayers and customs. Now he often doesn't remember what prayer is appropriate for the current holiday, where to find the prayer in his prayer book, or what observances occur on the holiday. Consequently, he doesn't want to attend services at all.
• Has his "pat" stories from childhood and WWII which he repeats constantly, but now they're getting a bit distorted, and some names elude him.

NINE

A woman in a white lab coat approached us in the waiting room and warmly extended her hand out to my dad.

"Hi, I'm Dr. Friedley. It's nice to meet you, Mr. Miller," she said.

"Likewise," Dad replied.

In a friendly tone she said, "Let's go back to the exam room so we can talk and have some privacy." As we followed her back, I was trying to remember the last time I was greeted by a doctor in an office. Dr. Friedley showed Dad to a chair and began talking directly to him.

I asked her if she wanted me to wait in the waiting room, and she asked Dad what he would like. He said that he wanted me to stay, in case there were things he couldn't remember. I promised myself I would remain silent. I would try not to interrupt with additional information, and would try to avoid the temptation of correcting him and putting his comments in the correct sequence. This took a certain amount of self-discipline. I found myself at times pressing my lips together so I wouldn't interrupt.

Dr. Friedley began by asking several questions, "Mr. Miller, tell me when and where you were born?... Do you have any brothers or sisters?... How many?... Are they all living?...What city do you live in?...What state do you live in?"

As Dad answered each question, he appeared to be quite comfortable, eager, and at ease. The doctor was looking straight at him and talking directly to him as if he was her next-door neighbor.

You could tell Dr. Friedley was really listening by the content of each question she asked. She allowed him to talk freely about his childhood, his army service, his work, his wife, children, and grandchildren. Dr. Friedley helped Dad clarify pertinent questions and never stopped him if he went off track. I was amazed how she remained totally focused on him, without taking any notes. I sensed her genuineness when she occasionally interjected with comments about herself and her family.

I glanced at my watch. We had been there over an hour and a half, and the doctor was still asking him questions. Dad didn't seem tired or be in any distress. I noticed that Dr. Friedley seemed to be incorporating questions from the Folstein Mini-Mental State Exam in between her inquiries. She was very subtle and cleverly included the questions in the conversation. I was somewhat familiar with the test having come across it while researching dementia.

"Mr. Miller, I'm going to name three objects: apple, penny, table. Can you repeat them for me?" Dad repeated two of the objects, but didn't seem aware that he couldn't repeat all three. I listened closely, knowing his short-term memory had really declined in the past year. He generally compensated very well when he knew he couldn't retrieve a word or the specific information being asked. He usually did this with humor and oftentimes said, "It will come to me" or "It wasn't that important anyway."

A few minutes later, Dr. Friedley asked Dad to tell her the three objects she named earlier. Dad didn't remember any of them, and Dr. Friedley reassured him and continued her evaluation.

Another half hour passed, and Dr. Friedley asked Dad if he was tired. He told her that he was fine and she said that she would like to examine him. Dad had no objections and responded favorably to her request. He appeared to be enjoying the attention.

"You will need to get undressed, Mr. Miller, and put this gown on. Do you need any help?" Dr. Friedly asked.

Dad replied he thought he was all right. She showed him the button to use to call the nurse if he had any difficulty. I let him know that I would be in the waiting room. Dr. Friedley said she would be back in about ten minutes. "Push the button if you need to, OK?" Dad nodded, indicating that he understood.

Dr. Friedley and I left the exam room and began to talk in the hallway. She let me know that she was going back to her office to read the packet of information I had faxed her before my father's appointment. She told me she liked to get to know the patient first before she looked at any files or reports. That way, she could remain unbiased and form her own perceptions without outside influence.

As I turned to go to the waiting room, I heard a door open. I saw Dad poking his head out of the slightly ajar door. He looked relieved to see me. He asked me if I would help him with the buttons on his shirt. With his swollen, arthritic fingers and permanently crippled thumbs, he had a lot of difficulty with small objects. After helping him with his shirt, Dad told me he could do the rest. I reminded him that Dr. Friedley would be in soon.

After about an hour, Gina, Dr. Friedley's nurse practitioner, told me I could go back to the exam room. When I entered, Dad was dressed and smiling. Dr. Friedley wanted to go over a few things with Dad. I could tell by her expression she wanted me to remain in case there was a need for clarification.

Making direct eye contact with Dad, Dr. Friedley told him, "I am a doctor with special training in working with older adults. After talking and examining a patient, I develop a plan for each of them. I also work closely with the patient's primary care doctor as well as with the patient's family.

"For today, Mr. Miller, I want to suggest a few things I would like you to do. I will write them down for you to take home in case you need to refer to them later. Our studies have found people your age get just as much pain relief from Extra Strength Tylenol as they do from taking

Darvocet. Tylenol has fewer side effects. What I would like to see you do is stop taking your Darvocet and use Tylenol instead for your PMR (polymyalgia rheumatica). You can take two tablets four times a day if you need to. Tylenol is much cheaper and won't interfere with your memory.

"I want you to continue taking Namenda in the morning and evening. I also want you to take your Seroquel only in the morning, and I'm going to recommend a new medication for you to take in the evening. I will give you a prescription for Zoloft. We have had success using these medications. I also think it is important that you exercise or walk every day and eat more fruits and vegetables."

I was thrilled that Dr. Friedley carefully analyzed all Dad's prescriptions and over-the-counter medications and was making appropriate changes. I read somewhere that it was very important to have someone with the proper credentials, like a doctor or a registered pharmacist, periodically review an older person's medications because older people metabolize meds differently than younger people. As people age, their metabolism slows down. This can often cause an adverse drug interaction. Most pharmaceutical companies do not conduct trials and studies geared specifically for the elderly, nor do they always take into account gender or race. Older people take a variety of pills —prescribed medications, over-the-counter medications, vitamins, and supplements. When you consider the complexity of this combination of pills, keeping track of the proper dosages, and when and how to take them, it is easy to see how possible harmful interaction can occur, particularly with older adults. These interactions can also mimic or mask other diseases and can affect memory. I was grateful Dr. Friedley was a gerontologist who dealt with medication issues all the time.

Dad told the doctor that he was somewhat hesitant to change to Tylenol, and she suggested he try it for two weeks and then call her to let her know how he was doing. Dad showed her the shoulder exercises he did and told her he walked a couple of miles each day. I knew that is what he had done in the past, but lately his walking was limited to the inside of his home and even that was hit-or-miss. I remained silent.

Dad's face lit up when Dr. Friedley handed him her written instructions and the prescriptions he was to take with him. I could see that she had written down all his prescriptions in large print under the headings *morning* and *evening*. She told Dad she wanted to see him back in one month to see how his memory was with the new medication. Dad told her, "This is great and I am so glad that I came today."

Dr. Friedley responded, "So am I."

Dad wasn't aware that we had been there for almost four hours.

Before Dad's next appointment with Dr. Friedley, I faxed a short update letting her know that Dad had been remembering to take his medications as directed. I told her he had complained about not having his Darvocet, and we had put signs around the house reminding him that he could take Extra Strength Tylenol up to four times a day.

I informed her that I thought his illness might be taking a different course because he often seemed more agitated, more paranoid, and more aggressive. It seemed that it was the little things that set him off, but Shirley claimed his aggressive episodes were infrequent. I felt Dad often resented Shirley's perceived parental role and no longer saw her as a loving partner.

I didn't know if it was the medication, depression, boredom, or all three that were causing his tiredness and need to sleep a good portion of each day. We were having a hard time motivating him to do things.

With all the negativity, I thought it was important to highlight some of the positive things that Dad could still do for Dr. Friedley. I wrote them down as follows:

Dad can:
- dress himself and make clothing selections that match most of the time
- care for personal needs; brush teeth, comb hair, see to toilet needs, sponge bathe (doesn't take showers very often), uses an electric razor
- recognize friends and family
- read but doesn't do it as often as before
- recognize monetary denominations
- read a menu and order what he wants to eat
- address an envelope correctly with help, knows it needs a stamp and address label
- spell and correct my grammar if I say something incorrectly!
- dial some telephone numbers correctly, but has

a difficult time hanging the receiver back on the base

- play seven-card rummy

"I don't have any more pain than usual since being off Darvocet," Dad told Dr. Friedley when they met next. He had been taking Tylenol two to three times a day for about a month and seemed very satisfied with the results. I found this revelation amazing, but knew how comfortable and confident Dad felt with Dr. Friedley. Shirley and I couldn't be more pleased with her. Shirley had noticed that since beginning the Zoloft, Dad tended to be a bit sleepier and she related this to Dr. Friedley.

I was glad Shirley came to that appointment so she could meet Dr. Friedley and see for herself what Dad and I had been raving about. It was not that Shirley didn't want to attend the first appointment, but Dad seemed to resent the parental role she had been forced into assuming. That role sometimes caused confrontation between them. Dad seemed more tolerant of me lately and my taking him to some of his appointments gave Shirley more time to herself during the day.

While Dad was undressing for his examination, Dr. Friedley talked to Shirley. I left so Shirley could have some privacy and give Dr. Friedley her perspective of what had been happening.

Later, Shirley told me how hard it was for her to admit to Dr. Friedley that Dad had been accusing her of having an affair, usually whenever she left him alone. He seemed to have fixated on this absurd accusation ever since she talked to a legally blind man when they visited a friend who had lost a spouse several months earlier. Dad didn't remember many things that happened recently, but this one stayed with him and he used it against Shirley when he became agitated or frustrated. Shirley and I talked about it, and she realized this was not really her husband speaking—but rather a symptom of his illness. Regardless, it was a hard pill to swallow.

Shirley remembered to ask Dr. Friedley the two questions Jessica wanted answered: did she think it was safe to leave Dad at home alone, and did she feel Dad was competent enough to make his own decisions? Dr. Friedley felt she could better answer those questions after Dad was evaluated at Copper Ridge in early January. She was delighted that Dad had an appointment there, because of its outstanding reputation for evaluating people with various memory impairments.

After Dad's uneventful examination, Dr. Friedley told us she thought it would be better for Dad to take his Zoloft in the morning and the Seroquel at night. She wrote down new medication instructions for both morning and evening and made copies for all of us. She told Dad, "I think you are going to like the people at Copper Ridge. I'm so glad you have an appointment in January. They are really good at what they do."

"I'll do whatever you say, Doc," Dad replied.

Shirley and I glanced at each other and smiled. I knew what we were both thinking. We wished we had met Dr. Friedley sooner.

TEN

I was up early exercising, when the phone rang. It was Shirley and I could tell by her voice that something was wrong. Shirley told me that after she and Dad played gin rummy last night, Dad got up to take his pills and suddenly lost his balance and began to fall backwards. Luckily, Shirley was right next to him, and she was able to catch him before he fell. As Shirley guided him over to a chair to sit down, Dad complained, "The kitchen is spinning." Shirley told me the episode didn't last long, but Dad was still dizzy afterwards. Later, she was able to get him into bed and he slept through the night.

"Is he up now?" I asked.

"No, I just checked and he's still sleeping," she responded.

I asked Shirley, "Did Dad complain of pain anywhere when he said the kitchen was spinning? Did his speech seem slurred? Did he have difficulty walking to the bedroom?"

Shirley answered no to the first two questions, but she said he had some difficulty walking and was leaning to one side. He tended to lean to one side at times due to his arthritis. Shirley asked me, "What do you think I should do?"

You should have called 911 last night, but that's not the issue now. "I definitely think he should be checked out to see what caused this. Call Dr. Friedley and have her paged," I said.

Shirley asked me if I would make the call based on the premise that she didn't want Dad to hear her on the phone if he woke up. I could hear the concern and tiredness in her voice, so I agreed to try to reach Dr. Friedley. I told Shirley I would be over as soon as I could get dressed. I could hear the relief in her voice.

I dialed Good Samaritan Hospital and asked to have Dr. Friedley paged. Five minutes later, she returned my call. I explained the sequence of events from the night before, as I understood them. Dr. Friedley asked me if Dad was having trouble walking. I told her Dad wasn't up yet. I was going over there soon and could then better assess the situation. She also asked me if we would be able to bring my father to Good Sam. She would meet us at ten. I told her to expect us, unless Dad was having difficulty and we couldn't get him there on our own.

On the way to Dad and Shirley's home, I called Dave and left a message. When I got there, I was surprised to find Dad in the kitchen, dressed, and having oatmeal. I was relieved. Dad repeated his account of what happened the previous night with unusual clarity, explaining just how he felt when "the kitchen was spinning." He told me, "It was the strangest thing. I never had anything like that happen to me before."

In between bites, Dad told me again about the spinning. I listened intently to every word, delighted there didn't seem to be any evidence that his speech was impaired in any way. We didn't want to rush him, so Shirley and I waited patiently for him to finish his breakfast. I was anxious to see how he walked.

He was very agreeable about seeing Dr. Friedley that morning. Dad didn't mind that Shirley and I were walking on either side of him on the way out to the car. His strides were slow, his balance was not the best, and he seemed to be leaning more to the left than usual.

Dad's face broke out in a big smile when Dr. Friedley greeted us in the waiting room.

"I heard you had some problems last night," said Dr. Friedley. "Can you tell me about them?"

Dad related what happened with the same lucidity as before. Dr. Friedley asked him a few more questions before wheeling him back to the exam room. Shirley was unusually quiet, the tension and anxiety apparent on her face. I took her hand but didn't comment. We were both absorbed in our private thoughts and relieved that Dad was here and in good hands.

Soon Dr. Friedley returned to the waiting room. She told us that from her initial examination she suspected

Dad had a mild stroke, his strength appeared diminished on one side, and she would like to admit him for further tests. She said Dad was in good spirits, very cooperative, and anxious to see us. Dr. Friedley wanted to arrange to have Dad admitted to the hospital.

When Shirley and I went back to see Dad, he was aware that Dr. Friedley felt he had a mild stroke. He was glad to be in the hospital and under her care. He was cheerful and very talkative. I told him I had already called Dave at work, and he would be coming to the hospital in a few hours.

It didn't take very long for a volunteer to take Dad to his room. Several doctors came in to examine him. I diplomatically suggested to Shirley that we leave his room. I wanted Dad's responses to be his own without any unsolicited coaching from either of us. I knew Dad often looked for help from Shirley or me, especially when his memory failed him.

Dad went for an MRI and CT scan in the afternoon, so we didn't see him much until dinner. This gave us a chance to have some lunch, make phone calls to family and friends, and cancel things that we had scheduled for the rest of the week. Both a physical and an occupational therapist visited Dad to evaluate his balance, gait, and vertigo. I was surprised Dad wasn't more fatigued, since for me this had been a very long day. He was upbeat, joking a bit, and eager to please any hospital staff that came into his room. I thought he was scared and this was his way of compensating. Since Dave was there and would be staying later, Shirley and I said goodnight and told Dad we would see him in the morning.

Dr. Friedley went over the results of Dad's tests with us the next day, and they confirmed her earlier diagnosis that he had experienced a mild stroke. There was also evidence that he probably had several silent mini-strokes over the years that we weren't aware of. Dr. Friedley had already seen Dad earlier that morning and told us, "He's quite a character! I always leave his room smiling." She told us he was not experiencing any of the vertigo he showed on admission, but their team of specialists recommended an intense inpatient rehabilitation program to help improve his mobility and to help him with daily self-care and activities. She explained that he would be receiving physical and occupational therapy daily. They transferred Dad to rehab after breakfast.

It seemed that there was a constant parade of doctors, nurses, therapists, and staff going in and out of Dad's room each day. In between, relatives and friends came to visit. Shirley and I took turns going to the cafeteria so someone would always be there in case a doctor came to report on Dad's progress or tests. With Dad's memory problems, we knew he would not be able to comprehend or remember all the information given and we didn't want to miss anyone. Thank goodness, we were both there when Dr. Friedley came in, since I had to excuse myself and quickly leave Dad's room when my own doctor's number came up on my cell phone.

My dermatologist was calling with the results of my oral biopsy taken almost three weeks before. I asked him to repeat the findings again as I headed for the nurses' station for some paper and a pen. "Mucous membrane what?" I asked. "Please spell the last word for me, so I can research it online when I get home. Pemphigoid? I never heard of it." He explained that mucous membrane pemphigoid was a chronic autoimmune disorder characterized by blistering lesions most commonly affecting the mucous membranes of the mouth and eyes. He also told me that it could affect other membranes of the body. He asked for my pharmacy's telephone number and said he would call in a prescription for tetracycline and a topical oral ointment. He ended the conversation by saying, "Watch the stress!" I had to laugh.

During Dad's speech evaluation, the therapist noticed Dad coughing when he drank liquids. Shirley told the therapist that Dad often had coughing spells at mealtime even before his recent stroke, and actually had to go to the hospital one time to dislodge a piece of meat that was caught in his throat. She also shared the fact that he refused dilatation of the esophagus against his doctor's recommendation.

The therapist couldn't keep a straight face when Shirley told her that Dad had asked his doctor, "What happens if your throat should tear during this procedure?" The doctor replied indifferently, "You die!" With that Dad commented, "Well, you know what rhymes with die, Doc. Good-bye!"

The speech therapist scheduled a video fluoroscopic swallowing test because of Dad's coughing, his slightly impaired communications skills, and mild dysarthria. Mild dysarthria is a speech disorder caused by weakness of the speech muscles.

Everyone was pleased with the progress Dad was making. He loved the attention he was getting and loved entertaining the staff with his humor. That was so like him, a master story and joke teller. He loved an audience and the staff loved taking care of him. We often heard descriptions like "delightful" and "charming," but that was Dad.

Being so close to Christmas, some of the nurses on his floor planned to sing carols via closed-circuit television so patients throughout the hospital could enjoy some holiday spirit. I took Dad out in the hallway to listen to their singing. Before long, they had Dad, in his robe and wheelchair, in the middle of their ensemble, singing carols along with them. He sang with such enthusiasm and fervor, remembering every word to just about every song. Other patients, family, and staff gathered to watch and listen. He was a real stitch, his face illuminated and his hands waving in the air to emphasize special words and phrases. I loved watching him, as did the crowd that had gathered.

Dr. Friedley was amazed when she came to the nurses' station and saw Dad singing away. When the nurses took a break, he continued to entertain the troops by going through his repertoire of World War II hits. Dad didn't want his moment in the sun to end, but when it did, no one could believe it when I told them, "Not bad, for an old Jewish guy."

The swallowing study confirmed that Dad had mild dysphagia or difficulty swallowing with silent aspiration when drinking thin liquids. Because swallowing is a delicate process, this condition may occur for many reasons, but the speech therapist believed his stroke aggravated the condition. The fluoroscope showed that when Dad swallowed thin liquids by spoon, he aspirated and some liquid went down his trachea rather than his esophagus, increasing his chances for developing pneumonia.

For someone Dad's age, this could be particularly dangerous. Dad did fine when swallowing solid foods if he took small bites, but thin liquids were the problem. The speech therapist worked with Dad extensively, showing him the necessary swallowing strategies to avoid aspiration. She felt the major problem with this regimen would be Dad remembering to follow her instructions.

Dad spent eight days in Good Samaritan Hospital. Before he was discharged, Dr. Friedley stopped by early to say good-bye and to reassure Dad that he was making good progress, but he needed to do some work at home to increase his strength and improve his balance. She told us to postpone Dad's outpatient appointment at Copper Ridge by a couple of months until he was stronger and could better handle an extensive evaluation. The floor nurse went over Dad's discharge instructions with all of us. Dad could continue on his regular solid food diet. At all times, Dad should only drink nectar-thick liquids in a cup, no bottles or straws. We needed to thicken all his liquids, including water. He should have one-on-one aspiration supervision when eating using the following strategies:

- Take only small bites and sips
- Sit upright for meals and for 60 minutes after eating
- No talking with food or liquid in his mouth
- Swallow twice after each bite
- Clear throat after a sip of liquid
- Alternate solid food with liquids:
  Bite of food, then swallow twice
  Sip of liquid, then swallow twice and clear throat
  Bite of food, then swallow twice

Holy Cow! I wasn't sure I could follow this regimen. How was Dad going to remember to do this every time he ate? Shirley was going to have her hands full. In three weeks, we should schedule another video fluorographic swallowing study at Good Sam. The nurse gave Shirley the numbers to call to arrange the study, and to set up physical and speech therapy at home.

I asked for a copy of Dad's hospital discharge summary when it was available, and the nurse told me I would have to call Dr. Friedley's office for that information. She asked Dad, Shirley, and me if we had questions or if we didn't understand any of the instructions.

Dad thanked this nurse and anyone else on the way out that he thought helped him during his hospital stay. We were all looking forward to going home, and grateful that this stroke hadn't caused more serious problems.

Once Dad was home, he tried hard to follow his swallowing instructions. He wasn't crazy about how the thickened liquids tasted. Shirley was even more conscientious when it came to his care. She thickened every drink she gave Dad with Thick-it, a common food thickener available at drugstores. She gave him gentle reminders about clearing his throat. It was a difficult routine for anyone to remember and Dad was trying his best. I was able to order nectar-thickened juices for him online. He liked these.

I also wrote down all his swallowing and physical therapy instructions and put them in a red folder, boldly labeled "Doctor's Orders," which made it easier for him to find. He kept the folder on his bed and referred to it often. I added, "walking is the best exercise," to his instructions, hoping he would spend less time in bed. Since I copied and pasted Good Samaritan Hospital's logo on each sheet, his order folder looked official, and he showed it to everyone who came to visit him at home.

The home health therapist determined that Dad's mobility was too good for him to qualify for home health care. She recommended he continue to have therapy at Good Samaritan as an outpatient.

Shirley drove him to every appointment. Her world centered on Dad's needs, and she was dedicated to helping him make the best possible progress. She worked hard to implement the suggestions made by the neuropsychologist who evaluated Dad when he was in the hospital.

This doctor had spoken to us prior to Dad's discharge, and gave us a list of behavioral management recommendations she thought would be helpful to caregivers coping with someone having cognitive memory problems. In fact, quoting the doctor:

Although some of these suggestions may not be relevant at present, they may become useful, especially as the disease progresses… Because cognitive problems are often just as, if not more, devastating and frustrating for patients' family members to cope with than for the patients, I encourage you to contact and utilize the community resources listed.

The neuropsychologist's plan outlined below was divided into the following four categories: agitation, paranoia, orientation, and community resources:

Agitation: Agitation refers to a range of behaviors associated with dementia, including irritability, sleeplessness, and verbal or physical aggression. Often these types of behavior progress with the stages of dementia, from mild to more severe. As a caregiver, the key is to identify whether the behavior escalates because it is event-related (i.e., a visitor arrives, dinner is served) or occurs suddenly, (i.e., unexpected noise). The strategies listed below often help to combat these behaviors:

• Modify the environment to reduce known stressors (e.g., increase lighting, remove mirrors, and minimize loud noises).

• Note patterns of behavior and subtle (and not so subtle) clues that tension and anxiety are increasing (i.e., pacing, incoherent vocalization). Dysfunctional behavior often increases at the end of the day as stress builds and your loved one becomes tired.

- Maintain structure by keeping the same routines. Keep household objects and furniture in the same places. Familiar objects and photographs offer a sense of security and can suggest pleasant memories.

- Try gentle touch, soothing music, reading or walks to quell agitation. Speak in a reassuring voice. Do not try to restrain the person during a period of agitation.

- Allow the person to do as much for himself as possible—support his independence and ability to care for himself.

- Acknowledge the confused person's anger over the loss of control in his life. Tell him you understand his frustration.

- Distract him with an activity or change the topic of conversation. Allow him to forget the troubling incident. Confronting a confused person may increase anxiety.

Paranoia: Seeing a loved one suddenly become suspicious, jealous, or accusatory is unsettling. Remember, what the person is experiencing is very real to them. It is best not to argue or disagree. This, too, is part of dementia. Try not to take it personally.

- If the confused person suspects money is "missing," allow him/her to keep small amounts of money in a pocket or handbag for easy inspection.

- Help them look for the object and then distract them into another activity. Try to learn where the confused person's favorite hiding places are for storing objects, which are frequently assumed to be "lost." **Avoid arguing.**

- Try nonverbal reassurances like a gentle touch or hug. Respond to the accusation and then assure the person (i.e., "I see this frightens you; stay with me, I won't let anything happen to you.")

Orientation:

- Mr. Miller will likely require intermittent supervision. Although leaving him alone in his home environment for one to two hours during the day is acceptable, he should **never** leave the home unaccompanied. Because of his difficulties with orientation and memory, he is at high risk for getting lost.

- Reminders about where he is, especially in new environments, may prove helpful. Point out landmarks for later reference. Avoid quizzing, as this may increase his agitation.

Community Resources: The Central Maryland Regional Office of the Alzheimer's Association can provide assistance and information about senior centers, adult day care programs, respite care services, and other supportive programs available in the Baltimore area.

Shirley tried her best to have a normal supportive home environment for Dad, providing opportunities for both physical and mental activity as well as social interaction. For the first month after his hospitalization, he was very positive, cooperative, and carefully followed his swallowing and exercise routine. As winter set in, he began sleeping more, frequently became disoriented in his own home, more overwhelmed, agitated, and frustrated with his memory decline, and less interested in his self-care and doing outside activities. This made things much more difficult for Shirley as his wife and primary caregiver. Each day presented new challenges, as Dad became less active, isolating himself more and more from family and friends. She often cancelled her own activities in order to spend more time at home caring for him.

Dad relied on Shirley more and more. At times, he was appreciative of her help, and other times out of his own frustration, he resented her *hovering and mothering*, and responded to her very unpleasantly. Unwanted confrontations sprung up more often between them. Even though Shirley was acutely aware that the illness caused much of his unpleasantness, there were many days when she was emotionally spent from the constant stress.

About three weeks after Dad was discharged from Good Samaritan Hospital, I received his discharge summary in the mail. I made myself a cup of green tea and sat down to read the packet. Although it was technically challenging and the numerical statistics were way above my comprehension, I was able to understand most of what was included. The medical terms I didn't know I researched on the Internet, making the report much more understandable.

Included in the packet was a detailed admission summary with Dad's past medical history, medication list, examinations, and a synopsis of his hospital treatment and tests. There was a final diagnosis, a list of discharge medications and instructions, diet recommendations and plans, and follow-up directions.

The neuropyschiatrist that evaluated Dad's cognitive and emotional status while he was at Good Samaritan Hospital had talked to us about her findings. Now that I was holding a copy of her very comprehensive analysis in which she gave specific examples from her interview with Dad and the neuropsychological tests she administered, I saw evidence of the things she told us with more detail and clarity. The conclusion of the report stated:

> On neurological testing, he demonstrated severe impairments across multiple domains, including verbal learning and memory, visuospatial construction skills (of or relating to visual perception of spatial relationships among objects), and confrontational naming (to name an object based on a brief description or definition). Behavioral observations suggest that he can also be irritable and defensive, and prone to verbally aggressive behaviors. The etiology of his cognitive difficulties is unclear at this time, although his difficulties with naming, visuoperceptual disturbance, and behavioral problems are consistent with Dementia of the Alzheimer's Type.

There it was, in black and white, "Dementia of the Alzheimer's Type."

PART TWO

Accepting the Challenge

ELEVEN

The door to the wheelchair van slammed shut. It was only because I called the ambulance company on my own that I was even able to travel with Dad. His social worker from the hospital was emphatic. "No one is allowed in the van with the patient when they are being transferred to another facility." There was no way I was going to let my eighty-five year old father, frightened and disoriented from vascular dementia and maybe Alzheimer's, travel alone.

The noise startled Dad. I was hoping the medication the nurse gave him before we left would have taken effect by this time. I was so glad my father was strapped in, because the Beltway seemed a lot bumpier in the van than in my car. My mind was racing, or was it the van? Dad looked up at me for reassurance. I leaned over and made eye contact with him. I took his hand in mine.

"Daddy, it's OK. I will be with you all the way. We're going to a different hospital that is going to help you with your balance. It's kind of far away so you just relax. It's all right if you doze off."

He closed his eyes. I was glad he could sleep.

I would have liked to have closed my eyes also and forgotten the past three weeks and the nightmare he had experienced in that psychiatric facility. I needed to revisit all the unnerving details from this traumatic hospitalization, so I could put this phase behind me and focus on what's next. I didn't realize so much responsibility would be placed on me when Dad asked me to be his power of attorney. I hated the fact that Dad had been involuntarily admitted due to a behavioral crisis. I hated that I had to be the one to sign him in, in the middle of the night, after a grueling, mind-numbing sixteen-hour ordeal in the emergency room of another hospital. I hated that I had to leave him all alone in a locked geriatric unit. What was Dad going to think when he woke up in that strange place? I hated that our family could only visit him one hour a day, sometimes in the evenings and other times in the middle of the afternoon. I hated the fact that the nurses kept trying to reassure me that all of this was necessary for Dad's well-being.

At this psychiatric hospital, I observed my dad in a community setting, where people with all types of psychiatric disorders were lumped together. I had my doubts about this being a productive environment. His confusion, disorientation, and outrage were understandable, considering twenty-three hours of each day were spent with strangers in a totally unfamiliar place. *Didn't the staff understand that Dad's apprehension, anxiety, and fears were mainly situational, due to his new circumstances that were beyond his control?* I hated the fact that during my visits Dad was strapped in a Geri chair like an infant, defenseless and not understanding why he wasn't allowed to get up. That was when I was there! *What happened when I wasn't there?* I hated that they put Dad in diapers, even though he was continent. *Can someone become incontinent overnight?* I hated that he had no privacy and many of the staff's requests were made in a degrading and insensitive manner. *Dad was not used to having nurses "standing guard," while he used the bathroom. He certainly had no problem voicing his displeasure.* I hated that they kept medicating him whenever his behavior didn't meet their criteria. *What was their criterion? Was everyone treated the same way? Was what seemed to me like overmedicating the norm? Was it clinically therapeutic for him or was it just to make things easier for the staff?*

Most of all I hated, that despite many requests during those terrible three weeks, I never once was allowed to meet his doctor and could only communicate with his social worker. I know I really, *really* needed to forget that woman and how crazy she made our family. Every other day she told me something else. "Your father cannot return to his present home." *Does she mean right now or ever?* "Your father needs to be in an assisted-living facility. You need to look at some now because a decision may need to be made soon." *What does she mean by soon?* After a week she told me "Your father needs to be in a nursing home. You should check those out because he could be released at any time." *What? We didn't even have a definitive diagnosis yet!* A week later, "Your father needs rehab." Four days after that she told me, "Your father doesn't need rehab."

I became more alarmed when she said, "Oh, by the way, the state may require your father to go before a judge because this was an involuntary admission."

I asked, "Does he need a lawyer? Can I be present if there is a hearing?"

"That is not necessary," she said. *Not necessary for whom?*

I asked, "You mean to tell me my eighty-five year old father is going to be brought before a judge, and his case is going to be discussed in front of him, and no one from his family can be present? You do realize that he can be very lucid, and he can read and understand English." Thank God, because of my vocal perseverance, his doctor was able to convince Dad to sign a voluntary admission form eliminating any need for a hearing and further degradation.

During that whole experience, I kept thinking how grateful I was that God gave me the fortitude and skills to be an effective advocate for my father, to speak up and intercede on his behalf. I'm sure the staff was delighted when Dad was discharged. It obviously bothered them that I asked a lot of questions and often challenged their judgment and skills.

I was sure of one thing. Before we moved him anywhere, we needed a more comprehensive diagnosis than we received from that hospital, a supposedly nationally acclaimed institution.

Thank goodness, I had a brainstorm in the middle of the night to call Copper Ridge to see if we could have Dad transferred there for their two-week short stay evaluation. Dad was already scheduled for an out patient assessment there in a week, and I was so relieved when Cindy, director of admissions, told me they had a bed open. I already knew Copper Ridge was in partnership with Johns Hopkins Neuro-Psychiatry and Memory Group, so I was confident Dad would be getting a more complete diagnosis. Those two weeks would also give us more time to check out other facilities and options. Our family was in agreement with this plan, and I arranged for Dad to be transferred to Copper Ridge.

Our noisy, bone-jarring ride continued. We were only half-way there, but Dad was already awake. How could that be? *Think fast,* I said to myself. Almost instinctively, I heard myself singing *You're a grand old flag, you're a high flying flag, and forever in peace may you wave.* Dad chimed in, remembering every word, even the line I could never remember, *Where there's never a boast or brag.* We joyfully concluded, *Should auld acquaintance be forgot, keep your eye on the grand old flag.* Together we sang any song I could think of until we finally pulled up in front of Copper Ridge.

I took a minute to regain my composure. As the van's ramp was lowered, I was relieved to see Shirley and a staff member from Copper Ridge warmly greeting Dad. I knew he was apprehensive and undoubtedly thinking,

"What's next?" So was I!

"This looks like a nice place," Dad said as we were led down the hallway to the Baltimore House. Dad smiled when we entered his room. He commented on how clean it was, and how he liked the fact he had his own bathroom equipped with handrails. I didn't think he had yet realized there wasn't a shower or tub in his bathroom. He was delighted to see familiar pictures and other things from his own room at home that Shirley had brought with her. He loved the view from the large window in his room and the window seat where we could sit by his bed. Originally, Copper Ridge planned to assign Dad to a room on the assisted-living side of the facility, but because of his high risk for falls and aspiration, they decided he needed the extra care he would receive from their comprehensive unit. I left so Dad and Shirley could be alone since they really hadn't spent much time together the past three weeks.

I spent the next hour talking to the director of admissions at Copper Ridge, signing contracts, and becoming familiar with what to expect during Dad's two week stay and evaluation. Cindy was easy to talk to. We had been talking back and forth over the telephone for more than a week. She always returned my calls, reassuring me, giving me her shoulder, and walking me through the transition process after a very difficult experience. I had already faxed her Dad's application for admissions, medical release forms, doctor reports, medication list and family observations. Cindy seemed surprised when I handed her the following list that I thought would be helpful for the staff at Copper Ridge.

1. Wears glasses/ requesting an eye exam
2. Has hearing aids, rarely wears them
3. Uses lactaid before eating dairy products
4. Because of swallowing problems, all liquids should be thickened to a nectar consistency
5. No straws should be used
6. Uses nitro, if needed, for occasional angina
7. Please, no ham or pork products
8. Family strongly requests that no Haldol be given at any time
9. Loves vanilla or chocolate Ensure or Boost
10. Has a sweet tooth!

Cindy assured me she would share the list with the staff and they would place it in Dad's file. She also gave me a *Family Handbook*, pharmacy information, and the date for Dad's comprehensive evaluation with the Copper Ridge team. As we walked around the building, Cindy introduced me to people on staff.

Copper Ridge is a non-restraint, 126-bed assisted-living and skilled nursing community exclusively dedicated to the care of people coping with the effects of memory-impaired illnesses, including dementia and Alzheimer's disease. The facility has an assisted-living side and a more comprehensive side for those residents needing additional medical care. The building was designed to accommodate all levels of care. There is carpeting throughout the facility including the resident's rooms, secure handrails in all hallways, and several courtyards and gardens that are accessible and secure. Copper Ridge is divided into five "houses," each unique in style and accessories, with familiar themes making it easier for residents to recognize their home. Each of the three houses on the assisted-living side has a community kitchen/dining room where meals are served and some activities take place. The other houses have only dining rooms. There are large community rooms where groups of residents can enjoy daily activities, special programs, and entertainment.

Cindy gave me the door code our family would need to enter each house throughout the building. She told me that at Copper Ridge, residents could have visitors anytime, and showed me the outside call bell we needed to ring when visiting after eight at night.

While touring I kept wondering what was happening with Dad. As I rounded the corner leaving Cindy's office, I saw Dad and Shirley sitting on the couch in the fireplace room, holding hands, and singing *If You Knew Susie*. Tears welled up in my eyes. I could hardly contain my emotions. I knew we had made a good decision in bringing Dad to Copper Ridge.

Shirley and I were in the Baltimore House sitting room waiting for Dad to have his dinner. I was exhausted and had dozed off, when I heard Dad's boisterous voice. Dazed and barely awake, I saw a nurse wheeling Dad down the hallway towards Shirley and me.

"I'm not staying here and no one can keep me here!" he yelled.

Evidently, he told a resident assistant in the dining room that he wasn't going to eat until his wife joined him. Because Dad was a new resident, the aide told Dad she did not know who his wife was. Dad became very upset, refused to eat, and told everyone in no uncertain terms that he "was not staying in a place that didn't know his wife!"

By the time he reached us, he was livid and fixated on this issue. Even seeing Shirley and hearing her loving acknowledgment of him could not calm him down. Dad was so incensed he wasn't able to focus on Shirley or what she was saying. He kept ranting, repeating the same thing over and over at the top of his lungs. There was no consoling him.

I got down on my knees on the floor to be at Dad's eye level, and gently placed my hands on his face so he could look directly at me. I tried desperately to reason with him.

"Daddy, I understand you're upset. I would be, too, if someone told me she didn't know who my husband was. The aide should have asked another staff member if they knew where Shirley was, or tried to find Shirley for you. She made a mistake, Dad. As you always tell me, 'she might not be the sharpest knife in the drawer.' " My attempts to settle Dad fell on deaf ears. He was beyond reason.

Dr. Onyike, Dad's Hopkins physician, had joined us in the hallway, intently listening to Dad's tirade.

Originally he came to introduce himself, talk with Dad, and examine him. It didn't take Dr. Onyike long to assess the situation. Dad didn't seem to have even noticed him. We all knew Dad was having a catastrophic reaction, common in many patients with dementia. I had read that often when a situation overwhelms or confuses a person with a brain illness or with limited thinking ability, they may overreact by crying, becoming agitated or angry, or by striking out at others. This was happening to my father.

Dr. Onyike, a stately, soft-spoken man about six foot four, got down on one knee and addressed Dad.

"Mr. Miller, I came to talk to you. I'm going to be your doctor while you are here at Copper Ridge."

I heard Dad reply, "That's very nice of you, Doctor, but I'm not staying!"

Dad went round robin again with Dr. Onyike, who was patiently and quietly trying to change the subject and distract Dad.

"Do you know where you are, Mr. Miller?" Dr. Onyike asked.

Dad looked up the hallway and responded, "I think I'm in a hospital, but it doesn't look like a hospital."

"Do you know why you are here?"

Dad appeared to be bewildered by the question. Dr. Onyike waited a few a moments for a reply. When Dad didn't respond, the doctor told him that he and the people at Copper Ridge were going to help him with his balance so he could walk better and become stronger.

Dad responded, "I'm not staying in a place that doesn't

know my wife!"

By that time I was shaking my head, thinking that just a few hours ago Dad seemed happy and resolved. I was so hopeful that the transition would go well. Now what?

Chris, the nurse on this shift, calmly approached and asked Dad if he would like some juice. She thought he might be thirsty. Dad thanked her and drank the thickened juice. It was at this point I realized the staff had determined Dad needed to be given some form of medication to help quiet him down. I wondered if it was disguised in this drink.

I watched Dad slowly drink his juice, hoping he didn't stop with just two sips. I felt ill, my mind was spinning. *Was this ever going to end? I'm dead tired. I can feel my stomach tightening. I wished I could blame this abdominal upheaval on the three peanut butter crackers I managed to get down for dinner, but I knew that wouldn't be a correct assessment. This was really, really hard. I didn't want Dad to see my frustration. I prayed I wouldn't lose it. God, could you give me a little assistance here, please? I'm at my wits end!*

Still sitting on the floor and choking back the tears, I took a deep breath and made a last ditch effort to get through to Dad. I took his hands in mine, gently stroking them.

"Daddy, you know I love you, don't you?"

"And I love you with all my heart," he told me.

"You know you're having trouble with your balance, and you are in a wheelchair so you won't fall until you get stronger. The people here at Copper Ridge are good at what they do, and they can help you walk better. Dr. Friedley recommended Copper Ridge because it has a good reputation and it's connected with John Hopkins."

Dad interrupted me to tell me, "It's Johns Hopkins with an 's.' Most people don't say *Johns.*" His lucidity and common sense made me laugh inwardly. He always did correct my grammar, my dangling participles, and my misplaced modifiers. But I really didn't expect it in the middle of all this.

"This isn't Hopkins!" he exclaimed.

"I know it doesn't look like the big hospital with the dome in downtown Baltimore, Dad, but it's connected with Hopkins. They just didn't have the space in the city to make a place with such a nice view and beautiful open-spaced gardens. You love Hopkins, Dad, You know they do great work and are world-renowned."

Dr. Onyike was still kneeling on one knee next to me, and instinctively I showed Dad his identification badge that said "Johns Hopkins" on it. Dad looked at the badge. I prayed he didn't notice it also had "Neuro-Psychiatry" printed on it. I realized immediately I might have made a big mistake. I quickly started talking, trying to redirect Dad's focus.

"Daddy, you know we all want the best for you, so please trust me on this one. Copper Ridge is a good place. I'm sorry one person didn't use good sense, but the people here really know what they're doing. I've talked to many of them."

I was hoping that if something was put in Dad's juice it would take effect soon because I was running out of things to say. To my relief, Dad was receptive when his nurse suggested that we all go back to the dining room together so he could finish his dinner. Dad told her that he was a bit hungry.

Shirley followed Dad into the dining room, while I stayed behind to talk to Dr. Onyike. I was a little embarrassed over Dad's behavior, but I realized it was good for the doctor to see some of the same behaviors that we had been dealing with at home.

Dr. Onyike said, "There is no need for an apology. Oftentimes an outburst like your Dad's is harder on the family than it is on the resident."

His plan was to begin gradually reducing Dad's dosage of Seroquel until it was at the correct level for his specific needs. The psychiatric hospital where Dad had previously been treated had increased his dosage until it was up to 300 milligrams. Dr. Onyike recommended Dad have physical therapy five times a week, and he wanted him to be evaluated by an occupational therapist who could help him get acclimated to his new environment.

Dr. Onyike gave me several of his cards so we could contact him if we had questions or concerns the personnel at Copper Ridge couldn't answer. I thanked him and headed for the dining room to see how Dad was doing. He seemed to be enjoying his dinner, talking to Shirley, the incident all but forgotten. I was so relieved and grateful. Dad never mentioned the episode in the hallway anytime during the rest of the evening.

Leaving Copper Ridge tired and drained, I drove towards Route 32. This had been the longest day. I was so glad Dave was there and I could finally go home. It was late but still light out. Only four blocks from Copper Ridge, I saw a policeman signaling me to pull over to the side of the road. Next to him was another officer pointing a radar gun directly at my car. I glanced at my speedometer. It's registering thirty. I had no idea what the speed limit was on Obrecht Road.

I took a deep breath. The officer looked at my license and saw that I lived in Towson. He asked me if I was familiar with this area.

I responded by telling him, "My dad was just admitted to Copper Ridge today and this is only the second time I've been here."

The officer replied, "The speed limit is twenty-five, and we regularly patrol this area." *They regularly stood at the bottom of this small hill with their radar guns!* After talking to the other officer, I saw him writing in his book. *Oh well, this is out of my control now. This just added to the drama of the day.*

The officer returned and gave me back my license. He handed me a warning ticket. He told me, "This is just to let you know we met today." Relieved I didn't have another crisis to deal with, I thanked him and headed for home.

TWELVE

I reached for the telephone, half startled, half awake, and squinting to see what time it was. I realized I must have finally fallen asleep. The woman identified herself as Chris, a nurse from Copper Ridge. *Now what?*

When getting Dad ready for bed the night before, his caregiver noticed multiple bruises on his body, one in particular on his left thigh was about eighteen inches long. They were disturbed about the bruises and asked if we were aware of them. Chris told me the bruises were different from the purplish black-and-blue marks on his arms, caused by taking prednisone for his polymyalgia rheumatica. I told her that we were only able to see my father for one hour a day at the previous hospital and he was always dressed. No one ever noticed anything unusual. I could hear the concern in her voice which frightened me a bit since I knew the bruises could only have happened at the other facility where Dad had fallen several times. I had received phone calls on those occasions when he had fallen, but no one had ever mentioned any bruises.

Chris reported that Dad had rolled out of bed last night, but he was checked by Lorrie, their physician assistant and was doing fine. I asked Chris what kind of night Dad had and she said, "He was a little restless, but he did get some sleep." I thanked her for calling and told her I would be in later. I told her I would talk to Shirley and Dave and let them know what happened.

The staff at Copper Ridge was very aware that Dad was a high risk for falling due to his poor balance and difficulty with walking. Being on the comprehensive side at Copper Ridge, he was given a bed that could be lowered close to the floor. As an extra precaution, a thick gym mat was placed next to his bed at night and a sensor was placed by his pillow to alert the staff when he was getting out of bed. I asked one of his nurses why they didn't use a regular hospital bed with side rails that could be raised to prevent falls. She explained that dementia residents often get disoriented and confused, and frequently try to climb over the rails, other times they get their arms or legs caught between the side rails, putting them in more danger. I had noticed that the mattress on Dad's bed was indented in the middle, making the sides somewhat higher to help protect him.

Shirley had been staying with us the past three weeks. Understandably, with everything going on with Dad, she was stressed out. When I peeked into our den to see if the ringing phone had awakened her, I noticed her bed was already made. I found her note in the kitchen telling me she had gone home to get a few things for herself and Dad, and she would see me later at Copper Ridge. Chuck and I really must have been sleeping soundly to not have heard her leave our apartment.

While staying with us, Shirley did her best to give us our privacy and was helpful with shopping and cooking some meals. She needed to keep busy and be around people, even though she had been by herself and alone when Dad had been hospitalized before. The current circumstances were very different and all of us were on edge because of the uncertainty of Dad's situation. Shirley tried to put up a strong front, but at times her tears just flowed. I knew she needed to get some of this out and suggested she call Jessica at Jewish Family Services, to try to get an earlier appointment. I was so glad Shirley was getting some counseling. She had been showing signs of caregiver's stress—denial, exhaustion, anxiety, sleeplessness, social withdrawal, and lack of concentration—for longer than she would like to admit. In a Health Alerts e-mail I received from Johns Hopkins Medicine, I learned:

> Being a caregiver for a family member or friend with Alzheimer's disease can be so stressful that doctors often think of caregivers as "hidden patients." Because caregivers are often faced with overwhelming day to day responsibilities,

many stop going in for medical check-ups, self-medicate their anxieties with alcohol, don't exercise, and eat poorly. Many experience a mixture of feelings, including frustration, sadness, anger, irritability, helplessness, guilt, and depression.

Wide awake and somewhat aggravated about the news concerning Dad's bruises, I decided to exercise, have breakfast, and clean a little before going out to Copper Ridge. I had tried to maintain my exercise schedule and eat properly during this whole ordeal, even though there were times in the past weeks that I didn't feel like doing either. Having lupus and some other autoimmune conditions, I knew it was important to keep my strength up and not let the stress affect my health. Despite being sleep deprived, I was more relaxed that day than I'd been in awhile, knowing that Dad was in a safe, caring place. In reality, I knew there were still big decisions to be made concerning Dad's care, but this two-week inpatient evaluation was a real reprieve for me.

The phone rang while I was trying to get ready to go visit Dad. It was Beth, Dad's physical therapist at Copper Ridge. She told me she had read the reports I'd given Copper Ridge, and she would be seeing Dad five days a week for physical therapy, usually in the mornings. My cell phone rang again just as I finished talking to Beth. It was another nurse named Sheila who told me that Dad had eaten breakfast, was dressed and shaven, and appeared to be calm and in no distress. I was still trying to get dressed and leave when the phone rang again. This call was from the dietician, who talked to me at length about Copper Ridge's nutrition goals and wanted to know Dad's food preferences. She also wanted to know if there was anything we thought he shouldn't have in his diet. She had already ordered thickened juice for him for each meal and for snacks. Now I was really running behind schedule, so the cleaning would have to be postponed again. It was unbelievable. I had received four phone calls from Copper Ridge on Dad's first day there. *Were they trying to impress us, or could this really be the norm?*

Shirley was in Dad's room when I entered. Dad had a big smile on his face when he saw me. It was nice to see him dressed and in his own clothes with a belt on, something he couldn't have done at the last hospital. There was a man talking to Dad, and he extended his hand as I approached. He introduced himself as Jim from occupational therapy. I suggested that Shirley and I wait in the sitting room for Jim to finish, and we assured Dad that we would be back soon. Dad seemed quite comfortable talking with Jim.

I asked Shirley what time she had arrived and if she had gotten any sleep. She replied, "At nine o'clock, and very little." A nurse told her that Dave had visited Dad after work last night and had stayed until Dad fell asleep. Shirley also said Beth from physical therapy had already been in to evaluate Dad and brought him a self-propelled wheelchair and a walker suitable for his height.

Jim came out to tell Shirley that Dad was asking

for her. He said he was finished his assessment and it was all right to go in. Jim wanted to talk to us, and Shirley seemed torn between wanting to be in two places at the same time. I told her I'd stay with Jim and relate everything he told me with her and Dave.

I took out my notepad. I'd learned to jot things down while they were still fresh in my mind so I could refer to them later. Lately, I've had more "senior moments" than I would have liked to admit. While Dad was in the previous hospital, I kept a log of things I observed. I made notes detailing conversations and phone calls I had with his social worker and his nurses. I also kept a record of the phone calls I made and the faxes I sent. It was the only way I was able to keep events in sequential order as to what happened when and who said what. I can say without a doubt that my log came in handy many times.

A crisis came up with another resident requiring Jim's immediate attention. He apologized for not being able to speak with me right then. He said he would try to get back to us later in the afternoon if we were going to be around. I assured him someone from the family would be at Copper Ridge, and if not, he could try to catch up with us tomorrow. I had a gut feeling that Shirley wasn't going home anytime soon.

Dad was in good spirits when I returned to his room. I thought he was enjoying all the attention he was getting. I believed having his family around and experiencing the staff's reassuring, understanding approach made a huge difference. Knowing Shirley was going to be with

Dad and Dave would be visiting later that evening, I was determined to leave Copper Ridge by four o'clock. I wanted to miss the Beltway rush hour traffic, and more importantly, spend some quality time alone with my husband. Even with the best of intentions, something always seemed to come up concerning Dad lately, which oftentimes changed our focus and plans.

Chuck had been my rock through this whole ordeal. He was so supportive and understanding, and my best advisor. It was so wonderful to have a loving spouse to vent my frustrations to, one who really listened. Even with his own health issues, he was there for me. Two weeks earlier he had his eighth angioplasty and the seventh stent placed in a left main artery. People say that God doesn't put more on your plate than He thinks you can handle, but having my father and husband in the hospital at the same time truly made my plate very full. I was very grateful that Chuck was doing well.

THIRTEEN

Even though there were a hundred different things running through my mind during the morning drive out to Copper Ridge, I felt more relaxed. It was no surprise what an enjoyable dinner out with my husband had done to boost my spirits and energy level. Last night we had vowed not to have any discussions about Dad during our evening. As hard as I tried, the subject of Dad still managed to come up. In reality, Chuck knew it would. The uncertainty of Dad's situation was weighing heavily on me, especially since I was the one handling his financial matters, tracking and ordering his medications from the Veterans Administration, and serving as an advocate for his medical treatment.

It was a thirty-minute drive from my home to Copper Ridge in Sykesville, Maryland. I was trying to concentrate on my driving while sorting out questions I wanted to ask at the meeting this afternoon. Carol, Baltimore House nurse coordinator, wanted to talk with our family. Since it was only Dad's fourth day at Copper Ridge, I couldn't imagine why she called this meeting. I was hoping Dave could leave work early to attend. I knew Shirley would be there.

I found Dad and Shirley in physical therapy when I arrived. Beth encouraged me to stay. She was working with Dad, showing him how to use his feet to propel the wheelchair. Beth also showed Dad how to get up from his wheelchair and back down again. Dad was very unsteady and needed a lot of cueing regarding where to place his hands on the armrests. He seemed to be better at pulling himself up than remembering to place his hands on the armrests to sit back down. Beth was teaching him how to back up until he felt the chair on the back of his legs and then sit down. Dad had a tendency to just flop and there was a risk of him not being close enough to the chair when that happened. Her directions were clear and given with only a single request at a time. Her patience was remarkable. Dad was being very cooperative and was trying his best to do what Beth asked.

Dad said, "I like having a pretty girl working with me." Sometimes he was able to follow her requests, and sometimes it seemed his brain and body were not in sync. At home his balance was not the best but it had improved considerably since his mini-stroke last December. Beth placed a special belt around Dad's waist so she could hold on to him as she walked with him. That day it looked like he needed to be told to put one foot in front of the other to walk. While observing I kept wondering, *Could this be further decline from the disease or the effects from overmedication at the other hospital?* I was hoping it was the latter, so it wouldn't be permanent.

It was about 1:15 p.m. I looked at the daily activity schedule that I picked up at the front desk when I arrived to see what activity was next. It was Baseball Week at Copper Ridge and many activities were planned around that theme. I knew this was right up Dad's alley. That day's activity, Orioles Reminisce, was scheduled for two o'clock in the Baltimore House. Cindy told us we could take Dad to any of the activities planned for any of the five "houses" while Dad was at Copper Ridge. She said, "This will give the staff a chance to observe him in a group situation, to see how well he participates in the activity, and to give us a better understanding of his cognitive ability." When I told Shirley earlier that I hoped Dad didn't have too much scheduled for that afternoon so he could attend this Baseball Week event, she just nodded and didn't seem too excited about the idea.

The three of us were in Dad's room. Again I mentioned to Shirley about taking Dad to Orioles Reminisce. Since there was no response, I thought maybe she didn't hear me. I repeated it a bit louder. Her answer was, "We'll see." Five minutes passed, and Shirley wasn't giving me any indication she was going to take Dad to the activity. I knew she was making her own adjustments in her life as we all were, so I was trying to be patient. I understood Shirley wanted to have Dad all to herself, but I felt this was important for him. I was trying to keep my composure, so I tried another tactic. I bent down and told Dad about Orioles Reminisce to get his reaction. He was a little hesitant at first, but when I reassured him we would be going along with him, he seemed fine with the idea. I waited for Shirley to move, since it was only three minutes until the event started. In my anger, I said to Dad, "Let's go!" and I just wheeled him out of his room, down the hall toward the activity room.

The group was already assembled when we entered. Steve, the activities director, was standing in front of the group dressed in an Orioles shirt and hat, talking about spring training and opening day being right around the corner. I glanced around the room and observed the other residents for myself. Some were sitting in chairs, some in wheelchairs, and others had their walkers nearby. Some were concentrating on what Steve was saying, while others were already out in *left field* somewhere. As a group, most were dressed appropriately, and they were clean and well-groomed.

The door opened and Shirley came in. She took a seat next to me. I took that as a good sign but I didn't apologize for my actions. This wasn't a power struggle between the two of us. It was about what was best for Dad. Since we were paying to have him evaluated, I felt the staff needed to observe him in different situations.

Dad was engaged and responded to Steve's questions. He was telling Steve about Brooks Robinson playing third base for the Orioles, and he pointed out that Brooks won the Golden Glove Award for so many years. "It was worth it just to go out to the game to see Brooks play," he told Steve. He emphasized that Brooks was such a fine guy. Dad had a lot to say. He was making Steve and some of the other residents laugh. He talked about Jim Palmer, Frank Robinson, and of course all the Ripkens—Cal Sr., Cal Jr., and brother, Billy. He even told Steve about the time Elrod Hendricks, the Orioles bullpen coach and former catcher, came to his grandson Craig's baseball practice to give the kids a few pointers. Dad shared the story of Elrod suggesting to a young right fielder, "You may just want to take your hands out of your pockets when the batter comes up to the plate." I had forgotten all about that. Dad was really enjoying himself, although he seemed to be monopolizing the conversation. This certainly was a refreshing change for us to watch after seeing Dad literally talking to a table on one of our visits at the previous hospital. I don't know who was happier at this point, Dad or me.

Shirley and I met Carol in her office around four. Dave called to tell us he couldn't make it, but to call him afterwards. He had to be at work until seven, and would come later. To my surprise there were several staff members meeting with us besides Carol: Bonnie from social work, Beth from physical therapy, Jim from occupational therapy, and Cindy, the director of admissions.

Due to Dad's high risk for falls, Beth felt Dad was safer with a self-propelled wheelchair. She informed us he was only to use the rolling walker with help, never alone. She was planning to work with Dad on how to use the walker from a sitting position. Jim told us that Dad was having a hard time remembering to use the walker in his room. In addition, he was having trouble finding his room, despite having his picture on the wall right outside his room, B-9. Shirley thought if he had a visual clue on his door it would help. She told everyone that she'd bring an American flag for his door tomorrow. The staff thought that was a great idea. I knew Dad, a veteran of World War II and very proud of the flag and his country, would love this.

Jim said that Dad was having difficulty coping with Shirley's absence. So he asked Shirley to schedule her visits later each day. He suggested she come after lunch around two o'clock, and leave before dinner. As I was taking notes, I was thinking this regimen would probably be hard for Shirley to abide by, but maybe I was being unfair. I asked Jim if he wanted all visitors to come after 2:00 p.m. and he said yes. This would probably be better for Dad as he is transitioned into the Copper Ridge environment, particularly since his mornings would be filled with physical and occupational therapy.

Jim also told us that Dad was very personable, cooperative, but his insight and judgment were poor. Dad wasn't sure of his own capabilities and often looked to others for guidance on how to do simple daily tasks. He trusted Jim, but was unsure of himself. Dad relied on Jim to do the task at hand. Dad was also having difficulty remembering the sequential steps needed for his daily personal care.

Carol told us that the staff had been talking privately about Dad's placement at Copper Ridge. Because he had very good verbal skills and was ambulatory at home, they were considering trying him on the assisted-living side as a trial. That had been their original plan before Cindy, the admissions director, talked with his social worker at the other hospital. They were very aware of and concerned about his high risk for aspiration. They told us that the residents on the assisted-living side had more access to thin liquids, were freer to move about on their own, and didn't require as much supervision. They gave Shirley and me a chance to ask questions and express our concerns. The staff felt that it was worth giving Dad a chance on the assisted-living side, and they suggested Shirley go with him to lunch beginning that weekend. Dad would still be sleeping on the comprehensive side of the building. At the time, I was thinking the idea was a bit odd since they just told us to come after lunch. Yet, at the end of the week, they wanted Shirley to go to lunch with him. I asked if they thought this would be too confusing for Dad, and everyone agreed it was worth trying. They were the experts so I put my trust in them.

I suggested to Shirley that if she had her mornings free, maybe we should check out some other facilities that were closer to where she lives. She nodded in agreement. Carol reminded us to be sure each facility we visited had a locked unit and was able to schedule Dad for physical therapy five times a week. She emphasized how important this was for Dad's progress.

The meeting was winding down. Everyone had left except Carol, and she asked us if we had any other questions or concerns. I made Carol aware that one of

Dad's doctors felt Dad may have an overactive thyroid. I told her for reasons beyond our control, we were not able to have a specialist check him for this possible condition. Carol noted this in Dad's chart. I also told her that Dad had poor depth perception as a result of cataract surgery that didn't go well. Carol asked if we could get his records from his ophthalmologist faxed over, and I said I would take care of it. She asked Shirley to please bring in Dad's hearing aids and batteries which she felt would really help him. Shirley said she would bring them tomorrow and wished the staff luck in trying to get him to wear them.

I was already in bed reading, trying to unwind when I received a call from Brandi, a nurse at Copper Ridge. I glanced at the clock while she was talking to me. It was nine-thirty. Brandi informed me that Dad fell twice, once in a patient's room and again after being put in a chair. She assured me that there were no injuries. Dad was given his regular meds, and he was ready for bed. Brandi expressed concern about the large bruise on his left thigh. I thanked her for calling and attempted to get back to my book, but I found myself unable to concentrate and just read the same paragraph over and over again.

FOURTEEN

For as long as I could remember, my father and I had always enjoyed talking to each other on a regular basis. His hospitalization hampered our lines of communication, and I sought ways to correct this.

Dad did not have a telephone in his room at Copper Ridge. Our family considered having one installed but decided against it for several reasons. We already knew he had difficulty hanging the phone back on its cradle. We also thought other residents might come into his room at any time to use his phone. This could lead to several problems beyond those caused by strangers invading his private space. Our biggest concern was that Dad might stay in his room waiting for a phone call instead of participating in the programs and activities that Copper Ridge offered.

When Dad had been at home, I called him often to

remind him of things or to just talk. He always flattered me by saying, "It is the best part of my day." Previously, it was reassuring to know I could share almost anything with him. Lately, I had become more careful about what I told him. I regretted that, at times, I felt it necessary to withhold the whole truth, to omit parts of a story, or to avoid subjects that might upset him. I noticed our phone conversations had grown much shorter. I knew he didn't hear as well, but I wondered if too much information confused him, making him afraid that he might embarrass himself with his response.

I was grateful that, no matter what kind of day he was having, he always took my calls. It made me sad to realize that those treasured moments had come to an end. I knew I would really miss those calls to my father.

I continued trying to think of other ways to communicate with my father. One night during Dad's first few days at Copper Ridge, I couldn't get to sleep. My mind was on overload, and I was physically and mentally exhausted from a very long day. In the middle of the night, an idea struck me. I could write letters to stay in touch, to help maintain our bond. I immediately got up and went to the computer and composed my first letter to my father, triple-spaced, using a very large font, Comic Sans MS 20, to make it easier for him to read.

These letters proved a godsend. They provided comfort to both Dad and me. For his part, he would read them over and over again. I believed, in some way, it helped him keep in touch with reality, both past and present. For me, they had a therapeutic effect. The mechanics of thinking and writing gave me insight into new ways of communicating with my Dad. I crafted each letter to include something to help spark his memory or to reassure him. Dad was delighted every time he received one. He always knew he was loved and not alone. *I wondered if the day would come when he wouldn't be able to read or understand my letters. I tried to put those thoughts aside.*

Dear Dad,

There are so many times during the day that I think about you.

Sometimes I think of something I want to tell you, like the score of the Orioles game or something funny that happened to me.

Other times I think about my childhood and all the wonderful things we did together.

Still other times I draw from your strength and your wisdom which helps me get through a difficult day.

But no matter when I think of you, it is always with love, and it always brings a smile to my face.

Love,
Susie

FIFTEEN

I was so grateful that I was sleeping much better, knowing Dad was being cared for at Copper Ridge. I wished I could say the same for Shirley. Oftentimes I could tell her light was still on in the middle of the night. She was a strong woman, but I didn't know how she was functioning with so little sleep. Not knowing what the outcome would be with Dad had caused anxiety for everyone but even more so for Shirley. I understood that her old normalcy had been shattered. The uncertainty of the future probably caused her tremendous pain and sadness, as she grieved for what they once shared. We were hoping for the best, but I think deep down inside we all knew, Dad wasn't going to return to his home.

While Dad was at Copper Ridge, I made several morning appointments for Shirley and me to visit assisted-living facilities closer to Shirley and Dad's home. Our family had visited several places when Dad was at the other hospital but none were acceptable to us. We knew it was extremely important to find the one that met his specific needs.

The magazine, *Guide to Retirement Living*, and their website at www.GuidetoRetirementLiving.com were wonderful resources for me at the time. They provided a comprehensive guide to services for seniors and their families in the state of Maryland including articles and senior living options. These options were categorized by sections: active adult new homes and condos, retirement communities offering continuing care, independent living, senior apartment communities, assisted-living homes and communities, nursing and rehabilitation facilities, and a section for maintaining independence at home. Each section was divided by county making it easy to locate facilities in our area. I felt I had everything I needed right at my finger tips—telephone numbers, location, number of units, monthly cost range, and what services each offered. This handy guide helped me pick and choose, and shop and compare before making any appointments.

I also did some research on the Internet by typing "what should I look for when shopping for an assisted-living facility" on Google. This search provided an overwhelming amount of material on this subject, as well as a list of questions to ask when visiting a facility. I chose things that I felt were relevant for both Dad and our family's needs and developed my own questionnaire and checklist to take with me. This proved to be an invaluable tool in helping me keep track of the things each facility offered, my observations and reactions to each, and things

I wanted to research more. (See the Facilities Checklist in the appendix)

I was convinced that there was no lack of talent in the marketing and design departments of each place we visited, whether they were run by large corporations or privately owned. Every facility had some type of colorful slick brochure or packet showing smiling residents engaged in all sorts of activities, with numerous bullet points highlighting their services and programs. Some of the brochures even included room and floor plans. All of them were designed to lure the consumer into thinking their facility was *the* place for their loved one.

Most of the people we spoke to were articulate in describing the design of their facility, their model of care, their services, and their costs. All were delighted to show us their daily activity and program board or list, in an attempt to make us aware of the wide variety of things in which Dad could participate. Some showed us a daily menu so we could become familiar with the type of meals Dad would be receiving. We were given a tour and were often introduced to personnel as we walked around each facility. Each person we talked to was confident that their facility could meet Dad's needs and we would be pleased once he became a resident.

I listened intently at each place, taking notes, and trying not to interrupt until all the facts were presented. When the tour was completed, I asked questions from my prepared checklist, focusing on those items I hadn't received answers to previously. These specific questions proved to be the most useful in helping us make decisions as to what was best for Dad.

I was keenly interested in many of the things I became aware of during my observations. I had plenty to digest and plenty to think about. One place had a beautiful lobby, comfortable and inviting resident rooms and what appeared to be a very *homey* atmosphere. Unfortunately, we only saw a few residents during our visit. *Where was everybody at eleven o'clock in the morning? It was obvious that they were not engaged in the activity that was listed on their activity board.* This same facility showed us their locked dementia care unit on the third floor. *How safe was this in an emergency?* Two highly traveled main roads surrounded this same facility. *How safe was this if a resident accidentally wandered off?* I noticed there weren't any handrails in the hallways, just small ledges that protruded out of the wall at arm level. *How much support would this afford someone who had problems with balance, arthritis, or difficulty with grasping?*

Another place had independent and assisted-living as well as a twenty bed locked unit for dementia care. The rooms were a nice size. They were clean and each had an individual bathroom. There was a small outside courtyard area off the dining room. Residents were limited when walking inside to only one long hallway which was lined with different chairs and rockers. Our tour guide told us the chairs were provided, "So the residents can sit down if they grow tired." *What about those residents with walkers and wheelchairs, or those with limited eyesight? How difficult would it be for those residents to maneuver in that cluttered hallway?*

At that place and at one other facility, I noticed all the activities took place in the dining room, not in a separate community room. *How many of the activities listed on their board actually took place at all, when residents had their meals in the same area? We knew this was not the fastest eating population, and that most residents required a longer than normal time for dining, and additional time would be required for cleanup and for setting up for the next meal.* Another site had a beautiful garden area which was locked when we visited. Their dementia/Alzheimer's unit was on the fourth floor. *How often did the caregivers really take their residents outside in nice weather? Not very often, I suspected.*

I was prepared and asked a lot of questions. Would Dad be able to have physical therapy five times a week? Was there a speech therapist to evaluate Dad periodically since he was at a high risk for aspiration? Not everyone was sure of the answers, and one person told us that therapists served not only their dementia care building but also their nearby assisted-living building. Were there any other charges that weren't listed on the price list? Only one facility's quote was all inclusive, except for medications. Others had charges for medical supplies, nursing ancillary services, special needs, companions, transportation, laundry, etc. One marketing director told us that medications were included in their cost. I knew that wasn't correct. She also didn't know whether their facility accepted medications from the Veterans Administration or not, and she had to make several phone calls to other people for the answers.

I wanted to know how their dementia unit differed from the rest of their facility. What was the resident-to-staff ratio for each shift? What was the coverage at night? What type of staff did their facility employ? Were there registered nurses, licensed practical nurses, certified medical assistants, or geriatric nursing assistants—and how many of each? Was there a physician or physician assistant on staff, or did one have to be called in? What was the staff turnover? From my research, I'd learned how important consistency and continuity of staff was for dementia patients. Residents responded better and were less fearful when they saw and worked with the same people. Was special dementia training required for all staff members, and did the staff have ongoing opportunities to attend workshops and training sessions to keep their skills current? Would the staff work together as a team to develop a care plan to meet Dad's needs? How often did the staff reevaluate each resident? What would happen if Dad's condition changed, if he moved to a different level, or if he became ill? Would the family be notified of changes in Dad's care plan? Did the facility use chemical or physical restraints and under what conditions were they used? Were there activities for the residents on weekends?

I could tell Shirley was also making mental notes. At times during some of our visits we looked at each other and both knew we were thinking the same thing—this is not the place we want for Dad. We tried to be objective. We became uneasy when we felt pressured to make a quick decision or when we didn't feel comfortable with the answers we were getting to our questions. Not all facilities had openings. Most had waiting lists during the time we were searching for somewhere appropriate for Dad. Even though we weren't certain about what type of care Dad would need or when he may need it, I was not prepared when we were told that Dad's name would have to be put on a waiting list, and we would have to give their facility a deposit to hold a spot for him.

Shirley and I discussed what we had observed and heard on the drive out to visit Dad. We eliminated some facilities and continued considering others. These decisions were not easy. There were so many factors to consider which made them extremely complicated. I empathized with what Shirley must have been going through. I wondered if she and Dad, like so many couples, had made a pledge years ago promising they would never put their loved one in a nursing home. I'm sure the anguish of such a promise made this decision even harder for many spouses. Spouses need to accept the fact that their loved one needs more help than they can give at a certain point. They need to realize that they have done their best, and now their loved one needs a higher level of care that they can give. They have not failed, they are not being disloyal, and they have not betrayed their loved one if they are not able to honor the commitment they made to each other.

Since Dave ran his own business, he wasn't always able to make every appointment at each facility. He would often walk in unannounced after work. His visits proved invaluable. They were impromptu, not staged, giving our family another perspective. He would call me afterwards to discuss what he'd observed, and we agreed on most things. The process of finding the right facility to meet Dad's specific needs was tough. It was mentally draining and, at times seemed overwhelming, but it was worth the time and effort. The decision had to be about what was best for Dad, not about what was good or convenient for us. Figuring out the finances was complicated, but not knowing when we actually might need a facility was even harder. I was hoping we would get some guidance from the Copper Ridge team at our conference at the end of next week.

Even though our family was going through the process of researching various facilities, I guess I hadn't completely come to terms with the reality of Dad's illness. I was still hoping against hope that things would improve so Dad wouldn't need permanent residential care outside his home. Dr. Onyike's last e-mail gave me a good indication of what to expect. It said:

> Your father is doing quite well. I saw him today, he was in cheer, and had no worries or complaints. The brain scan data and the history support a diagnosis of vascular dementia. More about this when we meet. Thank you for the information, especially your insightful observations. It is helpful. Eventually it will be helpful to have neuropsychological testing (a detailed assessment of cognition), but that is not a matter for now.

I was grateful I had direct contact with Dr. Onyike at Copper Ridge. It was so cool to be able to e-mail him and receive a prompt response to my questions and concerns. It was comforting, reassuring, and made this difficult process so much easier. What a superb doctor!

Dear Dad,

I spoke to Dr. Friedley on the phone today. She is very pleased that you are at Copper Ridge. She knows they have wonderful doctors and nurses there. They will help you get your strength back and work with you to improve your balance.

Dr. Friedley has been to Copper Ridge. She is happy that Copper Ridge and Johns Hopkins are partners. There is plenty of space for you to do your walking inside, and you can also walk in their beautiful gardens when the weather is nice.

Copper Ridge already knows which medicines you are taking. The nurses will give you your pills each morning and again at night.

You are very special to me and I love you very much.

Hugs and kisses,
Susie

SIXTEEN

I really didn't know how to approach what was surely going be a very touchy subject with Shirley. She had been staying with us for over a month. Although she had been a grateful guest and had respected our privacy, I was ready for her to return to her own home. I discussed this with Chuck. I knew he would be more objective because he wasn't as entrenched in this drama as I was. We both knew what a difficult time this was for Shirley and how tough it would be for her to go back to their condo without Dad. Chuck told me, "There probably isn't an easy way or good time to do this, but it may be helpful to jot down your thoughts before you talk with her. You just need to be straightforward with her."

After cleaning up from dinner the following night, Chuck went in the other room to watch the news and to read. I'm sure this was deliberate on his part, so Shirley and I could be alone.

I questioned Shirley about how she was *really* doing and what her concerns were. I was hoping our conversation would lead to the topic of her going back home. We talked for a long time, but to my disappointment, the subject of her leaving never came up. *It was now or never.*

I asked her, "Have you given any thought to when you might be going back home?'

I think I caught her off guard. She was silent for a minute and said, "When things get resolved."

Not losing my composure, I looked Shirley straight in the eye and quickly responded, "You know things may never get resolved—or certainly not right away."

I didn't want to pressure her. I realized she was under a tremendous strain. I also knew it would be much better if the decision came from her rather than us. I felt a little better knowing that at least the seed had finally been planted.

Two days later, Shirley told me that she would be going home the next day. She said, "It's time." I tried not to show my elation, but deep inside I was really pleased. Chuck and I needed to try to regain some sense of normalcy in our lives.

I reached across the kitchen table and took Shirley's hand. I assured her, "Our family is in this together. No one is abandoning you."

No decision had been made about Dad's placement. He was making progress at Copper Ridge. He seemed content and was grateful for the help he was getting from physical and occupational therapy. He adored both Beth and Jim, and tried his best to follow their instructions. He had become friends with Reverend Larson, Copper Ridge's chaplain, from the first day he met him. They instantly connected and both enjoyed their conversations together. Everyone at Copper Ridge was friendly, and most already knew Dad's name.

After being at Copper Ridge for only eight days, Fran, nursing coordinator for assisted-living and Cindy, director of admissions, recommended moving Dad permanently from comprehensive to the assisted-living side of their facility. They both felt that, despite Dad's high risk for falls and aspiration, they wanted to give him the opportunity to try the assisted-living environment so they could observe how he did during his short-stay evaluation. They had discussed these issues at length with the clinical team before approaching our family. We were all concerned what this additional change might mean for Dad, but Fran and Cindy assured us everyone would be watching out for him.

Shirley and I went with Dad to his new room in the Annapolis House, three doors down from the Annapolis House dining room. We reassured him we took all of his belongings from his other room, including his door flag, and nothing that belonged to him had been left behind. Shirley showed him each piece of clothing as she carefully hung items up in his armoire to ease any anxiety he might have about his things. She patiently asked Dad which things he wanted to put in his night table drawers, and which did he want to put in the built-in cabinet drawers.

No one really expected him to remember where his things were placed, but it was an effective way of making him feel comfortable, a part of things, and letting him know his opinion counted.

Dad's new room looked out on a garden with a sitting area. There was a small tree near his window. He commented about the nice view and was mesmerized by the birds flying past his window. Fran stopped by to see how things were going, and later Pam, the family liaison for assisted-living came in to introduce herself to all of us. Dad commented on "all the pretty ladies they have in this place."

While Shirley stayed to talk with Pam, I took Dad to the dining room for lunch. I reminded him to use his feet and legs to propel his wheelchair, and I pointed out easily recognizable items on the way. I asked a resident assistant if they wanted Dad to sit at a particular table. She pointed to a certain chair that one of the residents claimed as her own, but said that anywhere else would be fine. Glancing around the dining room, I saw a group of three men at one table. I thought this would be a good place for Dad to have some conversation and camaraderie with these new guys. Reassuring Dad, I left the dining room. I was able to watch him through the window in the Garden Room, since Dad's back was towards the window. I observed for about ten minutes. Dad seemed happy with his meal as did the other men at his table, but no conversation took place between any of them. They seemed only to respond when an aide addressed them, and then only with a *yes* or a *no* or a nod. My naivety and limited understanding of dementia were obvious. I expected things to be the way they used to be, with Dad initiating conversation or telling one of his jokes or stories. I realized Dad had lost some of his social skills. I recognized I had a lot more to learn about his illness.

Pam saw me watching at the window. I guess my expression showed my sadness. She asked me if I wanted to talk, and I shared with her what I'd just witnessed. We sat in the Garden Room, and with a reassuring smile, she told me, "Many residents, because of aphasia, do not initiate conversation unless prompted or questioned. Some may only respond with one or two words. Some of our residents have problems expressing language, while others have trouble understanding what is said. Unfortunately, some people have problems with both." *Is Dad going to be like this? Is there going to be a time when he won't be able to communicate with us?* I got a sick feeling in the pit of my stomach.

Pam said, "I'm here to answer your questions and to help you with your concerns." She wrote down her extension and e-mail address and said, "You can call or e-mail me anytime and I will try my best to get answers for you or put you in touch with someone who can."

I wanted to hug Pam. Teary-eyed, I thanked her for her time and understanding. It was obvious this past month had taken more of a toll on me than I would have liked to admit. I knew I needed to remain strong because some tough decisions still needed to be made. For now, I gave myself permission not to be the Jolly Green Giant.

SEVENTEEN

I went to visit Dad early, in hopes that I could take care of a few things I'd been neglecting over the past month. He was in the dining room finishing his breakfast. There were only a few residents still there. I pulled up a chair next to his, and leaned over to give him a hug.

"I'm so glad you're here," Dad said. "I didn't think anyone was coming today."

"I'll be here for awhile, Dad, and Shirley and Dave will be here later."

Dad was concerned I hadn't eaten and he offered me some of his food. That was just like him, thinking about me and always wanting to share or help. I assured him I had already had breakfast with Chuck, and he told me, "It wouldn't hurt if you ate a little more. All I ever see you eat is *grass* (his word for salad)."

"I'm really fine, Dad."

Dad noticed the bag I brought with me and asked what was in it.

I took out the checkers game and showed it to him. "I thought maybe we could play a game of checkers after you finish breakfast. Would you like to play a game together? It's up to you."

Dad contemplated his answer. "I don't want any more to eat. I'm not sure if I remember how to play."

"Let's give it a try," I told him. "I think it's like riding a bike. They say you never forget, even if you haven't ridden in years." I could have kicked myself for giving that analogy, but the words just seemed to flow out of my mouth before I could stop them. *Dad was forgetting so many things. I needed to be more careful about what I said to him.*

Moving his plate to the side, I took out the checkerboard and the black and red pieces. Dad's face showed his reluctance. *Were my good intentions setting him up for failure? Would a game of checkers cause him unnecessary anxiety?* I knew he trusted me, but I was a bit nervous about this.

I asked Dad if he wanted to be red or black. I gave him all the black checkers, and then began to set up my side of the board. Dad watched me carefully, and then started to set up his half of the board accordingly. I hoped his slowness was caused more by his arthritic fingers than his inability to remember the game. I asked him if he wanted to go first.

"You go first!" he said.

Dad was a master at covering his inadequacies

and using humor and his inherent quick wit to mask his shortcomings. I realized he was looking at me for guidance. I moved one checker forward. Then Dad moved his piece. We continued back and forth. Dad was relaxed, his hesitation had faded. Maybe it was just wishful thinking on my part, but he seemed to have a strategy. He told me how he used to play checkers all the time with his fraternity brother's father, Mr. Meyers, and what a terrific player that man was.

"I loved going over his house because Mrs. Meyers was a great cook, and no one ever left her house hungry."

We continued our game, Dad being sure he moved his checker to the square he wanted. Before I knew it he said, "King me!"

Wow! I knew he was right on track; he remembered. A small gain but oh how wonderful!

We alternated moving our checkers. Dad jumped me and double-jumped me whenever he could. He had many more of my red checkers than I had of his black. He was beaming when he legitimately beat me.

By this time two other residents had come to watch our game. I asked Mr. Hart, "Would you like to play a game?" Since I didn't know him very well, I took a big risk asking him to play.

Taking a few steps back Mr. Hart told me, "Oh no!" Then he went into a lengthy explanation on how he used to play checkers with his father. Dad and Mr. Hart began conversing and sharing their experiences, while the other residents seemed to be enjoying their banter.

No one was enjoying their exchange more than I. I was

hoping that bringing a piece of Dad's past would spark his memory, but this was much more than I expected. I'd been careful not to bring any game or activity that Dad would think was juvenile. I wanted to preserve his dignity and self-worth.

By our third game, we had attracted a few more residents, who seemed to be comfortable just watching and listening. Dad wasn't distracted by the extra audience. He won two out of three games, but looked like he is tiring. We headed back to his room, but not before he shook hands with Mr. Hart and the other gentlemen. He smiled at the ladies.

Dad was concerned that I left the checker game on the table in the dining room. I told him I left it there in case someone else wanted to use it. He was afraid someone might take it.

He laughed when I told him, "I bought it at the Dollar Store."

Dear Dad,

I just wanted to let you know that I am paying any bills that come in while you are at Copper Ridge. I just paid your Blue Cross and Blue Shield premium for this quarter. I also paid a small bill from the VA.

Your Social Security check is going directly into your account at John's Bank. He asked about you when I was in last week. He misses your jokes and stories.

All your finances are in order.

I'll see you soon.

Love you,
Susie

EIGHTEEN

With everything else on my mind, I needed to think about what to do for Shirley and Dad's birthdays the next weekend. Since their birthdays were one day apart, we always celebrated them together. Circumstances made things very different this year. *Would it be better to just let Dad's birthday pass without recognizing it? Would Dad really know? Was that fair to Shirley? What affect would a party have on Dad? Would he be overwhelmed? Would it confuse him?* Dad never forgot birthdays or anniversaries. He loved having his family around him. He used to be the life of the party, telling one joke after the other, making everyone laugh. I wasn't sure what to expect these days.

I talked about it with Bonnie, the social worker at Copper Ridge, and Carol, Baltimore House nurse coordinator. Both agreed that there were no guarantees, but they felt having a small party would be fine. Copper Ridge regularly planned celebrations for their residents, many that included families. They told me that Copper Ridge had a family dining room downstairs in the Eastern Shore House, and any family was welcome to use it. I only needed to reserve it with the receptionist at the front desk. Bonnie told me that if we needed anything as far as food or supplies, I could contact Lisa, the director of dining and nutritional services. *How wonderful. They were really helping to make my decisions much easier. It certainly would be nice to have some type of normalcy back in our lives.*

I left messages for Dave, Craig, Scott, and my stepbrother, Bob, about getting together for a birthday lunch the following Sunday. Shirley and Dad's other four grandchildren lived out of town. Before I left for Copper Ridge, I made a note to order a deli tray and a birthday cake.

I bumped into Dr. Onyike in the hallway when I arrived at Copper Ridge. He told me he had seen Dad and would continue to decrease his dosage of Seroquel by 50 milligrams a week until he felt it was at a comfortable level for Dad. "We have to do this slowly," he said. "We're looking for a specific mix of meds that is right for your father." He assured me that Lorrie, the physician's assistant, and the house doctors and staff would be observing and documenting any changes in Dad's behavior or mood. I asked Dr. Onyike if he thought Dad was overmedicated at the other hospital. He didn't dodge the question but commented that it was not unusual for residents to come from other hospitals or facilities on too much medication. I thanked Dr. Oniyke and told him I was looking forward to Dad's evaluation conference next week.

As the words left my lips, I felt my body become tense. Panic set in with the realization that our conference was only seven days away. That didn't give us much time to digest all the information we were trying to absorb. *What was going to happen after that? We hadn't made a final decision on a facility yet. How could we make that decision in just a week? How would Dad respond to being moved to yet another facility?* The conference was scheduled for April 13. If we chose another facility, would Copper Ridge expect us to leave on April 14? No facility we visited had a vacancy right away and most thought there wouldn't be any vacancies for a month or two. If a room did become available, we would only have a few days to move Dad into most of those facilities. Before I became too overwhelmed with those thoughts, I decided to see if Cindy, the director of admissions, could talk to me and answer my questions.

Luckily, the door to her office was open, and she signaled to give her a minute to finish her phone conversation. I waited in the hallway to give her some privacy. When she was finished, she was happy to talk with me about my concerns. Cindy hugged me, and reassured me that Copper Ridge would not be pressuring our family to leave on the fourteenth. She let me know that they offered respite care for up to thirty days, so Dad could remain there while a final decision was being made. Her voice was calming, and she told me their team would help us make the best decision for Dad when his evaluation was complete. They had lots of resources, and she let me know it was their responsibility to guide our family through the difficult process. Relieved and a bit tearful, I left her office to visit Dad.

Dad was happy to see me. I gave him a big hug and sat down next to him. He was engaged in a group activity called *sittercise*, exercises done in a sitting position. Dad tried to follow the activity leader's instructions. Sometimes he was successful. At other times, I believe he thought he was doing the exercise correctly, but his movements weren't in sync with the directions. Watching him, I was trying to decide if this was a result of a brain dysfunction caused by the disease, or was Dad not hearing what Chris, the activity leader, was asking? I think it was a little bit of both.

I did the exercises with the group and noticed many residents having difficulty following a simple exercise like marching in place, despite the clear instructions from Chris telling them to lift one leg and then the other. Some residents weren't participating at all, and others were catnapping. I guessed correctness didn't matter. It was enough that they were engaged in some type of limited physical activity.

Talking with Dad back in his room, he seemed in good spirits. I reminded him about his and Shirley's upcoming birthdays, and told him we would celebrate together at Copper Ridge. Dad was silent for a few minutes. I could tell he was trying to digest what I had just told him.

"I need to get a card for Shirley," he finally said.

"No problem, Dad. I will get a card and gift for you to give Shirley."

He looked up at me and said, "What would I do without you?"

I told him, "You would do the same for me if I was in the hospital."

I already knew I had several birthday, anniversary, and Mother's Day cards for a wife at home. I had found them, many still in the original store bag, when Shirley and I were straightening Dad's desk while he was in the hospital. Dad always took pride in selecting a special card for each person and occasion, one with just the right words and message. He didn't remember he had already bought a card and probably just purchased another one when someone took him to the store. Because of that, he had accumulated quite a collection.

I showed Dad the party reminder note I had quickly made on the computer before I left my house. We decided together where the best place would be for me to tape it up so he could easily see it. He helped me tape it up by his bathroom door. Dad appeared to be pleased with his decision.

I brought the wheelchair next to him and suggested we walk in the hallway. Dad was very receptive to the idea. I needed to remind him to place his hands on the armrests before he tried to sit down. I clipped the sensor on his wheelchair to the back of his shirt. Dad said, "I hate that thing. It's always buzzing and falling off every time I move."

I told him, "It's for your own safety, Dad, until your balance improves. It alerts the staff and lets them know that you are trying to get up on your own."

Dad looked up at me for guidance. I reminded him to use his feet to get started. At first he used the handrail to get himself moving. We walked together up and down the long, wide hallway. We paused awhile to look out the sitting room windows. Dad loved the picturesque country setting. Standing behind his wheelchair so I didn't block his view, I began to tell him a little bit about the history of Copper Ridge.

"Dad, in the 1930's all the land that you see, and then some, was part of a dairy farm called Fairhaven Farm. The farm was owned by the Beasman family for many years. Before that there were actual working copper mines located on this land."

Dad asked, "Is that how Copper Ridge got its name?"

I answered, "Exactly," and continued. Dad listened intently.

"The Beasmans lived in Carroll County and were very generous. Frank Beasman was especially concerned about good care for the elderly. In his will he specified his money and Fairhaven Farm would go to the Episcopal Church of Maryland after his wife died. He wanted the church to build a special place for aging men and women."

"That was very nice of him," Dad interrupted. "How do you know all this?"

"I read it on a plaque in the front hallway. I'll show it to you sometime."

I continued and told him, "The church used those

funds to build both Fairhaven in 1980 and Copper Ridge in 1994."

Dad seemed fascinated with this story. He paused and commented, "This guy must have been loaded!"

I find myself choosing my words more carefully when talking to Dad. I deliberately don't tell him that Fairhaven is a continuing care retirement community, and Copper Ridge is an assisted-living facility specializing in care for people with all types of memory impairments, including Alzheimer's. I didn't want to upset him. I knew it was in Dad's best interest not to mention this, but I also realized that my omission made our conversation much easier on me.

What I really found amazing was that Dad had never once mentioned anything about his ordeal at the other hospitals. No one in our family or anyone at Copper Ridge had ever heard him say anything about those terrible three weeks. Was that experience more traumatic for us than for Dad? Was the medication clouding his already diminished short-term memory, or was there a silver lining to this disease? I was just happy that awful experience was behind us.

Dad's hesitancy about being wheeled to another part of the building seemed to fade when he saw his children and grandsons in the Eastern Shore family dining room. Dad was all smiles, hugging and kissing each person as they came over to greet him, but not addressing everyone by their name. Even he was surprised by how many family members had been able to come. I was so glad everyone had made a special effort to rearrange their plans so they could be here. Their presence and support meant as much to me as it did to Shirley and Dad.

There was no indecision on Dad's part about what he wanted to eat. Corned beef had always been a favorite, and his face lit up when Shirley put his sandwich, chips, coleslaw, and a pickle in front of him. We were all chatting while eating, catching up and taking advantage of us all being together at one time, not an easy task to accomplish in recent years.

Chuck made me aware that we were leaving Dad out of the conversation. I didn't think it was deliberate on anyone's part, but I did think sometimes it was hard to think of things to say to bring him into the discussion. I signaled the people near me to try to talk to Dad more. Dad was right in the loop when the conversation turned to things from our past. The room filled with laughter as story after story from our childhood was told, with Dad adding his perspective on how things happened. He interrupted us several times to ask, "Does anyone know how to get back to my room?" His face showed his concern, and we tried to reassure him that finding his room wasn't a problem. He was satisfied for awhile, but then repeatedly asked us about his room again.

Dad forgot about going back to his room when I brought the cake over to Shirley and him. His eyes lit up and he sang *Happy Birthday* along with all of us. Dad had a real sweet tooth, so I didn't have to ask him if he wanted a piece of cake. He commented, "If I knew there was going to be cake, I wouldn't have eaten so much."

We all laughed because we all knew that no matter how full he was, he always had room for dessert.

I gave Dad the first piece of cake. While passing out slices to everyone, I tried not to let my annoyance towards Shirley show. It really bothered me when she didn't let Dad do things we all knew he could do himself. I knew he was perfectly capable of cutting his cake without her assistance, even with his arthritic fingers. I realized her role as wife and caregiver was changing, so I was trying to be more understanding and patient. At times it got to me, but I decided not to let it ruin this wonderful day we were all having.

Shirley's eyes welled up with tears as she read Dad's birthday card to her. I knew she appreciated my effort in getting Dad to sign it, even though his lettering and spacing were far from perfect. I knew he would want to sign the card I brought yesterday, like he always did. I had prepared a *cheat sheet* for him to copy just in case there were problems. It took some coaxing and a lot of patience, but once he got started, he was very determined. Dad was very proud of his accomplishment when he had finished. He wrote on the front of the envelope, "My Dearest Shirley."

NINETEEN

I felt the tension building inside me as Chuck and I drove out to Copper Ridge for our family's early morning evaluation conference. We didn't talk much, each of us immersed in our own private thoughts. All kinds of scenarios were going through my head in anticipation of what Dad's next step might be. Chuck sensed my apprehension and took my hand and gently kissed it. I looked at him and smiled. Words were not necessary. It always amazed me how he knew exactly what I need. How blessed I am.

Shirley, Dave, and many of the Copper Ridge team were already in the Institute conference room when we arrived. Other staff came in as we were seated. We waited for Dr. Onyike to join us. *I couldn't believe how many people were there. It was nice to see so many familiar faces, but I didn't anticipate eight staff from Copper Ridge to be involved.*

As Cindy, director of admissions, introduced the Copper Ridge team, Dr. Onyike came in and apologized for the delay. He had been at the Outpatient Assessment Clinic, and his examination had taken longer than expected.

Dr. Onyike began by asking Shirley, Dave, and me to give our impressions of what had been happening with Dad over the past few years, and what our concerns were. I was caught a little off guard by his request. I chose my words carefully, not wanting to overstate or understate the situation. I realized what an impact this might have on their assessment. Dr. Onyike took notes as each of us talked.

Dr. Onyike gave a brief summary of Dad's medical history and a synopsis of what he had observed during the past two weeks. According to him, Dad's main problems were dementia, frailty, impaired gait, and behavioral disturbance. He believed Dad had mild dementia due to cardiovascular disease with the possibility of having Alzheimer's also. *That really knocked the wind out of me. I felt the tears forming. I tilted my head down for a moment and covered my eyes with my hand. I took a deep breath. I needed to stay focused and try to digest all that was being said. This was really hard.*

When Dad was hospitalized with a mild stroke, I had read an Alzheimer's Association booklet that stated:

> Vascular dementia, often considered the second most common type of dementia, refers to impairment caused by reduced

blood flow to parts of the brain. One type may develop after a single major stroke blocks blood flow to a large area of the brain tissue. Another kind formerly called *multi-infarct dementia*, can occur when a series of very small strokes clog tiny arteries. Individually these strokes are too minor to cause significant symptoms, but over time their combined effect becomes noticeable. Symptoms of vascular dementia can be similar to Alzheimer's disease. They include problems with memory, confusion, and difficulty following instructions. In some cases, the impairment associated with vascular dementia may occur in steps, rather than in the slow, steady decline seen in Alzheimer's disease. It is not uncommon to see a combination of both. This combination is often referred to as *mixed dementia*, a condition in which Alzheimer's disease and vascular dementia occur at the same time.

Each member of the team, representing their different departments, gave their assessment of Dad's progress. Fran, assisted-living nurse coordinator, felt Dad was transitioning fairly well to the routines on this side of the building, but she was concerned about his frailty and high fall risk. Since being transferred to assisted-living, there had not been any behavioral disturbances, and Dad was usually very personable and cooperative.

Beth, Dad's physical therapist, felt he was making good progress, but he had a long road ahead of him. It was her goal to improve his balance and gait to the point where he would not have to use a wheelchair or walker. She said Dad was so eager to please and he tried hard when he came in for therapy, although he sometimes failed to understand even simple directions. He did much better when he was shown exactly what she wanted him to do.

I continued to take notes as each member of the team reported on their observations. Jim, Dad's occupational therapist, talked about the difficulties Dad was having with motor planning or dyspraxia, which impacted his ability to think, plan, and carry out simple tasks. Jim believed Dad was unsure of his own capabilities, and because he had a hard time remembering the sequential steps needed to perform his own self-care tasks, he was hesitant about trying. *Now I am starting to understand why Dad avoided taking showers at home. Just think how many steps there are and how many things you have to remember just to take a shower. It's second nature to most of us. We don't give it much thought. However, for someone suffering with dementia, taking a shower can be overwhelming.*

Dr. Onyike reviewed Dad's prognosis. He told us it was difficult to predict, but the average life span after diagnosis, especially with Alzheimer's disease, was eight years but it can be as long as twenty years. *Holy cow!* Dad's prognosis was influenced by both his frailty and *comorbidity*. I asked Dr. Onyike to define comorbidity, and he told us that it was the presence of one or more disorders or diseases in addition to a primary one. Dr. Onyike planned to decrease Dad's dosage of Seroquel gradually with the goal of maybe stopping this medication. Hopefully they could rely on Zoloft, which he believed would help increase Dad's mobility. He told us that Dad would need physical therapy five times a week to build up his strength and teach him how to be more proficient at using a wheelchair and walker.

Because dyspraxia affected Dad in many areas, Dr. Onyike wanted him to continue to have occupational therapy. That also dictated the need for twenty-four hour supervision, cues, prompts, and assistance. Dad would need residential and neuropsychological care either at Copper Ridge or at another facility. The team's consensus was that Dad could no longer care for himself.

My heart sank. Bottom line—Dad was never coming home.

Dr. Onyike excused himself to return to his patients at the assessment clinic. Before he left, he told us he would make a copy of his report for each of us. *I was so grateful and impressed with Copper Ridge's team. I couldn't help thinking how this conference was so completely opposite from the run-around I received at the psychiatric hospital where Dad had been previously. How could he have spent three weeks in that world-renowned facility and we received so few answers? Those people were supposed to be giving families direction. Instead, Dad was discharged without any guidance whatsoever.*

Cindy asked if we had any questions or concerns, or if we needed clarification on something that was said during the conference. I asked if the team thought we could take

Dad out for a few hours in a couple of weeks so he could attend our family's Passover Seder. They were familiar with what a Seder was, since Fairhaven, their associated nearby retirement community, held one every year for the Jewish residents in both facilities. The team wanted to know some more details before giving an answer. I explained that the Miller family had been getting together for the first Seder each year for over eighty years and between thirty and forty people attended. In the past, Dad always led the service until his memory began to fail him to the point he was uncomfortable and no longer wanted to have that responsibility. Because of his fragility and high fall risk, the team thought it would be too hard for him to attend, too hard on us, and too overwhelming for Dad to be around that many people. Dad would not be able to attend the Seder at Fairhaven for all the same reasons. I guess I really could have answered my own question after listening to all that had been said earlier at the conference, but I wanted Shirley and Dave to hear it directly from the team.

How disappointing this was for all of us. Dave had put together a DVD of pictures and video from past Seders to give to each family and he was looking forward to sharing it with everyone. Maybe next year, but I have a gut feeling that may never happen. I needed to come up with an alternative plan so we could all be together to celebrate the holiday in whatever way would be best for Dad. I had time to give this some thought. Now I needed to take advantage of this break before Shirley, Dave, and I met with Cindy to go over some financial matters.

Chuck said his goodbyes and told me he was going to the gym. He would meet me at home later. He thought the financial meeting should be just between the three of us. I went to the coffee shop to grab a snack before our next meeting began.

Cindy reviewed the cost for the various levels of care at Copper Ridge, as well as other items that were an extra expense. *No one realized that I had asked Cindy to please do me a favor and moderate this meeting with all of us. I didn't know when we would all be together again. As Dad's power of attorney I needed everyone to understand his present financial picture and to be aware of things for the future. We had some huge decisions to make, and I didn't want everything to rest on my shoulders alone. I needed everyone to be on the same page. I needed to know they were willing to accept some of the responsibility for Dad's total care.*

To my surprise, Cindy told us that Dad needed to qualify if we chose to have him stay at Copper Ridge. She handed me more financial forms that had to be completed. I never thought about Dad not qualifying for admission to any facility, but knowing his financial picture, I worried he might not be accepted. *Then what?*

Cindy thought the fact that Dad had a long-term care policy would be an asset for him being accepted, but there were many other factors for Copper Ridge to consider. I asked her, "What happens if Dad runs out of funds?" She told us a little bit about Medicaid, but said it was only available to residents on the comprehensive side of Copper Ridge, not the assisted-living side. She said Copper Ridge had personnel to help with that process if it developed down the road. We all listened intently while Cindy presented all her information.

My mind was racing. While my brother and I both shared the responsibility of having Dad's power of attorney, I had been the one taking care of his finances for the past two years, since I had more time to devote to that responsibility. I was very aware of Dad's circumstances. Even though Dad had a long-term care insurance policy, there was a significant gap between what it covered and what Copper Ridge charged monthly. That gap would widen as the length and level of his care changed.

I was really taken aback when the discussion turned to what the role of the power of attorney was, and who is obligated to pay Dad's bills if and when his funds were depleted. Shirley was under the impression that the power of attorney was responsible for using his or her own funds to pay for Dad's care. I looked across the table at Dave. He looked like he was going to jump out of his chair. I tried to remain calm. We were all tired and stressed. The discussion got intense. I was so glad Cindy was there to clarify what the durable power of attorney for financial matters actually entailed. She told us having someone's durable power of attorney allows one, as the person's representative, to make decisions about that person's money and/or property. Copper Ridge could *ask* the power of attorney to use that money to pay for the person's care, but could not *require* the POA to use his or her own money to pay for that care.

Dave, in a firm and surprisingly composed tone, asked Shirley if she was clear on what Cindy has just told us.

Without making eye contact with any of us, Shirley nodded yes, but didn't comment any further. The room was silent. I glanced at Cindy, and I could tell she was waiting for me to speak.

Finally I said, "No matter what our emotions are right now, we still need to resolve this financial matter whether Dad stays at Copper Ridge or goes to another facility." *I definitely needed this matter resolved that day so I could plug in the numbers and make it work.* After a very draining and passionate discussion, the three of us decided to use Dad's savings to make up for any monthly deficits. I told Shirley and Dave I would keep them informed concerning Dad's financial status. A secretary politely interrupted so Cindy could take an important long distance phone call. Dave excused himself and left for work. He told me he'd call me later.

That left just Shirley and me in the conference room. I didn't want a confrontation, but I sensed one coming. Shirley attempted to clarify her remarks. I realized she was under more strain that any of us, but her explanation did not satisfy me. I remained steadfast as to what we all heard. I made it clear what my legal responsibilities were as Dad's POA, what I was willing to undertake both as his POA and his daughter, and what I was not. *Shirley didn't expect me to be so self-assured. I even surprised myself.*

Before Shirley could respond, Cindy returned and apologized for having to leave. She couldn't have picked a better time to come back. She went over a few more points, before we concluded that stressful meeting.

I told Shirley I'd see her and Dad later. I had a slight

headache. *I needed some space and some time to think and relax. I decided to grab lunch at Zi Pani Cafe and walk around Kohl's Department Store before returning to Copper Ridge.*

Dad was in physical therapy when I returned. I sat on the couch next to Shirley and waited for him to finish. The subject of the POA was never brought up again.

Later that evening I reviewed the notes I had taken at our conference. I transcribed and saved them to Dad's folder on my computer. I was still unclear about the possibility of Dad having both vascular dementia and Alzheimer's disease, so I e-mailed Dr. Onyike for clarification. His response to me was the following:

> It is my opinion that your father has vascular dementia, but the possibility exists that he has Alzheimer's disease or both (the separation of the two is not always clear cut). His dementia is mild (yes, broadly speaking the clinical staging is similar, since the focus is on the clinical appearance rather than the actual pathology).

I had a difficult time falling asleep that night.

TWENTY

As the days and weeks passed, each of us got into more of a routine. I liked to get up early, exercise, have breakfast with Chuck, and then go visit Dad. Sometimes Shirley was already there, but most of the time she arrived at Copper Ridge after me. She stayed most of the day and sometimes into the early evening. Shirley chose to do Dad's laundry at home rather than use the laundry service at Copper Ridge. This not only saved money, it gave her the opportunity to play an active role in his caregiving. Shirley didn't say much about it, but I imagined it must have been difficult for her to relinquish many of her caregiver responsibilities to the Copper Ridge staff, even though intellectually she knew she was not able to care for Dad by herself. Dad had been dependent on her for so long, and suddenly all that was gone.

Dave visited many days after work. When Dave

stopped by late at night, Dad was often ready for, or in bed. He would frequently lie on the safety gym mat next to Dad's bed, and they'd talk and reminisce. Dave told me sometimes he would be talking away, not even realizing that Dad had fallen asleep. He added, "I treasure these visits because we have some of the best conversations, just the two of us."

Many times Dave brought his dog, Tymber, along with him during his visits. Tymber was a sheba imu, and because the dog rarely barked, she was the perfect breed to bring to an assisted-living facility. Copper Ridge allowed dogs to visit the residents as long as the visitors provided the proper papers and immunization history for their pets. They also had a program where volunteers regularly visited with their dogs. Dad was not the only one that liked Tymber. Many of the residents responded favorably when Tymber was around. One lady liked to walk Tymber up and down the hallways. Dave said the lady didn't say much, but came over when she saw Tymber, took Tymber's leash, and away they went. Tymber seemed to like all the attention.

Dave brought a small television for Dad to keep in his room. Remembering how to work the TV and keeping track of the remote could sometimes pose a problem. Dad always liked to watch *The Price is Right*, and re-runs of *Mash* and *The Lawrence Welk Show* at home. Dave thought Dad's having a television in his room at Copper Ridge might provide some company for him when we weren't around.

Dad's days were filled with physical and occupational

therapy. He didn't mind it because he knew his balance wasn't the best. His eyes always lit up when Beth, his physical therapist, came to get him. He enjoyed working with her. Shirley and I often went with him. Beth wanted us to see his strengths and weaknesses so we could chart his progress. She was working on helping Dad remember to back up to a chair until he felt it on the back of his legs and getting him to use the armrests to help him sit down. He was having a difficult time with this, but with enough repetition, he could hopefully master this skill. At times, Beth showed us things we could do with him in his room to help build up his strength. Before Dad left physical therapy each day, he always said to Beth, "It's been an honor and a pleasure."

Jim, Dad's occupational therapist, usually worked with Dad in his room showing him the best way to get in and out of bed, how to use the bathroom, and how to maneuver about in his room. He also worked with Dad in the Copper Ridge hallways to help him find his own way to and from different locations. Dad was very fond of Jim and they had an excellent rapport.

Although his therapy was very important, the staff encouraged Dad to participate in the daily planned activities whenever possible. Copper Ridge had a well-planned monthly calendar of activities which usually centered on a weekly theme that included sittercise; sing-a-longs; music therapy and entertainment; reminisce; and physical, sensory, or intellectual stimulation. Most of those activities were done in either small or large groups, and it was a time when residents could be together in a positive, creative way, no matter what their capacities for participation. Residents had a chance to socialize, react, express, and be involved. It wasn't about them "getting it right," it was about giving them opportunities to feel valued, to be honored and appreciated, to boost their self-esteem.

At Copper Ridge the activity team prepared an activity assessment on each resident and noted their leisure interests, hobbies, and whether they enjoyed television, movies, music, collecting, parties, museums, sports, travel, games, cooking, gardening, etc. They wanted to know if the resident did any volunteering, was a member of a club or organization, enjoyed being around children, liked animals or had a pet? Often that information could be obtained through conversations with the resident, but for those with diminished verbal skills and poor recall, discussions were held with the family. The team also kept a log on each resident's participation in each activity, so they could track ability level, likes and dislikes, and plan other activities geared specifically for that individual.

The staff at Copper Ridge encouraged families to participate in the activities with their loved ones. There were always daily activity schedules at the front desk so a visitor could easily locate their family member or plan to go to an activity with the resident while they were visiting. An activity calendar was included in the Copper Ridge newsletter that was e-mailed or mailed to each family monthly. This advance notice provided family members with the opportunity to plan their visit ahead of time. From the variety of activities on these sheets,

I could only imagine the amount of planning involved for the staff working with this type of population in a communal-living setting.

Often people were uncomfortable about visiting residents with dementia because they didn't know what to say, what to do, or how to act. Copper Ridge provided activity books at the front desk for family and visitors to borrow when they visited. These books were filled with ideas and pictures to engage the resident, making the visit more stimulating and meaningful for both the resident and their visitor.

Dad liked when we went with him to an activity. He loved to sing, and he remembered all the lyrics to most of the songs from the '30s and '40s. Music brought him such joy and pleasure, as it did for most of the residents. Dad's face was so animated when he sang, especially if it was a patriotic song or one from World War II. He adored the programs with accordionists, guitarists, and other individuals who visited on a regular basis. Special entertainment was scheduled periodically within each month. *It was such a delight to see him involved. At home he spent a good part of the day sleeping. I guess that was just easier for him.*

While watching the other residents, I noticed that many who seemed so removed and so totally oblivious to what was going on, responded well to music. For those that were confused or upset, music was soothing and seemed to calm their fears and anxieties. They seemed to become whole again, even if it was only temporary. It was really a powerful phenomenon and fascinating to watch.

The music therapist regularly used rhythm instruments with the residents. I was astounded the first time I saw her walking around the circle giving out tambourines, rhythm sticks, maracas, and other musical instruments to everyone. *I pictured myself, as a kindergarten teacher many years ago, giving out the same types of instruments to five-year-olds. What a defining moment that was for me, with the realization that I had come full circle in the life process.* There was nothing juvenile or degrading about this experience for the residents. Just about everyone participated, and the room was alive with a conglomeration of sounds and smiling faces. *It didn't get any better than that.*

TWENTY-ONE

It was two days before Passover. Dad was sitting in his lounge chair admiring the photo of a family enjoying a *Seder* that I'd taped on the wall next to his bathroom. I brought a chair and sat down in front of him and we talked a little about the holiday. It didn't surprise me when he told me he didn't realize it was Passover already. I told him we were all going to have Seder at Copper Ridge in the family dining room. He didn't mention the traditional Miller family Seder at all, and I didn't dare bring it up for fear that he would become upset.

I didn't plan to stay very long that day, since I had so much to organize and cook before our family could observe the first and second Seder at Copper Ridge. Getting ready for Passover was always involved since no bread was eaten, only *matzah* (unleavened bread). Special foods were prepared or purchased. A separate set of dishes, utensils, and pots were used for cooking, and the house was cleaned so that it was free of any *chometz* (bread products). I'd already finished the food shopping. I had planned an easy menu and had made a list of what I would need to bring to Copper Ridge. I would definitely be using paper products. I went to the Jewish bookstore to purchase a condensed version of the Passover *Haggadah*, which tells the story of the liberation of the Jews from their slavery in Egypt along with the rituals of the Seder. The store manager suggested a child's Haggadah, but I didn't want to use anything Dad would think was too juvenile. I managed to find a Haggadah that was condensed and more user-friendly.

Lisa, the director of dining services at Copper Ridge, was just wonderful. She had no problem with Shirley bringing Passover food for Dad. They even volunteered to keep it on a separate shelf in the refrigerator in the Annapolis House. They knew to use only paper plates during this holiday. Lisa told me I could use the microwave in the employee lounge to heat up anything needed on the two Seder nights. They would supply the matzah, paper goods, and water for us. I was really grateful for how accommodating everyone had been, since I was really tired. My motto that year was, "Whatever works!"

Chuck and I looked like bag ladies coming into Copper Ridge with all the packages we were carrying. We came early to set up for the First Seder. The receptionist saw us and immediately made a call to someone to find us a cart so we could get all the bags downstairs in one trip.

I remember the first time I went downstairs to see what the Family Dining Room was like in the Eastern Shore House. I stood motionless in the hallway, taking it all in. I was not emotionally prepared for what I saw. Some residents were in wheelchairs, geriatric recliner chairs, or Merry Walker ambulation chairs. Some had lost the ability to walk without assistance, to sit without support, or even to hold up their heads. Few were fully ambulatory. Some lay in fetal positions. I realized that most were in the last stages of their disease. I heard a few mutter words. Some cried out, shouted, or made unintelligible noises, having lost the ability to communicate coherently.

I walked towards the resident's dining room and stood in the doorway. I had read that often people in the more advanced stages lost the ability to feed and care for themselves because swallowing had become impaired, reflexes had become abnormal, and muscles had grown rigid. There were several assistants feeding certain residents with what looked like baby food to me. I realized their meals were probably pureed. Some other residents were just sitting at the table, probably waiting their turn to be fed.

I didn't have to remain there but something pulled at me, telling me not to leave. *Who were these people before this disease ravaged their minds and now their bodies? What kind of lives had they led? Did they have families? Were they suffering? How long did it take for them to deteriorate to this level?*

I continued to walk around the Eastern Shore House.

The rooms were the same as on the upper floor. I passed the nurses' station. A few residents sat watching two birds frolicking about their cage. They seemed transfixed. I continued up the long hallway. I heard music coming from somewhere and walked towards the sound. There were about eight residents in the community room listening to a young, energetic woman playing a guitar and singing a *hello* song, greeting every person by name. Some people were smiling, others moved their lips.

My mental wanderings were interrupted when a frail woman, using a Merry Walker, reached out to me. A bit surprised, I looked at her and smiled.

"Nice to see you," I said. No response. "That's a very pretty blouse you're wearing. I love the colors." Still no response. She took my hand. I placed my hand over hers. "Your hands are nice and warm," I told her. She looked up at me and moved on.

I stood there a little while longer, wondering if Dad would be here someday. I said a silent prayer, praying it wouldn't happen. Of everything I saw that day, I think the residents' faces affected me the most—the vacant, expressionless stares. Some looked bewildered, some sad, some anxious, others looked frightened. All seemed distant, lost in their own limited world. I will never forget those faces. *Even though each of those people was but a shell of their former self, I knew there was still a person inside. They were someone's mother, father, grandparent or other relative, who was entitled to end-of-life care filled with dignity and understanding.*

I could see the anxiety on Dad's face as Shirley wheeled him into the dining room. *Was he afraid that we might ask him to lead the Seder?* I immediately showed him where he was going to sit, and told him that Shirley would be sitting on one side of him, and I would be on the other side, close at hand. I reassured him that we were all going to participate in the service together. "It's so much nicer when everyone can take part in the Seder," I said. He looked at me with a reluctant smile. He was so delighted to see his son and grandchildren, but I could tell he was still apprehensive.

Right away, he noticed the Haggadahs were different. I told him, "I think it's about time we had some new ones without wine stains on them." He laughed and agreed, and we began the service.

Shirley lit the candles, and the plastic wine glasses were filled. Dad had thickened grape juice. We sang the prayer together over the wine. Dad remembered almost every word. The pace of the service was slower. We read the story of our people's being freed from Egyptian bondage that happened so long ago. Scott, the youngest grandson present, read *The Four Questions*, and asked "Why is this night different from all other nights?" We performed the traditional rituals of dipping a vegetable in salt water, eating bitter herbs, and spilling a drop of wine on our plate for each of the ten plagues forced upon the Egyptians. Dad interjected with explanations about different parts of the service, just as he did when we were growing up. It didn't matter that some of the names and the sequence were not exactly correct. We listened intently; no one was bored, because that year his account was even more meaningful. That night while we honored our ancient traditions, we also honored Dad, the patriarch of our family.

We sang many of the prayers and songs. Dad's enthusiasm really showed when we sang *Dayenu*, probably the most familiar Passover song. He tapped his left hand on the table to the beat of the music and used his right hand like an orchestra conductor. All of us loved his fervor, so we sang it again. It felt like old times. My eyes were so glossy I could hardly read the next paragraph in my Haggadah. We all said the blessing over the matzah, and then began the festive meal. Dad almost seemed like his old self, but very frail.

Thank goodness dining services left us a cart to use to go back and forth to heat different courses in the employee lounge. Shirley made the matzah balls for the soup. She really does make the most delicious, light, and fluffy matzah balls. We served chicken soup from improvised soup pots, tortilla holders I had bought at the Dollar Store. I brought a Gladware container filled with our family's special recipe for soup farfel, which consists of small pieces of matzah baked with eggs and *schmaltz* (chicken fat). It took awhile for us to heat the food between courses, but Dad just loved having his family around him so he didn't seem to mind. Everyone tried to engage him in conversation.

We were finally ready for Dad's favorite part of the Seder meal—dessert. Shirley brought some cut-up fruit, and I made chocolate chip mondel bread and chocolate nut-covered matzah candy. Shirley brought the traditional half-moon shaped candied fruit slices. Dad commented, "The red ones are my favorite." I could see the tiredness in Dad's eyes, so we sang a few more songs and said our goodbyes.

As tired as I was, Chuck and I still stopped at my cousin's house to see all my relatives at their Seder and to give everyone the DVD that Dave had made. It was great seeing my cousins and aunts and uncles, but I wished I had gone straight home like Dave and Shirley. I was besieged by everyone asking, "How's Bim? How's Uncle Bim doing?" (*Bim was the nickname Dad had since he was a small boy. In fact, it wasn't until kindergarten that he really knew his birth name was Leslie. While calling roll, his kindergarten teacher called out "Leslie" several times before my grandmother realized what was happening and said, "Bim! Bim! That's you!" My father's family and close friends called my dad Bim, but everyone else referred to him as Leslie.*) I certainly appreciated my relatives' concern, but I was overwhelmed by their questioning and didn't have the energy to keep repeating things over and over again. I wished I had made a single announcement to the whole group when I first arrived.

We repeated the same scenario at second Seder the next evening, but things seemed to go much smoother and were definitely more efficient. I guess having a dress rehearsal the night before helped. All of us were pleased that Reverend Larson from Copper Ridge was able to join us, for his first Seder.

Dear Dad,

It was so nice being together at the Mother's Day Brunch at Copper Ridge. I'm so glad Drew (youngest grandson) was here from Phoenix. The picture of all of us that Copper Ridge took really looks nice on your night table.

I'm helping out with the Turtle Derby at the Johns Hopkins Children's Center this week. The medical students really do race the turtles. I sponsor a turtle every year, and name it "C & S Pride" for Craig and Scott. I've never won, but it's just exciting to see the children's faces and hear their squeals when each race starts.

I remember all the times we went around Baltimore together in your truck to pick up donated merchandise for the Children's Center. You were such a big help to them.

See you soon.

Hugs,
Susie

TWENTY-TWO

It was pretty late at night when I retrieved Shirley's urgent message, telling me to call as soon as I got in. *Something must have happened to Dad.* I nervously dialed her number. As I listened to the rings, I became calmer. I realized that if something had happened to Dad, Copper Ridge would have called me immediately, since I was Dad's POA. They had several numbers so they could reach me. *But what if I had my cell phone on vibrate, and missed the call?* Thank goodness Shirley answered.

"Is Dad all right?" I asked.

"Dad is fine," she replied.

"So what's so urgent?"

Shirley had received a phone call from a friend who lived in the independent-living building of one of the other facilities we'd looked at and were considering for Dad's placement. I had put a deposit down to hold a place for him on a waiting list since they were not taking any new residents at the time. Shirley's friend told her that someone had passed away and there would be an opening in their dementia unit. *How eerie was that? Someone had to die so your loved one could have a room.*

Shirley was in a panic. She was rambling so fast it was hard for me to concentrate on what she was saying. She was terrified that the administration would call to let us know there was an opening, and not only would we have to make a decision, but we'd have to make arrangements to have Dad admitted there within three days.

I tried to remain calm, but I knew their procedure and she was right. We only had three days to move him to there or we'd lose his placement. *Was this definitely where Shirley wanted Dad to be? She had been silent regarding her preference for Dad's placement, and I hadn't pushed her to make a decision. I knew it was much closer to where she lived, and had a more Jewish connection, but I was hoping Shirley would choose Copper Ridge. I felt Copper Ridge was certainly a better facility, since their model of care was recognized both nationally and internationally for its excellence. When you combine this reputation with the efforts of the Copper Ridge Institute, the education and research arm of Copper Ridge working in partnership with the Johns Hopkins Neuropsychiatry and Memory Group, the decision would be a no brainer for me.*

I told Shirley that I had not received any phone calls and there hadn't been any messages from them either. Then I asked the question of the day: "Is this where you want Dad to reside?" She told me she wasn't sure. *There was hope.*

"Let's not panic until we're sure there's an opening," I told her.

I promised Shirley that I'd call as soon as I heard anything. I encouraged her to try to get some sleep, but gently reinforced the idea that we needed to make a decision soon and couldn't remain in limbo indefinitely.

What would I have decided if I were in Shirley's shoes? Copper Ridge was certainly an outstanding facility, on the cutting edge of research for Alzheimer's disease and other dementias. Would I want to travel that distance when I was in my eighties when there were two other facilities only ten to fifteen minutes from my home?

At two o'clock in the morning I was in the den glancing at last month's issue of *Good Housekeeping* magazine. Lately, I hadn't been able to focus long enough to read a book. Sleep eluded me. I couldn't turn my brain off. The questions kept reverberating. *Dad was adjusting well and making progress at Copper Ridge. What effect would yet another move have on him? Would Dad even go? Should we make the decision on what was best for Dad or what was best for Shirley? I wasn't pleased with some of the things I had seen at many of the facilities we visited, and was even more concerned about what we hadn't seen at those places when I revisited them unannounced. Do we choose better care over religious affiliation? Then there was the financial aspect of his placement. Copper Ridge was more expensive.*

The phone call never came. I guess Shirley's friend was mistaken about an opening or the opening probably was in their assisted-living building, not in their twenty-bed dementia unit. Despite having that knowledge, it didn't keep me from being anxious every time my phone rang.

Dave and I continued to visit Dad as much as we could. Shirley was at Copper Ridge every day, and there was no convincing her to take a day off. I thought she needed time to do some things just for herself—or just do nothing if that was what she wanted. She, however, insisted her place was with Dad. I couldn't convince her that one of the benefits of having Dad at Copper Ridge was that we trusted Copper Ridge without any reservations. I knew her nerves were shot, so I didn't mention to her that Dad might not even remember if she visited him or not. *Dad may become more independent if Shirley wasn't there everyday and if Dave and my visits were not as frequent.*

I was coming down the hallway when Sharon, a resident assistant, approached me about Dad needing a haircut. She told me the barber was there and he had a few openings that morning. Unfortunately, Sharon said she wasn't able to talk Dad into getting his hair cut. He was adamant about not going to the barber. Sharon asked me if I could try to convince him, and I said I would. Sharon smiled and wished me luck. *Haircuts were another thing Dad had stopped getting recently, so Shirley began trimming his hair as best she could. I guess it was just another thing that overwhelmed him.*

When I arrived at the Annapolis House, I saw Dad walking with Beth, leaning on his walker with an American flag taped to it. He was all smiles when he saw me. Dad used the walker for short trips and the wheelchair for longer distances. His biggest problem was remembering to use one or the other. Beth told me that they were almost finished, so I waited for him in his room.

When Dad arrived, we hugged and Dad sat in his chair where we talked awhile. *I was half listening to his conversation as I tried to figure out how to approach the subject of getting a haircut.*

"Dad, when I was walking to your room, I saw that the beauty and barber shop are open today. Did you know they had one here at Copper Ridge?"

"No," he answered.

"I think I should see if they have an opening so you can get your haircut. It's been awhile, and it's getting too long and thick, especially in the back." *Dad was always so well-groomed, and he took such pride in the way he looked. Now his attitudes had changed about so many things.*

"Maybe another time," he told me.

I stooped in front of his chair so I could make eye contact with him. I took his hand, really not knowing what I was going to say next.

"How about if we surprise Shirley when she gets here and you get your hair cut? I think she will really like that."

Dad was silent for a minute. "I don't have any money," he told me. *Not having any money bothered him a lot. He often brought up the subject, and we talked about it at length. He thought it was better not to have money at Copper Ridge, because someone might steal it.*

"No problem, Dad. I'll write a check and take it to the

office." *I knew Copper Ridge would bill me for his haircut.*

"That's the best thing I ever did," he told me with a smile, "having you write checks for me."

"It doesn't take me that long to write a few checks once a month. It's my pleasure, Dad," I reassured him. "What do you think about surprising Shirley and getting your haircut? I'll go with you."

To my surprise, he said yes. He probably liked the idea of surprising Shirley. I gave Sharon a thumbs-up as we passed her in the hallway. Dad seemed more at ease when he saw another gentleman getting his haircut. I told Dad I was going to go pay for his haircut, and I'd see him in a little while.

As I left the shop, I saw Cindy approaching with another resident who was also using a walker. I said hello, and the lady asked me if I wanted to see her babies. I told her I would love to. She undid a white blanket that was in the basket on her walker and showed me several Beanie Babies. Searching for something to satisfy her I said, "They are so cute."

Cindy discreetly told me that she was trying to coax Mrs. Harvey into the beauty shop." I told Mrs. Harvey, "I just took my father in there (pointing to the room) to get his haircut."

Mrs. Harvey told us, "I can't go in there today because I have to feed my babies." We all took a few steps closer to the door and Cindy told her, "You go on in Mrs. Harvey, and I'll go get some milk for your babies."

The beautician greeted a reluctant Mrs. Harvey at the door, and again Cindy told Mrs. Harvey about getting the milk for her babies. "You won't forget, will you?" asked Mrs. Harvey. I laughed to myself.

Cindy said, "I'm going to get it right now."

I looked up at Cindy in amazement. "How did you come up with that one," I asked

"All in a day's work," she said smiling.

It always amazed me how effective the staff was at defusing a difficult situation by talking to a resident in a soothing, reassuring tone, and redirecting their attention. They acknowledged the resident's statement and their feelings of confusion, anger, or fear, and tried not to correct them. A resident assistant told me that trying to reason with someone with dementia or Alzheimer's would get you nowhere fast and would usually just escalate the situation, causing more agitation, hostility, or fear.

I had personally seen how well redirecting worked. All Copper Ridge personnel including nutrition, clerical, housekeeping, and maintenance staff were experts at it. From observing and listening to them interact with the residents, I'd become better at redirecting not only with Dad, but with the other residents as well. I'd learned what to say and what not to say. Since our family visited so often, some of the residents probably thought we were part of the staff, and they came to us for the solutions to some of their problems.

One time, Alice appeared to be distressed when I said good morning to her on the way to Dad's room.

She said, "It's not a good morning for me."

"Sorry to hear that, Alice," I replied.

"I keep getting these letters telling me I haven't paid my bill for a very long time and I know I have," Alice told me. "I've been shopping there for years, and these letters are very upsetting."

"I don't blame you for being concerned," I told her, "especially since I know you are the type of lady that takes care of things. You never wait until the last minute."

"I certainly don't," she replied in a huff.

"Alice," I said, looking directly at her, "I'll be glad to call and see if I can straighten this out for you, but I won't be able to do it until tomorrow since its Sunday and their offices are closed. Reverend Larson will be conducting church services soon and I know how much you enjoy going to church."

Alice responded by telling me that she would love to go to church, and would I please come get her. Nothing further was mentioned about the unpaid bills.

Allowing Alice to feel like I was taking care of the problem, helped relieve her anxiety. I didn't correct her. I just tried to understand her predicament and offered her a possible solution. Her perception was her reality, whether the problem was real or contrived. All the while, I sought to preserve her dignity.

Dad was not in the barber shop when I returned, so I headed for his room. The door was open and I found him at the sink, admiring himself in the mirror. He turned towards me when he saw my face in the mirror.

"Oh, Dad, you look so handsome. I think this haircut makes you look ten years younger. Shirley's going to be so thrilled."

Beaming, Dad said, "Not too bad for an old fart." He

looked back at his image in the mirror again before he moved towards his chair. He was just tickled with the way he looked. He seemed in a really good mood. *Many residents don't recognize or are confused or frightened by the person they see when they look in a mirror. For them, that person looks old, grey, and wrinkled—not anybody they know or recognize. Their disease has tragically robbed them of the present. Their brain is focused somewhere in their past, when they looked much younger and where their current history and their family may or may not exist.*

I asked Dad if he wanted to sit or take a walk, and he chose to walk. I needed to remind him to use the walker, even though it was right next to his chair. As we walked towards the Garden Room, I saw Shirley approaching. Dad didn't notice her, since he tended to look at his walker, keeping his head down. Beth had been working on trying to get him to keep his head up when he used the walker so he could see where he was going. He did well when she was with him. I gave him a gentle reminder to look straight ahead.

He spotted Shirley and before I could say anything, he left his walker to greet her.

"Wow!" she said, "Where have you been this morning? You look wonderful!" She gave Dad a big hug. I caught up with them with the walker. Shirley told Dad that she brought a picnic lunch, and I figured this was a good time for me to leave. I kissed Dad and Shirley, and told Dad I'd see him soon. *I tried not to give an exact time or day when I would see him next, on the slim chance that he might remember and become upset if I didn't show up.*

I was halfway up the hallway when I heard Chris comment on Dad's haircut. I heard Dad reply, "Not too bad for an old fart."

Shirley called that evening to tell me that Dad was so thrilled with his haircut and all the nice comments he was getting from the staff. She said, "He was so cute about it, and kept checking the mirror to see how he looked." I laughed.

There was a pause in our conversation. She told me, "I've decided that I would like your father to remain at Copper Ridge." *Hallelujah!*

I made several phone calls the next morning. The first was to Cindy, director of admissions, to tell her the good news. She told me to stop by the office the next time I came to visit because I would need to sign different admission forms. My next two calls were not as pleasant. I called the other two facilities where I'd put down deposits to reserve a possible spot for Dad. I was amazed at how long it would take both places to refund my deposit. One facility said my refund request would have to go through their corporate office out of state, and the other facility said I would have to wait until their accounting department could process my request. One would take a month and the other could be up to two months. *Wasn't it ironic that they were so eager to take my deposit initially but not so enthusiastic about promptly returning my money? This really ticked me off.*

Dad had always been a master storyteller. It was a gift. Growing up he seemed to have an endless array of tales to keep Dave and me engaged and laughing. Wherever he went or whomever he came in contact with, Dad always had an anecdote to share.

He had lost most of that talent by this time, so I brought him a story I wrote and shared it with him.

Just Yesterday

I pretended I didn't hear my mother calling me from across the street. I hated stopping our game of "spud" now, especially since I was winning. I only had an "s," while my friends each had "spu." Again I heard her call my name. I knew I'd better get home. Before I left, we made a pact to pick up our game after dinner. Skipping home, I carefully jumped every number on the chalk hopscotch on the sidewalk near our front steps.

The sun was setting when we all met again. To my disappointment, no one really wanted to finish our game. Instead we played two rounds of "Mother May I," and "Red Light, Green Light." It was getting darker, but these warm summer evenings meant there was still plenty of time left to have fun.

Each of us had gone inside to get some money to buy a delicious, icy snowball. Together we walked through my backyard, up the alley, across our neighbor's lawn to the next street, past the Eldorado Food Market, and then up to Doc Robbins' Pharmacy at the corner of Liberty Heights and Eldorado Avenues.

The pharmacy was a small store, but full of wonder. Of course, there were all kinds of over-the-counter medicines and remedies, first aid stuff, medical equipment, and the pharmacy counter where Doc Robbins always stood. Yet, in this tiny space, there was still room for comic books and magazines, paperbacks, cigarettes and cigars, cosmetics, candy and gum, and a six-stool soda fountain selling ice cream. There were pretzels, snowballs, and coddies (a ten-cent fried Baltimore treat combining codfish flakes, mashed potatoes, and onions that's served between two mustard-slathered saltines).

It seemed my whole neighborhood decided to get snowballs on that sultry evening, so there wasn't any room for my friends and me to sit down. After getting my grape snowball, I waited for my friends outside. We laughed and people-watched, while sipping and slurping, checking each other's tongues as they changed color.

We could spend hours playing jacks, playing step ball or wall ball with a pinky (a fifteen-cent classic pink rubber ball with a big bounce). We loved working intricate patterns with a piece of string, climbing trees, bike riding, roller skating, racing our homemade orange-crate scooters, or just sitting around and talking on the wicker rockers on my great-grandparents' front porch. Those were great times—much simpler yet very fulfilling. I can only imagine how boring this *techno* generation would think those times were. They'll never know what they missed.

After reading the story, Dad and I had a lively conversation about our old neighborhood, our neighbors, and old Doc Robbins. Of course, my questions were the catalyst to getting the dialogue started and Dad thinking about the past. I told Dad that when I was a child, I always thought that Doc Robbins lived at the pharmacy because no matter what time of day or night I went there, he was behind his pharmacy counter. Doc knew every customer by name, what type of work they did, and even their children's names. He was a friend to our entire neighborhood, and both Dad and I enjoyed talking about those wonderful times.

TWENTY-THREE

As spring slipped into summer, Dad had made phenomenal progress. His balance had improved so much that he wasn't using a walker anymore. Beth felt he no longer needed physical therapy, unless he became symptomatic again. Dad had become more independent. He was able to move more freely around the assisted-living corridors, although there were many days the staff had to coax him to come out of his room. He was able to enjoy the beautiful outside gardens, the walkways, and the fountain on his own if he chose to do so.

Shirley and I discussed Dad's improvement and adjustment at our update meeting with Fran, assisted-living nurse coordinator, Chris, activities coordinator, and family liaison, Pam. A partial team met semiannually with each resident's family, either in person or by phone. Although Dad had only been at Copper Ridge three months, they were more than willing to meet with our family.

At this informal meeting, Chris gave us a record of Dad's daily activities and told us how much Dad enjoyed the men's breakfast and the monthly Jewish Awakenings class. She informed us that the lady who regularly did Jewish Awakenings would no longer be coming to Copper Ridge to do that program. Chris didn't know if she had a scheduling problem or if there were budgetary restraints. She just knew that this month would be Janet's last one at Copper Ridge. *How unfortunate for the residents.*

Chris said, "Leslie is the best singer on AL (assisted-living), and he knows most of words to the oldies from the '30s and '40s. He just lights up when he hears music." Pam told us how much she enjoyed talking to Dad and how he loved to talk about his family. Pam said that she often found him reading my letters when she made her rounds. She added, "He's a real *hoot* and has a great sense of humor."

Pam e-mailed me once to tell me about one of her visits with Dad. She said she was walking down the corridor to his room and heard all this laughter. When she peeked in, Dad was engaged in a lively conversation with four of his Delta Kappa Pi high school fraternity buddies. All were in their eighties. What a Kodak moment that was for her!

When everyone had finished giving their reports, Pam asked if we had any questions. I asked Fran, "To what do you attribute Dad's transformation?"

Fran said, "Several things come into play. We have found the right medications and the correct dosages that work well for your father, and we know he is getting them properly and at the correct time prescribed." She elaborated by saying, "Many people do not take their medications correctly, they skip doses, mix up their meds, or don't take them at all on any given day. That becomes quite a problem for both the person and their caregiver. Our nursing staff dispenses all medications, and residents are more receptive to taking them without any complaints or arguments." I looked over at Shirley, and we both knew she was right on target on that one.

Fran continued by telling us, "The staff has eliminated most of the anxiety from the things that used to overwhelm your Dad when he was home, like showering, dressing, eating meals at a reasonable time, etc.

Chris added, "Your father is more engaged here because there are activities and programs throughout each day for him to get involved in. He's on more of a routine and is kept awake more during the day so he sleeps better at night."

I asked, "I know this is a progressive disease and is different for each person, but can you give us your best guesstimate on when we might expect a further decline in Dad's cognitive ability?"

Fran's answer to us was, "It's hard to predict. It could happen next week, next month, or in a few months—maybe even a year from now. But it will happen." *Listening to Fran, I wondered when Dad's time would come.*

I told Fran, Chris, and Pam that I was so glad my Dad was at Copper Ridge. Shirley thanked them and expressed the same sentiments.

Although Dad's improvement was a welcome change for everyone, other issues arose. Dad questioned us on why he was still at Copper Ridge. He no longer believed our story about his being there for his balance. He recognized that his balance was much improved. *Although it wasn't easy to admit, there were some days that I wished he wasn't as aware as he now appeared to be at times.* He often challenged us with his questioning. Some days that made leaving him much harder, particularly for Shirley. Dad usually understood I had to leave because Chuck was at home and Dave worked and was very busy. However, he often chided Shirley by asking, "What kind of marriage is this? You're in one place and I'm in another." At other times, he was all right with her leaving, but he would tug on her heartstrings by saying, "This is the hard part."

It wasn't always easy to spontaneously respond with the right words to appease and satisfy his questioning or to stop him from becoming upset when we left. The staff was more than willing to intercede and redirect Dad's attention when those problems arose. They seemed to know the exact words to say to him, and if one staff member wasn't making any headway, another person was ready and willing to intervene. They knew each resident and his/her personality, quirks, idiosyncrasies, likes, and dislikes. Some residents just responded better to one person than to another. No one was offended if another person was more successful in dealing with a resident, because the entire staff worked as a team to meet the needs of each person entrusted with their care.

Dad usually responded well towards the staff. He

appreciated what they were doing to help him. He always thanked them for whatever they did to assist him. They appreciated his verbal skills and enjoyed his quick humor. He adored Basil, his geriatric nursing assistant, who often cared for him in the evenings. Basil called Dad *Boss* after talking with Dad about his job and what it entailed. He found his own ways to relate to my father. Basil once told me, "You never know what will work at any given time, but you keep trying by trial and error." They had a wonderful rapport. I frequently heard laughter coming from Dad's room when I approached. It was usually Dad and Basil having an animated exchange.

When Lulu, a certified medicine aide, brought Dad's Tums to him, usually after lunch, Dad would always greet her by singing the jingle, "Tum-t-tum-tum— Tum!" The resident aides knew Dad. Some would call him Mr. Miller, some Leslie, and others would say, "Hi there handsome!" That would make Dad retort, "Have you been to the eye doctor lately?" He felt comfortable with just about everyone who cared for him. *I believe a trust was built between the residents and their aides, because the staff rarely changed and the residents saw the same faces most of time. That was reassuring for both the residents and their families.*

Not to say that Dad didn't have his moments. He frequently got agitated when he thought it was time for Shirley to be there and she wasn't. Many times he paced the hallways looking for her. Sometimes he would get annoyed when some residents didn't respond to his warm overtures or greetings. *I believe Dad's outgoing personality threw many residents off guard, since many were incapable of responding to his "good mornings" or "hellos." He thought some residents were a bit peculiar and had a hard time comprehending that some folks weren't on his cognitive level.*

Understandably, Dad got excited when another resident wandered into his room by mistake when he was alone. One woman shouted and scratched his face when he told her to get out. The staff had to intervene. Occasionally, residents would enter his room in error when I visited, and Dad would glance at me with his *hairy eyeball* look. *That was what I called his look as a child.* I often walked a resident back to their correct room. One lady habitually walked up and down the hallways trying to open any door with a knob on it. *Was she hoping one of doors would open, so she could leave? I could only imagine her frustration. Where did she want to go? Was she searching for her previous home or for a home that, because of her dementia, no longer existed? Was she trying to find someone from her past?*

It surprised me how many residents, who seemed perpetually dazed, managed to find their rooms without any difficulty at all. *Did they recognize the objects that Copper Ridge had strategically placed in their "house" so they could easily find their room? Did they recognize their picture or their names outside their room? Was it the objects and pictures from their past that their family had placed in their room or did they recognize their room as a safe place to be?*

Dad told me that a man frequently came into his room to use the bathroom. I never knew if he was hallucinating or if someone really did use his bathroom. He told me it really didn't bother him that much, because "If a guy needs to take a whiz, he needs to take a whiz."

As the weeks passed, we were able to take Dad on short outings outside of Copper Ridge. We took rides in the area, or went out for lunch or dinner. Sometimes we went as a family, but at other times we took Dad out one on one. The outings were a welcomed change for all of us. Sometimes Shirley took Dad to Wal-Mart to pick up a few personal items, and it gave him a sense of independence. Dave occasionally took him out to breakfast on Sundays.

Dad enjoyed his excursions with me. I would tell him we were going out for a short "Susie and Me Day." He loved that—it was a reminder of the past. When we went out to lunch, I'd bring his wallet with enough money to cover a meal and the tip. I thought it would be comforting for Dad to know he had money with him. It was also reassuring for him to see his medical cards, personal identification, and the pictures in his wallet. Dad had always paid when we went out before, and I knew he would be upset if he thought I paid for our meal during our excursions.

Although he loved the beautiful countryside and the farms we passed, he was a little nervous when we went for a ride. He repeatedly asked me if I knew how to get back to Copper Ridge, and I continually assured him that I did. None of us ever had a problem getting Dad to go back to Copper Ridge. He always returned willingly and never asked to go back to his previous home.

I believe Dad became so comfortable at Copper Ridge, he considered it his home. One time my aunt called me to tell me that Dad's brother wanted to talk to him. Because of his own ailing health, his brother couldn't come to visit. During my next visit, I dialed my uncle's number on my cell phone, and gave the phone to Dad. He seemed eager to talk to his brother. I overheard my uncle ask Dad, "When do you think you're coming home?" My heart sank as I heard Dad respond, "I'm probably not coming home. I have my little apartment here with my own bathroom. They treat me very well and bring me my medicines." I had to turn away so Dad wouldn't see my tears. I think Dave summed it up the best when he said to me, "Dad's world is narrowing." Even though I knew Dad was in a safe place, getting the best of care, it was still difficult watching him struggle with his dementia. I was grateful for the monthly support groups Copper Ridge sponsored for residents' families and the community. Copper Ridge hosted the Carroll County chapter of the Alzheimer's Association of Maryland. This support group gave us an opportunity to learn more about dementia and ways to cope, as well as informing us about the latest research. We heard excellent speakers discuss a variety of topics, watched informative DVDs, and participated in round table discussion groups.

For me, the support group was a safe place to vent, a place to ask questions in a caring, non-judgmental environment. Pam and Cindy facilitated the group meetings. Pam told us before every meeting, "Whatever is said in this room, remains in this room." People were relaxed. People felt comfortable. People opened up because they were with others who were going through similar situations.

I remember Tim. He was a tall, gentle, private man who asked questions but rarely spoke about himself or his wife who was at Copper Ridge. At one meeting he voiced his disappointment in his family, friends, and his church after his wife was diagnosed with Alzheimer's. "People we've known for years who've been part of our lives for what seems like forever have forsaken us. They never visit, rarely call anymore, and never ask if they can help out. I know my wife has declined, but there still is a person in there and *I'm* still here," Tim said sadly. "I am angry. I feel abandoned."

After that, to my surprise, Shirley spoke up. She was an attentive listener in the group, but rarely said anything. She haltingly said, "When my husband first came to Copper Ridge, a few of his nieces and nephews came to visit, as well as his sister and brother-in-law and another sister-in-law. My husband has one brother who is too ill to visit, but he also has another brother who is in good health and has never been here. It has been a few months now and there have hardly been any extended family visits—and it hurts. It hurts deeply."

Pam, who was a great facilitator, asked if anyone else had a similar experience. Two other people relayed their personal stories. Pam waited until everyone was finished to give her response. "We have to understand that there are some people who just hear the term *dementia* or *Alzheimer's*—and it scares them. Some, out of their own ignorance, are misinformed and believe dementia is somehow contagious. Others don't know how to react, what to say, and are really uncomfortable being around the other residents, so they stay away. Still others shy away because they see their own vulnerability and mortality. For whatever reason, don't judge these friends or family members too harshly; they mean no harm. They just can't handle it."

Pam reminded the group that because people don't know what to do, it may be helpful to give them a specific task to do to help you out if they should ever call or ask. For example, she suggested we might call someone and tell them we have a doctor's appointment on a certain date, then ask if they would consider coming over for a couple of hours to stay with our loved ones while we went to our appointment. We might ask a neighbor to pick up a few things at the grocery store or a prescription, or go to the bank for us, since we aren't able to get out. Pam suggested that the caregiver prepare a list of things ahead of time that a friend or family member could do to help out if they volunteered. "If you keep the list of needed tasks near the phone or have it memorized, you won't be caught off guard when someone offers to pitch in. You should be specific as to what you really need at that particular time." Pam believed this could be very helpful when enlisting the help of others, especially for those people who wanted to help, but weren't comfortable being left alone with a person with dementia.

I was so glad Tim, Shirley, and the others opened up. Sharing their individual situations was a release for them, and the support they received from Pam, Cindy, and others in the room was both comforting and useful.

Reverend Larson spoke at one of the support group meetings on the topic *How to Make the Most of Your Visits*. Afterwards, I was able to talk to him while everyone was having refreshments. I asked him if Copper Ridge ever had a Rabbi who came to visit the residents. He told me, "I think they did before I came aboard. Do you know of anyone who might be interested?"

I said, "Sykesville is much further away and isn't exactly in the area that the rabbis I know would visit. I do know of a rabbi whose synagogue is Beth Shalom of Carroll County, which is further out on Liberty Road. You might consider giving her a call. I've never been to a service there, but I have heard her speak, and she is very knowledgeable and articulate. I'll e-mail you her name and other contact information."

Two weeks later Wayne, the name Reverend Larson wanted everyone at Copper Ridge to call him, e-mailed me and said he had lunch with Rabbi Scheinerman. She agreed to visit the residents at both Copper Ridge and Fairhaven once a month. *Referring to Reverend Larson as "Wayne" was difficult for me, since I've never called any member of the clergy by their first name.* I couldn't believe Reverend Larson was able to make that happen so quickly.

My cell phone rang as I was leaving to go to Copper Ridge's Father's Day barbecue. Jenny, Dad's nurse, told me he had fallen and hit his head. "He has a cut that doesn't require stitches, but because of where it is, we are having a difficult time keeping a bandage on. Don't be scared when you see him. We needed to wrap his head with gauze to keep the bandage on. It looks worse than it is."

When I saw Dad, he seemed in good spirits. With the bandage wrapped around his head, he reminded me of those pictures you would see of wounded soldiers coming back home after the Civil War.

Dear Dad,

I loved watching you and Shirley sing and dance to the accordion player's music at the Father's Day barbecue. You looked like you were having a great time together. Chuck took a picture of you and Shirley, and I'll bring it to you the next time I come.

Of course, it was that huge hot fudge sundae with all those maraschino cherries and whipped cream that topped off the day!

It was a fun afternoon.

Love you,

Susie

TWENTY-FOUR

In the introduction to her book, *Creating Moments of Joy,* Jolene Brackey writes:

> When a person has short-term memory loss, his life is made up of moments. We are not able to create a perfectly wonderful day with those who have dementia, but it is absolutely attainable to create perfectly wonderful moments—moments that put smiles on their faces, a twinkle in their eyes, or trigger memories. Five minutes later, they won't remember what you did or said, but the feeling you left them with will linger.

Using her philosophy, I tried to make those *moments* happen when I went to visit Dad. I planned each visit ahead of time, thinking about what I could bring to stimulate him when he wasn't involved in an activity. I wanted to be prepared so my time with dad would have more meaning for both of us. I kept activities simple. I knew with each visit I needed to be flexible, to accept Dad as he was on that particular day. I had to let go of any negative thinking about what once *was* or what *could have been*, in order to embrace what *is happening right now*.

More than anything else, I wanted my visits to be a celebration of our bond and spirit. I was careful not to impose my will on Dad. I brought several things to share with him during each visit. I tried to give him choices, by letting him decide what he wanted to do. I wasn't disappointed if Dad wasn't receptive to anything I had planned or brought. Over time I learned that what Dad really needed most was companionship, love, and assurance that he was still valued as a human being. Although his cognition certainly wasn't what it once was, he could still think for himself, he still had periods of lucidity, and he still had much to offer despite his decline.

I kept a box in my trunk which contained family photographs, memorabilia, and large interesting picture books that I thought Dad might enjoy. I called them *story starters*, things that were readily available, things I could use more than once.

Dave made a huge poster for Dad's wall. It consisted of four-inch-square black and white photos of family and friends from Dad's childhood and colored photos of our childhood, his years with Shirley, and his grandchildren. It was a wonderful collage of the people and events from Dad's life history. The poster was a great story starter that was accessible for all who came to visit, as well as the Copper Ridge staff.

Dad liked seeing old photographs of his family. I once brought a few pictures of me in costume from my ballet recitals. We reminisced about some of my recitals being held downtown at the Alcazar Ballroom and others at the Lyric Opera House. I told him that he never missed one of my performances and how much that meant to me. We talked about how bored David (he was David then, not Dave) was with the whole thing. Dad knew sitting through an entire dance recital was of little interest to David, so he used to take him over to Mount Clare station to watch the trains until the recital was over. That was their special time together.

We laughed about how I had to jump in his truck quickly after ballet class at Wally Saunders Dance Studio when the horse races were being run at Pimlico Racetrack. The policeman directing traffic on Reisterstown Road would blow his whistle and yell at Dad for stopping if I wasn't standing outside when he pulled up.

I reminded Dad about the little choreographed ballet routine he used to perform on his tiptoes to make me laugh when I was a little girl. I stood up and did a *plié*, then a *relevé* and a pirouette on my tip toes just like he used to do.

Then I took him over to the collage poster Dave had made, and we looked for pictures of me in my dance costumes. I was so skinny back then. There was a picture of me standing on point in toe shoes, where it looked like my thighs were the same size as my ankles. I told Dad I looked like Popeye's Olive Oyl. How we laughed that morning. *Would Dad remember our conversation later in the day or tomorrow? Most likely not, but for me one picture was worth a thousand words. I knew I had to make today matter for him.*

Another time Shirley brought in Dad's favorite book, Harry Golden's *Only in America,* a compilation of anecdotes and stories drawn from Golden's Carolina Israelite newspaper. Most stories were about one page or less in length, which made them ideal to share with Dad. Golden's common sense, wisdom, and humor provided us with many moments of fulfillment, nostalgia, and laughter, as did his other books, *Ess, Ess, Mein Kindt (Eat, Eat, My Child)* and *So What Else is New?* I'd bought those two books for Dad earlier that year for his birthday.

Many years ago I gave Dad a small book, *Children's Letters to God* by Stuart Hample and Eric Marshall. I brought it to Copper Ridge along with Art Linkletter's *Kids Say the Darndest Things!* I didn't always plan to read to Dad when I visited him, but these were the old *reliables* that I could always pick up to engage him, provided I could find them in his room. How could anyone not laugh at Jennifer's letter to God: *Dear God, In Bible times did they really talk that fancy?* or Dennis' letter: *Dear God, My Grandpa says you were around when he was a little boy. How far back do you go?*

I often downloaded biographical sketches from the

Internet of some of Dad's favorite sports players, authors, historical figures, and movie and television personalities to share with him. Nothing got Dad laughing more than Yogi-isms, the terse comments and witticisms of the great Yankee player and manager, Yogi Berra. Sometimes we were laughing so loud that the Copper Ridge staff would come to see what all the commotion was about.

When the weather was nice, I frequently walked out in the garden with Dad. He would always say, "The sun feels so good on my shoulders." *I remember my Saturday walks with Dad as a child, trying to keep up with his long robust strides, feeling his strong grip around my tiny hand. Now I was leading the way and he was following.* Most times I had to initiate any conversation to get him talking. When there were pauses in our talk and I couldn't think of other things to say, we would sing as we slowly walked around the path.

I often read to him after our walks. Many times I would encourage other residents to come sit with us, or we would join a few who were already sitting on the bench outside. *What a treat it was to see a resident's face light up when something I was reading triggered a memory for them. Some would talk about their experience, others might say a few words, and some would just smile, letting me know that they enjoyed being with us. What they got out of the experience didn't matter; it left them with a good feeling knowing they were part of something. Simple things, but so rewarding.*

Since Dad grew up in Baltimore, I brought in the book, *Baltimore Then and Now* by Alexander D. Mitchell.

It was filled with black and white photographs of many historical attractions, neighborhoods, museums, and places of interest, showing how they looked years ago and how they looked today.

Two residents, Mr. Watson and Ned, seemed interested in what Dad and I were doing, so I asked them to join us on the bench. We browsed through the book slowly. I talked about each picture, while Dad sometimes added comments about things he remembered, like washing those famous white marble steps in front of their Oliver Street home or working at Hutzler's Department Store. Mr. Watson just said, "Just beautiful! Oh how beautiful!" as I turned each page. With an animated smile, Ned would point to most of the pictures and say "And that!" letting me know he recognized what he was looking at, even though he couldn't express his excitement in words. It didn't matter. The four of us were having our *moment*, each of us enjoying something different.

When we came to the picture of Fort McHenry, birthplace of the *Star-Spangled Banner*, Dad began to sing *Oh say can you see...* as did Mr. Watson, Alice, and some other residents who were near us. Ned nodded to the music. Nolan, who always wore a navy blue hat embroidered with WWII, the Korean War, and Vietnam on the front, slowly stood up at attention to sing with us holding on to his walker. *I know I was supposed to be the one creating the "moment," but on most days it was the residents who gave me my "moment."*

Dad never seemed to mind sharing our moments with the other residents—and neither did I. Some residents were curious; others had very short attention spans and would come and go. Many seemed to be unaware that we were even there, but they stuck around anyway. Initially I wasn't comfortable having others join us since I didn't know what to expect, but with time I learned what each resident really wanted was to feel valued. For whatever reason, I was filling a need in each one of them, even if it was often short-lived.

One warm, breezy, summer morning, William Proxmire, former U.S. Senator from Wisconsin, sat down next to us. At the time I was reading excerpts from another of Dad's favorite books, *The Wit and Wisdom of Harry Truman: A Treasury of Quotations, Anecdotes, and Observations* by Ralph Keyes. Senator Proxmire did not respond to anything I was saying, even when Dad said boisterously, "Give 'em hell, Harry!" He just took my hand and held it while I read. He had a strong grip, but I did not pull my hand away. *Did I remind him of someone from his past? Maybe, maybe not.* I didn't mind, because I knew for that moment, holding my hand was what he needed. It just made it a bit harder for me to turn the pages with my left hand.

I remember when I was first met Senator Proxmire while touring Copper Ridge. I knew of him, but it wasn't until I Googled in his name when I returned home that I realized how much he had accomplished during his thirty-one plus years in Congress. This former giant in American politics had been reduced to a shell of what he once was. I realized then that this disease knows no boundaries and how devastating it could be. Not even a United States senator who advocated proper nutrition and exercise, who had written several books on keeping fit and healthy, could escape the heartbreak of this illness.

I put together a songbook for Dad, filled with pages and pages of lyrics from his old favorites. I copied and pasted the lyrics from the Internet and put them in a blue binder labeled, "Leslie Miller's Songbook." When all else failed, I would rely on the songbook to help change his mood. How can anything be wrong when you're singing? Actually, it was a gift for him, but I used it to remember titles and the words to songs written before my era. I could always count on a song to lift Dad's spirits and get him involved.

I wondered what activities I would plan when the day came and Dad failed to recognize or couldn't communicate with me. Even though I didn't want to think about it, that possibility was always very real.

It had already happened once to Shirley, and it terrified her. When Shirley arrived at Copper Ridge one day, Dad was pacing up and down the hallway looking for his wife. He didn't respond to Shirley's "Hi Honey" and told her he was looking for his wife. *For that moment did Dad think she was someone else? Was he looking for the blonde he had married, not recognizing the lady with grey hair standing before him? Or was his mind so far back in his past that he thought he was still married to my mother, his first wife, who had black hair?* Thank goodness this episode didn't repeat itself, and Dad returned to *his* present day reality later that afternoon.

Knowing the progression of Alzheimer's disease was

unpredictable, I decided that if and when there was a further decline in Dad's cognitive and verbal abilities, my role would be the same as it had been. I would still continue to read to him and bring pictures and props to engage him, even if there was little or no response. My approach might be different and my words more guarded, especially if he didn't recognize me. Despite that, he'd still be my dad, and we'd still have our moments together.

Dear Dad,

I read an article in the *Reader's Digest* about dads and how they are so important to a child's development. It talked about how they are different than moms, and that's a really good thing for a child. Dads are more "rough and tumble" with their children than moms.

I remember when you first took me out of town in your truck. You didn't have to wake me up early because I was so excited, I was ready to go. I felt so grown up, even though you had to lift me up to put me in the truck. Sitting in your truck, I could see everything because we were higher than all the cars on the road. That was really cool. It was our special day and I loved it! It was so special that I didn't even mind when

David was old enough to come with us.
Our rides were wonderful. We passed
farms with vegetables, dairy farms,
and horse farms. Sometimes we went
through small towns, and other times we
went through Baltimore City to make a
delivery or pick up bags.

You would point out scenery,
architecture, and scores of landmarks
that Baltimore is so famous for. There
were so many monuments erected for
historical figures that Baltimore is
named "The Monumental City". Baltimore
was the first city to plan a monument
to honor George Washington in the
Mount Vernon neighborhood. We saw
neighborhood after neighborhood of red
brick row houses with their short flight
of white marble steps out front. How
often did we see people scrubbing those
steps, taking such pride in their home
and their city? We rode through Little
Italy with its bustling trattorias and fine
Italian restaurants, and Highlandtown,
a blue-collar neighborhood filled with
people of German, Irish, and Polish
ancestry. I'll never forget the images
and smells of Corned Beef Row on

Lombard Street, with its Jewish delis and bakeries, chicken cages and produce stands lining the street.

We saw new things, met new people, and had experiences the other kids didn't have. We learned how they made potato chips at Utz and Senefts' and pretzels at Quinlain's. We saw how they bottled soda at the 7-Up, Coca-Cola, and Pepsi bottling plants. Those huge vats of syrup smelled sickening sweet to me. We went to Domino Sugar at the harbor. We often went to Littlestown Hardware and the D.E. Horn Farm Supply in Pennsylvania. At Superfine Cannery, there were huge open trailers filled with tomatoes, corn, and string beans. I never saw so many vegetables in my whole life! One of my favorites was Footz's Candy Company where they made jellybeans. I still remember the deafening sound of all those jellybeans tumbling in those copper vats. I didn't mind, since they always gave us samples. Hauswald's Bakery was another favorite because I loved the smell of fresh baked bread.

Oftentimes you would load your truck yourself, and I was amazed at how high you could stack those bags or bales above the sides of your stake body truck. Then you would tie the load down with ropes or put the canvas on if bad weather was predicted. You knew how to make all kinds of rope knots. You tried to teach me how to make them, but I didn't have your knack. David was definitely better at it.

Talking with your customers was your forte. You always had a story or a joke to tell them. You knew about their families, and they knew about yours. The Orioles and Colts were always a favorite subject. You liked your customers and they adored you. You were genuine. They knew your word was your bond and a handshake meant something. We learned how you made deals, how to compromise and bargain, and even how to write a check. Those things weren't taught in school.

Sometimes we brought lunch and had a picnic, and other times we stopped at the local restaurant. I really loved that, because you didn't care if I had two pieces of homemade blueberry pie, or three scoops of ice cream. It was our secret.

It seemed to me, that wherever we were, you managed to come home by Old Pimlico Road. It was our favorite, so hilly and curvy. When we came to a bump in the road, you always went a little faster and we would laugh out loud as we bounced up and down in the truck. There were no seat belts then, but it didn't matter. We always talked along the way and sang songs you knew we liked. We had so much fun.

Many times we came home with a fully-loaded truck. We would ride down the alley behind Springdale Avenue. You had a special spot to park your truck near the garage. I was always amazed that you were able to back it in perfectly each time. Sometimes you asked us to get out of the truck and tell you when you were near the end of the space. I loved yelling "HALT!"

If we came back early enough, we would

head straight to "The Place," better known as the Miller Bag Company. You and Henry, and later Bo, would unload the truck, and we got to go into the office and talk with Uncle Herman. He let us use the typewriter and play with the adding machine and check writer. We also got a soda out of the old Coca-Cola cooler. We liked to jump on the old Maryland license plates that were nailed to the floor in the back. We spent time with Mary, who mended the bags on the sewing machines. I loved collecting those hard cone-shaped spools from the thread she used. Henry showed us how to clean cotton and burlap bags in the long blower and how to make bales. He was so little. I never knew how he was able to work the baler. For a little guy, though, he was really strong.

When I was about twelve, you thought the guys at the places we went were looking at me too much. After that, you didn't want me to go with you as often. I was a bit crushed but I accepted your decision. I had no choice. You were probably right but I didn't think so at the time.

Even though I didn't ride with you anymore, I always listened for the sound of your truck coming down the alley— because then I knew you were home.

Love,
Susie

I decided not to mail this letter to Dad because of its length, mostly caused by using such a large font and double spacing. I also wanted to see his reaction to my writing. I placed it in a green folder and labeled the outside, in bold letters, "The Truck Story."

Dad was sitting in his easy chair when I gave it to him during my visit. I sat next to him. At first Dad placed the green folder in his lap. I was wondering if I was setting him up for failure or frustration. *Could this be the day when further evidence of decline from in his disease surfaced? Would he still be able to read this and comprehend what I'd written? If not, I would read it to him.*

Dad opened the folder and began to read. I watched his reaction intently. He seemed pleased, smiling and commenting as he read further. My goal of sparking his memory seemed to be working. He paused often to talk about a point or event. He said, "I forgot about that," or "This is great, Susie." We reminisced. We laughed a lot. Inside, I was remembering the Dad I once knew. Many times I had to find his place for him after he looked away from the paper. I didn't mind. I loved sharing those moments with him. It was so special for both of us.

Dad closed the folder and looked towards me. "I love you Susie. You bring me such joy."

I replied, "You always taught me, you get back what you give. You've given me so much. Now it's my turn."

The green folder was still on his lap. He glanced down and asked me, "What's this?" My heart sank but I answered, "It's a story I wrote for you. You can read it if you like."

Dad opened the folder again, not remembering he had just finished reading it a few minutes ago. I didn't say a word and just listened as he read my words to me again. He stopped several times to comment or share a particular event, as if he was seeing it for the first time. I was just glad my words were putting a smile on his face, if only for a moment. When Dad finished "The Truck Story," I placed the folder on his bed.

We took a walk outside in the garden. It was a beautiful summer day. When we returned to Dad's room, he immediately noticed the green folder on his white bedspread. We sat together once more, and I pretended to listen intently as my father began to read. Although this was the third time he'd read the story to me, I was grateful. There were many residents at Copper Ridge who had a form of aphasia that caused them to lose their ability to read. Others found it difficult to understand what they read, especially if what they were reading was long or complicated.

How distressing it would be for Dad if he couldn't read, since he always felt reading was relaxing and stimulating. He consistently said, "There's nothing like a good book." Shirley had noticed that in the past months he might glance at a magazine or look at the pictures in the sports books his grandsons gave him. Rarely, though, did he pick up a book, not even his prayer book. *Was Dad becoming aphasic? Was reading too overwhelming? Or was it just that he couldn't remember he had books to read?*

I let these thoughts pass. I left Copper Ridge energized. It was a very good day.

I thought a lot about that visit with Dad on the drive home. I remembered when Dad was finally diagnosed with vascular dementia and Alzheimer's disease. I walked around my home in a fog, my head filled with worst-case scenarios and my heart filled with sadness. I imagined that was how most families felt when their loved one was given a similar diagnosis. But by this time I was entrenched in the drama of this disease. I thought differently. Magical visits like today helped me see the disease in a new light. Being diagnosed with Alzheimer's disease should not be looked at as an immediate death sentence. Generally speaking, Alzheimer's is a slow, insidious disease that progresses in stages. Within these stages there can be periods of near normalcy—a lucidity which can bring joy, humor, and pleasure for everyone involved. Who would have thought that a disease that can bring such tremendous heartache could also bring such great rewards? I learned one can truly find joy in the shadows, if you take the time, make the effort, and remember that you need to be the initiator.

TWENTY-FIVE

I knocked and entered. Dad was facing the wall, rummaging through his dresser drawers. "Hi Dad," I said. Without turning he replied, "Oh, hi, Susie." I made a mental note that Dad still knew me by my voice. *This was very significant, since the devastation of vascular dementia and Alzheimer's was gradually eroding his memory.*

We hugged. Even with a shirt and bulky sweater, he felt thin and bony in my arms. "I'm looking for my electric razor. I just had it." Once again I helped him look through his dresser drawers. He was amazed when I found it wrapped between his undershirts. He moved it to his nightstand. How many times had Shirley or I searched for his razor? Relieved, my father turned to me with a bewildered stare. "What am I supposed to do now?' he asked.

"It's Friday night, Dad. I thought we could share

Shabbat together."

"It's Friday?" he asked, looking puzzled. "I don't think I know what prayers to say."

Reassuringly, I eased his fears by telling him that we would say the prayers together. He smiled.

I asked Dad to honor me by standing by my side while I lit the Shabbat candles. I closed the door to his room. I was concerned that Copper Ridge might not be happy with me lighting candles, even though I'd taken precautions to bring tea lights and heavy foil to place them on. I waved my hands over the candles and covered my eyes with my hands. I recited the ancient prayer, and then silently asked God to let me share this ritual with my father for many years to come. Dad was transfixed on what I was doing.

Next, I filled his Kiddush wine cup with his thickened juice. With my arm around him I lifted my plastic glass, and began to sing in Hebrew, "And it was evening, and it was morning, the sixth day... and He rested on the seventh day from all his work which he had made." I looked at my Dad as he joyfully joined in, singing every word of the prayer. Tears welled in my eyes, as I told him he could drink his thickened grape juice.

I directed him to his easy chair. Sitting beside him, I took out my Hebrew School *siddur* (prayer book) because the font was very large. I open to the *Shema*, one of the first prayers a Jewish child learns. With his eyes closed, he sang in Hebrew, "Hear O Israel, the Lord our God, the Lord is One." He continued, and together we read the entire prayer. Then we sang songs and other prayers from the Shabbat service. Dad sang with animated fervor, clapping his hand against the armrest. We held hands, and he looked directly at me. Between songs, he told me, "You are my diamond. Ever since I saw you in the nursery, I knew you would bring me happiness and you have."

I smiled and we hugged. How fortunate I was to still have him in my life.

Sitting here with Dad, evokes a childhood memory of him sitting in his chair quietly reciting his prayers from his small grey siddur or reading from his larger navy blue Chumash (Bible). Dad always seemed so comfortable, so absorbed, so in touch with his faith. I hope he still feels that pleasure tonight.

Chuck often brought me out to Copper Ridge on Friday evenings. He didn't want me to drive home late at night or in the dark as the days grew shorter. He would visit with Dad for awhile and then went out to the lobby to read his book. He understood how special this Shabbat ritual with Dad was, and he wanted just the two of us to share that experience.

I often brought a brief summary of the Torah portion for that week or an appropriate Bible story to read to Dad. I had to gauge how much detail I went into with him, and it usually depended on how focused he seemed or how tired he appeared. Every Friday night was a little different. Different—but still wonderful. *I don't think I ever felt as close to Dad as I did during those quiet evenings that we sat side by side, sharing the rich traditions of the Sabbath.*

It bothered Dad that he didn't say his daily prayers as often as he had while he was still at home. When he told me that, I responded by asking him if he said prayers before he went to bed now. His answer was always yes. I explained to him if he was doing that, then he was praying. *I thought Dad still knew most of the prayers, but he wasn't saying them because he often couldn't remember he had his prayer book in his nightstand. If he remembered where the prayer book was, he couldn't find the correct place in it. The dementia had robbed him of his sense of time and place, his initiative, his ability to start new things, and also his memory of how to do familiar tasks on his own.*

During one of my Shabbat visits, I brought a favorite poem of Dad's that I had put in a picture frame so he could keep it on his night table in his room. It was written by Yehudah Halevi, a famous Jewish philosopher and poet. I thought it might help ease Dad's concerns.

> Lord, where shall I find thee?
> High and hidden to thy place;
> And where shall I not find thee?
> The world is filled with thy glory.
>
> I have sought thy nearness,
> With all my heart I called thee,
> And going out to meet thee
> I found thee coming toward me.

When I gave the frame to Dad, he asked me to read it to him. *Was he not able to read anymore, or was he too tired to make the effort?* I read the poem slowly trying to enunciate every word loudly and clearly. When I finished reading and looked up at Dad, there were tears in his eyes. I hugged him and said, "It doesn't matter how you reach out to God. It just matters that you do. And if you reach out to Him, He will reach out to you no matter where you are."

On several occasions during our Shabbat singing, Dad would pause and become somber. He would look up at me and say, "You know, Susie, there is going to be a time when I won't be here." My response would be, "I know that, Dad, but none of us knows what's in God's plan." He would tell me that he didn't want me to cry when he was gone. I said, "I can't promise you that, Dad. You know I cry at the singing of the *Star-Spangled Banner*, and I didn't even know Francis Scott Key." We laughed together and got back to our singing.

How fortunate I was to have both Chuck and my Dad in my life.

Like the other residents, Dad loved Rabbi Amy's (the name the residents affectionately called Rabbi Scheinerman) monthly visits and programs. He was so pleased when I started leading monthly Shabbat programs at Copper Ridge. The first time I led the program, I didn't know what to expect or how receptive the residents would be. I had six Jewish residents and several non-Jewish residents who liked to come to all the activities no matter what was happening. We talked about the Christian Sabbath being on Sunday and the Jewish Sabbath beginning at sundown on Friday. We discussed how many of the Jewish Sabbath rituals took place in the home. I told the group about the history behind my Shabbat candlesticks and showed them the pair I used when I was a little girl. "When I was young, we lived in a big house upstairs from my great-grandparents. Every Shabbat I would go downstairs to light the candles first with my great-grandmother, and then I went back upstairs and lit the candles beside my mother."

As I lit the candles, I asked the residents to please join me in the prayer. We sang the prayer together in Hebrew and I read its meaning in English. Many residents gazed in fascination, and others, to my surprise, sang the prayer along with me. We sang *Shalom Aleichem* together. Some people only moved their lips, while others hummed the tune. It was a familiar song and sparked a memory for many.

We talked about how it was customary for fathers to bless the children before we recited the Kiddush (prayer over the wine). I told them how I remembered my dad blessing my brother and me when he came home from synagogue. I glanced over at Dad who was sitting beside me. He was beaming. A rush of nostalgia flowed through me, filling my heart, and I got a little choked up.

As Shirley and Chris filled the resident's cups with grape juice, I showed the group my son's silver kiddush cup, the one he received at his Bar Mitzvah, when he was thirteen years old. The residents liked the personal stories I told them about celebrating Shabbat with my family. Before we said the prayer over the wine, I said, "The seventh day is consecrated to God. With wine, our symbol of joy, we celebrate this day and its holiness. We give thanks for all our blessings—for life, for health, for work and rest, for love and friendship, for one another. On Shabbat, we raise the cup in thanksgiving." After that we said the prayer over the wine together.

I showed them the challah (twisted bread used on Shabbat) and the embroidered challah cover that my sons gave me as a gift. I passed the cover around so everyone could see and touch it. Then we said the *motzi* prayer over the challah. I sliced several pieces and gave a piece to each resident. Marie, one of the residents who was not Jewish and hard of hearing, began to tell us about how she used to live next door to a Jewish family in Chicago. Marie was invited to all their Jewish holidays. She loved all the different foods her Jewish friend made, especially gefilte fish, her chicken soup with matzah balls, and rugelah (pastry). I asked questions about the many traditional foods. A few people were motivated enough to tell us about their likes and dislikes of some of the foods I named. I distributed the kosher cookies I'd brought. Everyone seemed eager to eat something sweet.

In between, we sang and clapped to other Shabbat songs: *Ein kelohenu, Adon Olam,* and *Oseh Shalom bimromav.* The room was alive with tradition, most residents were engaged, and many sang the traditional songs exuberantly. As the program came to an end, I asked if anyone had a special song that they would like to sing. Before I got a response, Claire, who was over ninety years old and usually left most activities early unless she fell asleep, spontaneously began singing *Bei Mir Bist Du*

Shein totally in Yiddish. She ended the song with several loud "Um-pah-pahs" that were uniquely her own. Her solo performance was enjoyed by everyone, so I asked her to sing it again as we clapped along together. As the residents began to leave, I personally thanked each one for coming. I gave Dad a hug and he told me, "This was great!" *What a delightfully gratifying afternoon.*

Dear Dad,

I am reading a book called, *To Life- a Celebration of Jewish Being and Thinking* by Rabbi Harold Kushner. It talks about what being Jewish means to him. When Rabbi Kushner talks about the Sabbath, he talks about the father blessing his young children after the candles are lit. The rabbi said, "When my children were young, this was my favorite moment of the week. There is something deeply stirring about a parent blessing his children, telling him that he loves them and wishing them well."

Dad, I remember when you blessed David and me each Friday night. Sometimes we were in our pajamas, and you were in your maroon, wool-striped robe. Sometimes you had your wool Army hat on to keep your hair down after it was washed. I loved that special time that we had together. I can still picture it in my mind after all these years, so you know it had a great impact on me. I even wrote a poem about it for my poetry class.

I hope you like it.

All my love,
Susie

The Blessing

A humble prayer evokes stored memories
Of simpler times, a little girl and boy
Standing silently each Friday evening,
Gazing up at a handsome young father
Placing his hand over our heads saying-
"May the Lord bless you and keep you,
May He make his face to shine upon you
And be gracious unto you, may the Lord
Turn his face unto you, and give you
peace."

I reach for those words,
On gray days and in the silence of the night.

TWENTY-SIX

The summer drifted by slowly. Dad was doing fairly well but seemed more fragile. All of us were on an emotional roller coaster knowing we were slowly going to lose the husband and father we knew. The only question was *when*.

Whatever was happening to Dad was hidden inside his brain. Although there were certainly subtleties and behaviors that gave evidence of vascular dementia and Alzheimer's, the path that the disease would take for Dad was still unknown. It is a disease that affects everyone and every family differently.

Seeing the slow decline of a loved one was a heavy burden. I often had difficulty falling asleep. I would lie awake at night with a myriad of thoughts saturating my mind, with troubling brain *intruders* that I called my good and bad "H's".

I *hated* this horrible disease. I *hated* what it did to people, destroying the very essence of what they once were. I felt *helpless* at times knowing there was nothing we could do to stop its progression. Despite all their efforts, it seemed there was very little medical science could do either.

Occasionally I was plagued with the *hows*. *How* did Dad really feel about all this loss? Did he feel powerless because he was not only losing his memory, but also his independence, his personal life history, his social circle, and maybe his confidence and self-esteem? Did he feel he was losing control over his life?

How would his disease progress? Would the day come when he wouldn't recognize me or couldn't communicate with me? I read somewhere experts refer to this as anticipatory grief—grief that occurs prior to the actual loss. This grief can impact a person physically, emotionally, intellectually, and socially. At times, I felt like a silent mourner, wondering when the axe would fall and there would be an even further decline in Dad's cognitive abilities.

Then there was the big HOW—*how* were we going pay for all of Dad's care? Would Dad outlive his savings?

Even though I knew Dad was in a supportive facility, it was sometimes *heartbreaking* to see him living with such limitations: a 12 x 13 bedroom, a few hallways, a dining and activity room, a couple of walking paths and gardens, plus a few outings with family. Dave had been so right. Dad's world was shrinking.

Ironically, while this bothered me, Dad seemed more content in this limited environment. He had adjusted very quickly and definitely was a more willing participant in the activities offered to residents.

Now and then, good old Mrs. *Hindsight* would slip in, stealing my precious sleep with her guilt and *if onlys*. *If only* we had recognized the symptoms earlier. *If only* we had sought out help sooner.

If only we could have predicted the negative impact of replacing Dad's old beloved desk would have on him, when he and Shirley moved to a new building with an elevator. Something that seemed so insignificant to us really upset him. *Dad felt comfortable and secure at his old desk. For years that desk was where he paid bills, did his paperwork, wrote letters, and kept some of his files. It was what he knew. It was his domain and where he had control. Even though his new desk was beautiful as well as practical, it wasn't familiar. It wasn't what he was used to. Dad became frustrated and agitated when he couldn't find things. It caused him much pain and anxiety. Looking back, would it have been so terrible to have kept that old desk? It was such a simple thing. If only we had known.*

The *if onlys* were endless. Intellectually, I knew second-guessing was useless. No one can go backwards or change things that have already happened, but oftentimes the *if onlys* in my life plagued me.

I knew this was selfish, but there were times when I did not look forward to the *hassle* of rearranging my schedule, changing appointments, or juggling my time because a situation or crisis arose concerning Dad. I knew I was wearing too many hats at once. I was geriatric care manager, liaison for my family, decision maker, POA, and accountant. At the same time I was trying to be a wife, mother, and just Susan. I have to admit that, on some really difficult days, wearing only one hat would have been just fine.

The amount of time spent taking care of Dad's financial affairs or making phone calls on his behalf was unbelievable. I spent hours developing spread sheets detailing Dad's expenses at Copper Ridge and his income and savings. I would make copies for Shirley and Dave so everyone would be aware of Dad's financial picture. I was really annoyed when my efforts were totally ignored, without any response or feedback from either of them.

My biggest nightmare was the fear that this disease could be *hereditary*. I spoke to Dr. Alva Baker, executive director of the Copper Ridge Institute, about this. His answer to me was, "If you ask me about Huntington's disease, I would say there is a definite genetic correlation. With Alzheimer's you are at greater risk, just like you would be if one of your parents had heart disease or diabetes."

I tried not to let these *intruders* disrupt my sleep, but instead, I tried to focus on what I could control. I sought ways to *honor* my father by being a loving and caring daughter, accepting and respecting him at the level he was at on any given day.

On page 124 of his book *In the Arms of Elders: A Parable of Wise Leadership and Community Building,* Dr. William H. Thomas, founder of the Eden Alternative, writes:

The notion of honoring people with dementia seems strange to me. I was taught to see them in terms of what they have lost. After all, losing one's memory is the result of chronic, irreversible brain damage. How can we possibly honor brain damage? ... Demented elders are purely themselves— they travel backward and forward through time in a way that the rest of us can achieve only in dreams. For the people, this is magic, and all magicians hold honored places here.

I also wanted to bring *happiness* into Dad's life by creating opportunities that might bring him pleasure while preserving his dignity, sense of independence, and self-worth. Lastly, it was my *hope* that Dad's illness, if it had to progress, it would progress slowly. My greatest wish was that one day soon medical research would find a cure for this tragic disease that affects millions. *Intellectually I realized it was probably too late for a medical breakthrough to help Dad, but wouldn't it be wonderful if medical science could prevent this disease in future generations?*

On those restless nights I closed my eyes and focused on three words—honor, happiness, and hope. Finally, I would drift off to sleep.

Shirley came to spend time with Dad almost every day, and Dave and I visited several times a week. People often chided Shirley by saying, "Why do you have to run out there every day? He's not going to know if you are there or not." Her answer to them was always the same, "Because I still have him."

As the months passed, only a few people came to visit Dad other than his immediate family. I think many people had the mindset "Why go?" since Dad wouldn't remember their visit anyway. When I talked to family, I often tried to mention how much I knew Dad would love to see them. Then I came to the realization that most people rarely do what they really don't want to do, no matter how many hints you give them.

People fear what they don't understand. Many were afraid to visit Dad because they didn't know what to expect. They didn't know what to say, or they felt uncomfortable being around other residents whose dementia was more advanced. I also knew that people were busy with their own lives and had valid reasons for not visiting. Intellectually, I accepted this premise, but emotionally, their absence saddened me. I knew that if one of our relatives was in a similar situation and Dad was well, he would have made every effort to visit them more. That was just who he was.

Dad's dear friend and fraternity brother, Irwin, came many times to see him, sometimes alone and other times with his wife, Betty. Their special friends, Dolores and John, would visit and take Dad and Shirley out in order to put a little normalcy back in both their lives.

Nothing made Dad's face light up more than when Chuck's two grandsons came to visit him. Charlie was five and Will was three. They lived in Richmond, Virginia, and each spent a week with us in Baltimore during the summer for their special time at *Camp Garbett*. I had discussed taking them out to visit Dad with their parents, who were supportive of the idea.

Charlie and Will knew Dad from previous visits before Dad became ill. They remembered making a dirt cake from crushed Oreo cookies, chocolate pudding, and gummy worms. *I'll never forget Dad's expression when he bit into a gummy worm in the middle of his cake. Charlie thought that was the funniest thing and Dad overplayed his discovery to the hilt.*

Since Charlie had visited his great-grandmother, who also suffered with Alzheimer's, he was well prepared and had no qualms about going. *If only adults had the acceptance and fearlessness of children.*

When we arrived at Copper Ridge, Dad was with a group who were singing patriotic songs in the Garden Room. Charlie jumped right in and sang a couple of his school songs. The residents loved having a child among them. They showed their delight by clapping when Charlie had finished his repertoire.

Charlie was anxious to see where Dad's room was. He easily recognized the pictures of Will and himself, along with the photos of his cousins, Cal and Cameron, displayed on the wall. Charlie asked Dad, "Why do you have a flag on your door?" Dad told him, "It helps me find my room. This place has a lot of doors." Charlie was full of questions, and we responded with simple, honest answers that we thought were age appropriate. *I don't think children need a great deal of complex, detailed information that may overwhelm them. They are curious and need a simple explanation of what they don't understand. A parent must judge how much information their child can handle, based on their age and maturity level. A child knows something is different, something is not right, and they are good at reading adult body language. It's important to reassure them and keep the lines of communication open when their questions, fears, or doubts arise. Remind the child that it's the illness affecting the person's memory, responses, or behavior. The best thing you can do is to comfort and support them with your love.*

Because Will was only three and had less experience with people with dementia than his older brother, we thought it would be better to bring Dad to the coffee shop instead of taking him back to Dad's room. Will was a bit timid at first, but he warmed up when we got ice cream sandwiches for him and Dad. Chuck and I initiated conversation by asking Will to tell Dad and Shirley about the things he was doing at our home and the places we had taken him. He brought one of his animal magazines to share with Dad. Will, who was our animal and nature lover, knew more about some of the animals than I did. Dad loved being with Will and thanked him for coming and bringing him a picture that he had colored.

Shirley told me later that after we left the coffee shop, Dad was staring at her, mesmerized, not ready to go back to his room. He said, "I just want to look at you and remember what you look like." *Did Dad realize that his memory was getting worse and he might not recognize her one day? Whatever the case, his words tugged at her heartstrings.*

I never told Shirley, but during one of my visits I remembered Dad gazing at the picture of her on his bureau. He asked, "Who's that person in the picture?" When I brought the picture closer to him and said it was Shirley, he said, "Funny, it doesn't look like her." I didn't press the issue and hoped that tomorrow would be a better day.

Did it really matter that Dad most likely wouldn't remember anyone who came to Copper Ridge to visit him? His visitors, no matter what their ages, created their own "moments of joy" for and with him if only for a brief period. That is what really was important. They each made a difference, and I was truly grateful for them being there for him. I only wished others could have been more responsive.

TWENTY-SEVEN

The temperature had risen to eighty-five, giving little credence to the fact that autumn was supposed to begin in two days. Only a few leaves had begun to change color, and the nights were relatively warm for September. Although Dad didn't have any knowledge of the date, he enjoyed being able to take his walks around the gardens at Copper Ridge despite having grown more frail.

Our pace had become much slower. At times Dad barely raised his feet when he walked. He tended to shuffle, but that didn't stop us from taking our walks. I made my adjustments as we moseyed along. We also seemed to be chatting less lately. Dad had to concentrate more—just on the task of walking. When I tried to engage him in conversation, he answered in a few words or with a simple *yes* or *no*.

On one of our loops around the path, Dad said, out

of the clear blue, "Craig (his eldest grandson) is going to have some good news soon." Astonished, I looked at him and asked, "What's the good news, Dad?" He told me Craig came out to Copper Ridge before he left for his trip. Craig told Dad he was going to ask his girlfriend, Sonel, to marry him. *I knew Craig was invited to go to Lithuania with Sonel and her parents, who hadn't been back to their native country in over thirty years. I was aware of Craig's intentions, but had no knowledge of his visit with Dad. I was really touched that my son wanted to share this milestone in his life with his grandfather. I knew they shared a special bond, but was very surprised that Dad remembered Craig's visit.*

"I guess you'll have to dust off your tuxedo," I said to Dad.

Dad looked at me and smiled, "I hope somebody knows where it is."

"We'll find it, Dad," I told him. "Craig and Sonel haven't set a date to get married yet, so I know we have plenty of time."

Craig told me how important it was for him to have both of his grandfathers attend his wedding. His other grandfather was ninety-one. I hoped that Dad would be able to go, but I knew people with dementia didn't do well in crowds or in strange new environments. I was already thinking about hiring one of the resident assistants to be a companion for Dad.

A few days later, Craig called me from Vilnius, the capitol of Lithuania, to let me know he had proposed to Sonel. The actual proposal took place on top of Gediminas

Castle, which was built in 1419. After congratulating both of them, I told Craig, "Zaid remembered that you were going to propose to Sonel." Craig screamed to Sonel, "Zaid remembered!" Craig and I were over 4,000 miles apart, but the tears flowed on both sides of the Atlantic.

Chuck and I were waiting in the Kershner Room at Copper Ridge for Dad, Shirley, and the rest of our family to arrive. Tonight was the first night of Rosh Hashana, the Jewish New Year. Copper Ridge was sponsoring a dinner for the Jewish residents and their families, plus the Jewish residents at Fairhaven.

In August I had approached Marcie Koenig, director of Copper Ridge, about hosting this dinner. After presenting my proposal, Marcie did not give me the top ten reasons why they couldn't hold this event. Instead, to my delight, her response was, "What can we do to help with this effort?" She called a meeting with Steve and Chris from activities, Lisa from dining services, and Reverend Larson. After an enthusiastic and productive discussion of what was needed, the plan moved forward.

Chuck and I greeted people as they came in. Beatrice, who was very knowledgeable about the Jewish religion and an articulate resident, strolled in with her son at her side. She was eager to introduce him to us and glad to have him with her. I complimented her on her outfit and her new hairdo. *The resident assistant told me earlier that Beatrice had wanted her hair done for this occasion, and she had been looking forward to coming all day.* Beatrice commented on how beautiful the room looked, all decorated in fall colors and cornucopias with assorted plastic fruit. Turning to welcome the other guests, I spotted Dad, wearing navy dress pants and a plaid shirt. I gave him and Shirley a hug, and asked him if he would honor me by sitting by my side while I conducted the service. I showed him where I was sitting and told him I'd be back after I went to get another resident. Dad was fine with me leaving since Dave and my children were there to talk to him.

I approached Harriet, a wheelchair-bound resident in the Baltimore House, with a smile and bent over to be at her level. "So good to see you, Harriet," I said. She looked at me hesitantly and said, "Do I know you?" I knew she tended to be a bit nervous, so I talked with her for a few minutes explaining who I was before asking her to come to the Rosh Hashana dinner.

"It sounds very nice, but I just don't know if I can make it. I have to go to see my mother soon," she said.

I looked at my watch and told Harriet, "You know, Harriet, we have time to do both. I'll take you to the dinner, and make sure you get back in time to see your mother."

"You can do that for me?" she asked.

"I'll be happy to do that for you," I replied, "and I will keep an eye on the time while we're at dinner."

I thanked God for helping me find the right words to satisfy her and calm her fears. I disliked the fact that I constantly told these little "white lies," often referred to as judicious fibbing, whether I was talking to another resident or to Dad. Reverend Larson told me, "God understands, don't feel guilty about it. It's a necessary alternative when talking to people with memory loss."

I was ready to begin the service. It was wonderful that the Jewish residents from Fairhaven were in attendance with us. We read in unison a Rosh Hashana prayer in English from the booklet I had prepared for each guest.

With thankful hearts we have come together, to join in this Rosh Hashana celebration. We are grateful for the opportunity to worship together in accordance with our tradition. We are grateful for the freedom to worship as individuals and as a community. We are grateful for the strength to come into God's presence, to acknowledge our blessings, and to find greater meaning in our lives. We are grateful for the days which have come and gone, and grateful for the hopes we cherish, and for the days that lie ahead.

Before lighting the candles, I told some personal stories about lighting the candles when I was young. Several residents and guests said the prayer with me. We filled the wine cups with grape juice, and I said "In Your love, You have given us this Day of Remembrance, to hear the sound of the *Shofar* (ram's horn), and unite us in worship as we say the Kiddush, the prayer over the wine, in Hebrew and then in English." Since tonight was the first night of this two-day holiday, we added the *Shehecheyanu* prayer, thanking God for allowing us to reach this season.

Dad was beaming, loving every minute of it, saying the prayers with me. Mr. Bernstein, a gentle man who was in a wheelchair, was sitting next to his daughter. His head was down and his eyes were almost closed. Until I stooped down next to him while reciting the Kiddush, I thought he might be asleep, but I saw he was silently mouthing the words. His daughter was overwhelmed with emotion, as was I.

I held up the *challah* plate with its white-fringed cover for everyone to see. I then showed them another cover I had made over fifty years ago in Hebrew School. It didn't matter that it had a few age spots on it. They liked hearing that I made it when I was a little girl.

Challah is traditional braided bread used on Shabbat and festivals. We talked about why the challah used on Rosh Hashana is round. It is round like a circle without an end, hopefully bringing a spiritual renewal in preparation for the New Year. The *Hamotzi*, is the same blessing recited over all bread: *"Baruch atah adonai, eloheinu melech ha'olam, hamotzi lechem min ha'aretz.* Blessed are you, Lord our God, King of the universe, who brings forth bread from the earth." Everyone oohed and ahhed when I showed them the tiny, round challah I also brought. "It's a challet," I told them, "I had never seen one before, and I couldn't resist buying it at Goldman's bakery because it was so cute."

There were sliced apples and a bowl of honey on each table. Chris, Chuck, and Reverend Larson passed the apples around. We each dipped our apples in honey and hoped for a sweet new year. We said the prayer over fruit together and I taught them a short song, to the tune of *My Darling Clementine.* My friend Helaine, who teaches preschool at a synagogue had taught it to me over the phone:

Dip the apples in the honey
Make a *bracha* (prayer) loud and clear
L'Shana Tovah Umetuka
Have a Happy New Year.

I knew it was not wise to try to teach people with memory illnesses new things, but I thought this simple, peppy song would lift their spirits and would be something they would enjoy. The group loved it so much, we sang it three times.

While we ate the traditonal festive meal of chicken soup, salad, baked chicken, red bliss potatoes, and stringbeans, Dad looked at me and asked, "Whose idea was this?" I asked him, "Whose idea do you think it was, Dad?" Smiling, he replied, "Yours." I moved closer to give him a hug and said, "I had a great teacher!"

I looked around the room. Everyone was enjoying the delicious meal that dining services had prepared. Beatrice was having a lively conversation with her son. Bessie was talking with her daughter and granddaughter. Marla was asking her daughter for seconds. Claire who had a short attention span and a family who rarely visited, was still sitting and enjoying being with the group. Shelley, who was upset and almost crying when her aide first brought her in, was sitting in a Geri Chair relatively calm except for uttering a few unintelligible sounds. She seemed unaware of anything we were doing, but her eyes lit up when she heard the prayers. Each time I passed Harriet she told me, "I'm so glad I came. This is really so nice." There was no mention of her wanting to meet her mother.

We sang many of the familiar Jewish songs, while enjoying desserts of fruit, honey cake, and *rugelah* ("little twists" in Yiddish that refers to yeast dough rolled around a sweet filling). To hear the residents' boisterous voices and see their expressive faces was so fulfilling. It didn't matter that we sang the same songs over and over. The Fairhaven residents didn't mind, especially when Harriet belted out all the words to *Ei Keloheinu*, not missing a beat.

In synagogues throughout the world the *shofar* (ram's horn) is blown on Rosh Hashana and at the end of Yom Kippur (Day of Atonement), trumpeting a spiritual awakening, renewal, and repentance. I had checked with activities to make sure it was OK to let the residents hear the shofar blown. Because it was loud, I didn't know if the blasts would frighten any patients. After showing the shofar and discussing its heritage, Chuck waited for me to announce the Hebrew words to signal when to blow one long blast, three short blasts, or a staccato of nine blasts. Everyone was mesmerized. Most Jews know that blowing the shofar is very difficult, and most people can't get a sound out of it. Silence filled the room as everyone looked and listened to the shofar. Chuck blew about twenty sounds. People applauded when he was finished and he took a deep bow in appreciation. Dad got up to shake his hand and hug Chuck. I laughed when I heard Chuck say to Dad, "Not bad for a *goy.*" In Modern Hebrew and Yiddish the word goy is the standard term for gentile.

Before the residents returned to their rooms, I gave each person a New Year's card to take back with them. I thought maybe seeing a picture of the candles, wine cup, challah, and apples and honey might help to keep the memory of that night alive. It might have been wishful thinking on my part, but I knew they would like something to hold on to.

Some residents thanked me, some gave me hugs, some smiled as they left. I wished each one a *L'Shana Tovah*, a Happy New Year. Beatrice told me, "You really thought of everything. This was so wonderful. I never thought anything like this would happen here." I responded by saying, "It was my pleasure. I'm so glad that I got to meet your son. Hopefully, we can celebrate together again next year."

While the staff was cleaning up, I said good-bye to my family and thanked them for coming. I knew I didn't have to thank them, because I knew in my heart they wouldn't have thought about being anywhere else that night. Dad gave me a big hug and told me, "Susie, I am so proud of you." I could hardly hold back the tears.

I left Copper Ridge on a real high. I was so very grateful.

I was at Copper Ridge by eight o'clock the next morning. I came early to say some Rosh Hashana prayers with Dad before I went to our synagogue to be with my children. Taking Dad to synagogue was not an option because of his fragility, the distance, and the length of the service.

Dad was dressed and was sitting in his lounge chair when I entered his room. He was so glad to see me.

Surprisingly, he mentioned last night's dinner. We talked about it for a few minutes and then I took out his tallis and yarmulke from his drawer. He placed his yarmulke on his head and I helped him put his tallis around his shoulders. I opened the *Mahzor*, the High Holiday prayer book, and began with the morning service. Together we read psalms and prayers in Hebrew and I read many in English. Dad appreciated that I was helping him stay on track and turning the pages for him.

I glanced up and noticed Karen, a resident assistant, respectfully standing in the doorway waiting for the right moment to interrupt. She asked Dad if he wanted to have his breakfast or whether they should hold it for him until later. *Dad told me he had already had breakfast, and I didn't make an issue of this. I knew Shirley kept a full supply of snacks and candy in his night table drawer, so I was sure he had some of those earlier and thought he had eaten.* Dad thanked Karen for holding his meal, and we continued. I was amazed at how much Dad remembered. He often said the prayer from memory without looking at the book. We were in the middle of the morning service and I saw that he was tiring. I skipped a few pages, maybe more than a few, and we concluded the service singing some well-known prayers and songs.

When we were finished Dad said, "This was great, Susie. I love you so much."

"It was good for me too, Dad," I told him, "I'll be back tomorrow morning and we can pray together again. I'll leave the Mazhor here for you to look at later, if you want to."

Dad chose to lie down rather than go eat breakfast. I covered him with a blanket and kissed him on the cheek. He took my hand in his and stared at me with an intense look. I saw there were tears in his eyes, but I didn't comment. "*L'Shana Tova* Dad," I said to him. He kissed my hand and said, "*L'Shana Tova,* my dear sweet daughter."

Dear Dad,

I paid Wachovia for your safety deposit box. It will not be due again until next year. I'm going to bring you a list of what is in your box, like you asked me to. We will go over the list together.

Your bank statements are correct. Everything is OK with your money.

See you soon.

Love,
Susie

TWENTY-EIGHT

I read a lot to learn more about dementia and Alzheimer's disease to help Dad, but also to help myself. Some books were written by leading doctors and nurses in the field of neuropsychiatry and geriatrics. Many were highly technical and difficult for me to get through. Others were written so I could more easily understand the progression of this terrible disease. I read books written by caregivers who recaptured the ordeals and trials they personally went through in caring for their spouse or loved one. The most heart-wrenching stories were the ones written by the people suffering with the disease, especially those who had early onset Alzheimer's. They chronologically summarized their own decline and struggles.

I also reviewed articles and stories I found on various Internet websites that often linked me to other sites online. The Alzheimer's Association had a wonderful website with a wealth of information, articles, and resources that I found to be extremely helpful. I could easily find and be linked to the Alzheimer's Association chapter and support group in my area.

Their website offered information on Medic Alert and Safe Return programs. According to the Alzheimer's Association, six out of ten Alzheimer's patients wander or get lost, often putting the person in danger and causing tremendous stress for caregivers and families. Enrolling in the Medic Alert and the Alzheimer's Association Safe Return programs brought peace of mind to the caregiver by providing a twenty-four hour nationwide emergency response service for individuals with Alzheimer's or related dementia.

An optional caregiver membership was also available for an additional fee. If the caregiver had a medical emergency, it would alert authorities or first responders that the person was caring for someone that couldn't care for themselves. *We were fortunate that Dad was not a wanderer, and now that he resided at Copper Ridge we didn't have that extra worry. I think this program fills a great need for so many.*

The Alzheimer's Association also has a twenty-four hour helpline. It provides encouragement and advice for caregivers and families even in the middle of the night when there is no one else to turn to. Many chapters provide care consultations by phone, email, or in person to assess the needs of the person with Alzheimer's or other dementias, assist with planning and problem solving as the disease progresses, and provide support for the caregiver. You can also take the "Brain Tour," an easy-to-understand interactive explanation of how the brain works and how the disease affects it. I only wished I had explored their website years earlier, when we first started seeing signs of a decline in Dad's cognitive ability. If I'd only known then what I know now, things might have been different.

Although the knowledge I was gaining by reading was valuable, I believe I learned the most from visiting Copper Ridge. As the months passed, my observations and conversations with the staff, doctors, and residents, truly enlightened me and unleashed a desire to learn more about these crippling illnesses. By interacting with the residents and participating in many of their activities, I was better able to come to grips with the disease. With time, I had a greater sense of acceptance. I discovered so much, and in that discovery, I learned more about myself. I learned to base my actions on Dad's needs, not my own, on his reality, not mine. I began to realize that Dad's reality was often quite different from mine. I went with the flow. I learned you don't have to have a great memory to have a great time. I recognized Dad still had unique abilities, gifts, and life experiences to share with me. He just needed my help to bring them to the surface. I approached each day as a gift, a chance to enjoy it together as fully as we could.

I recognized sometimes all that was needed was me being there—that it's OK to say nothing, rather than trying to force a conversation. Sometimes a smile, a gentle touch, holding hands, or thoughtful silence was the best communication.

I once saw a stone marker strategically placed at the entrance to Arden Courts, a comprehensive facility for dementia and Alzheimer's disease. A resident's daughter gave it to the facility after her mother died. It read—*Love heals and it comes in many forms, The greatest of which may be silence.*

I thought a lot about that endearing and moving passage. It reminded me of what I learned in a class I took on the Twenty-Third Psalm. Rabbi Adler explained that the line, "He leadeth me beside the still waters," refers to God wanting *stillness* in our lives. He wants us to take the time to stop and reflect, to regroup, to relax, and to enjoy the beauty around us and in each other. We must recognize that with our hectic schedules and electronic obsessions, we frequently forget this concept. Consequently, we need to plan to put stillness back into our lives. I learned that stillness is often just what a person with dementia needs. Stillness or silence can be calming, requiring no response from the person—a response that may be impossible to obtain because of the advanced stage of their disease.

Is stillness why we often daydream? Why we often go within our own little world, to get away, to dream, to hope, or to connect with ourselves? I've often wondered if what looked to me like a blank stare on the faces of so many people with Alzheimer's could be their way of daydreaming, of trying to come to grips with who they still are at a particular moment. There is probably no medical rationale for this view, just my own inner thought.

Several times during my day, I would consciously try to put stillness in my life. Other times those attempts were more spontaneous. To help me cope and prepare for what often was an ever-changing day, I began my morning by sitting quietly on the edge of the bed for a few minutes, allowing myself to be in the present, acutely aware of my breathing and the freshness of the day with its new opportunities. Throughout the rest of the day, I would find myself pausing to take a few deep breaths, closing my eyes, allowing the myriad of thoughts that clouded my mind to settle down. Before bedtime, I often wrote in my journal. *How therapeutic it was to put my thoughts down on paper. For me, it was a release from the tensions of the day.* Some nights I would read an inspirational poem or meditate to help me fall into a more peaceful sleep.

As time passed, even my untrained eye could recognize the decline in some of the residents at Copper Ridge. Residents who usually talked to me could no longer converse intelligibly. Others, who took walks with Dad and me, were now confined to a wheelchair. People who walked relatively erect were now shuffling along with their heads down. Still others had lost the facial animation I was used to seeing.

It was the times when I visited and I didn't see Mr. or Mrs. Whomever that filled me with sadness. The staff would tell me that the person was no longer on the assisted-living side because their decline made it necessary to move them to either the Baltimore or Eastern Shore House for care that was more comprehensive. I never feared that I would find Dad moved to another house when I came to Copper Ridge. I was sure the staff would bring our family together to discuss their decision before making such a move. They were excellent in keeping us informed, and that is something I really appreciated.

Some of the residents I observed puzzled me at first. Sarah, a young woman who was probably in her late forties when I first met her, was one of those residents. She appeared to be too young to be at Copper Ridge. I later found out she had early-onset Alzheimer's disease, which affects people under the age of sixty-five.

People with early-onset Alzheimer's exhibit many of the same symptoms as those whose disease occurs later in life. This dementia affects 5-10% of all Alzheimer's sufferers. Sometimes this type of Alzheimer's runs in families where a genetic predisposition leads to the disease. *What is it like for those younger adults who are still caring for children, who are still working, or who still have other ongoing responsibilities? How do they cope with such a devastating diagnosis?*

Although I didn't know much about her, Sarah fascinated me. I often found her reading the newspaper in the dining room, going through the stacks of magazines and papers in her room (she was a hoarder), or compulsively raiding the Annapolis House refrigerator whenever she could. Even with coaxing from the staff, Sarah rarely participated in group activities other than arts and crafts, unless there was food involved. Sarah used to be very athletic, so she did enjoy playing ping-pong with the staff or volunteers on the table provided by her family. She also liked using the pool at Fairhaven, the retirement community around the corner from Copper Ridge.

Occasionally I would sit with Sarah in the dining or garden room and she would ask personal questions like: *How old are you? Do you work? Are you married?* She never seemed to want to talk about herself, and I wondered if that was because she knew she was losing her own identity. *Did Sarah connect with me because I looked more like her than the older residents in assisted-living? What was it like for her to have to deal with life changes caused by the disease in her prime of life? Did she realize that her hopes, dreams, and aspirations were vanishing?* I'll never really know what was going on in Sarah's mind, but for me it was disturbing to see someone that young declining more and more over time.

At times, I wondered why a few residents were at Copper Ridge, since their intellectual and verbal skills seemed relatively *normal*, and their memories didn't seem that much worse than most seniors their age. *Of course, I never knew if what some residents were telling me really happened, but sequentially their stories and conversations made sense.*

My thinking changed when I once visited Dad in the late afternoon and stayed towards evening. Suddenly a resident with what seemed to me as normal behavior became increasingly agitated, demanding, and disoriented. She began shouting and cussing about things that she was seeing but no else could see. It was as if a switch turned on, and this relatively calm woman became frightened and enraged.

I couldn't figure out what triggered this behavior, and I was later told by a nurse that this type of behavior is referred to as *sundowning*. Why it occurs is not understood. Experts suspect that people with dementia may be mentally and physically tired at the end of the day. Another possibility is that their internal body clock is upset, causing confusion between day and night. Sundowning occasionally flares when light is reduced at night and people can't see as well. They become confused or see shadows, which upset them.

As I think back, Dad exhibited some elements of this type of behavior occasionally when he was at home. There's another one of those "if onlys" again. If only we had been more aware and recognized this behavior as sundowning, we could have made things less hectic during those times, by diverting his agitation or confusion. It could have been as simple as taking a walk or engaging him in a quiet activity, anything to change his train of thought.

If only we had been able to implement all the suggestions the neuropsychiatrist at Good Samaritan Hospital gave us after Dad's stroke. Would they have made a difference for Dad and for Shirley? Is it fair to expect Shirley or any caregiver to be able to remember and apply all those recommendations? After all, they themselves are so fatigued and stressed from dealing with the many daily changes that occur while caring for someone with dementia—such expectations may be unrealistic.

I truly believe that the majority of caregivers are trying to give their all and are doing their best under what can be very difficult circumstances. It is easy for others to judge, when they are not drowning in this drama themselves.

I frequently watched and listened as other families came to visit their relatives. I found the dynamics both fascinating and troubling. *What must it be like for the person whose disease has progressed to where they don't recognize their loved ones? Are they fearful or just puzzled? Are they glad that someone, anyone, comes to spend some time with them? Or has the disease stolen their ability to react at all?*

On the flip side, what was it like for the visiting wife, husband, daughter, son, or grandchild who first encounters their loved one and comes face to face with a stranger? Their precious loved one, the person who is such an integral part of their memories, no longer exists. Yet, they still come to visit, trying to reconnect—with a smile, by gently holding a hand, or by trying to carry on a simple, one-sided conversation. I tried hard not to let this reality sink in. At any time, I could easily be in the same situation with my father. Some days it was hard for me to keep such thoughts at bay.

I wanted to be there when Dad opened my latest letter because of its content and length. Dad's face lit up when he saw me. He lost his balance trying to stand to give me a kiss, and plopped back down in his chair. I slid my chair next to him as he opened the envelope. Looking at me for reassurance, he cautiously began to read.

Dear Dad,

Chuck and I went for a ride this weekend. We drove by Springdale Avenue, so I could show him the house where I grew up. Chuck took this picture of what our house looks like today. The color has changed and there aren't any shutters on it anymore, but it looks pretty much the same.

I have always wondered who lives in my room now.

Hugs and kisses,
Susie

Together we looked at the picture of the house that Dave and I grew up in. Dad and I talked about the missing shutters and the trees that were no longer there. We reminisced about the time my Bubbie (great-grandmother) had all the shutters painted pink and how awful it looked. We joked about how we never had to give our address to people to find our house. We just said, "Look for the green house with the pink shutters." No one had a problem finding it.

I told Dad how I hated my job of getting those wooden laundry poles out from underneath the house on laundry day when I was younger because it was dark and full of cobwebs. Dad couldn't believe that I still remembered those poles. "That shows how much I disliked having that job every Monday, Dad. I'm so glad we have dryers now."

"Did you have a washing machine when you were little?" I asked.

Talking about a simple thing like laundry evoked a conversation about Dad's past. He told me that his mother and oldest sister scrubbed their clothes on a galvanized steel washboard, and then hung them out to dry on pulley cords erected in their backyard. He remembered a really heavy iron that had to be heated up on the stove before you could press your clothes. His family did get a wringer-type washer later on, that had two rollers on top to squeeze the excess water out of each piece of clothing.

During these spontaneous conversations, I learned more interesting tidbits about my father. For me, the joy came from being Dad's motivator, initiator, and engager, tapping and sparking his memory and hopefully helping to keep it alive.

When I couldn't think of any more memories to talk

about, I slowly read the poem I wrote about that house
to him:

Once more...

Seeing you today,
I picture—
me skipping down the sidewalk
ponytail flying, book bag in tow
running through the back door
through the kitchen and dining room—
a quick *Hi!* to my great-grandparents,
racing my brother
up those linoleum covered steps
to our second floor apartment.

Seeing you today,
I imagine—
me skating from the back alley
winding around curves—
my skate key proudly hanging from my neck,
past the cherry tree we used to climb,
the storage alcove that housed my
turquoise bike,
speeding by "The Miller" side entrance
down the hill, only able to stop
as my hands landed squarely on
the blue Chrysler parked in front.

Seeing you today,
I recall—
family and friends eating snowballs
on the enclosed front porch

white wicker rockers and love seats
pillows piled high, a forest of planters,
playing step ball and "Mother May I"
on the wide stone steps
delighting in "spud" and "red light"
in the front yard,
waiting by the curb for the ice cream man.

Seeing you today,
you appear—
so much smaller now
your colors have changed
your shutters and numbers are missing
the swing set is gone
the two huge front blue spruce are no
longer there,
yet to me you still seem majestic.

It was good to see you once more—
my treasured childhood home.

Dad appeared to enjoy my words. I wondered if he grasped everything we talked about. It really didn't matter. It was just the two of us enjoying cherished memories and each other's company.

Afterwards, we looked for pictures of Dave and me on the large photo collage on the wall. I pointed to the one of us standing in front of the house on Springdale Avenue I referred to in the poem I'd just read. The picture was in black and white. Dad said, "I'm sure glad I don't have to walk up all those steps." It was such a great visit.

TWENTY-NINE

Dad was standing in the middle of the room when I entered. He looked so handsome in his grey dress slacks, maroon and white pin check shirt, and navy blazer. I kissed him and gave him a big hug.

"Good morning and good Shabbos, Dad. You look so handsome today."

"Thank you. Not bad for an old bird!"

One of his resident assistants came in and greeted him warmly with her usual, "Hi, handsome!"

My father smiled, and said, "I know I was supposed to do something today, but I can't remember what it was."

The resident assistant said, "You've been telling me all morning that you can't wait for your daughter to get here to take you to synagogue." She pointed to the reminder sign on his wall.

I told Dad, "We're going together to Beth Shalom,

Rabbi Amy's *shul.* I figured if she is nice enough to come here and teach classes, it might be nice for us to go to her synagogue and see what it is like."

"Gee, that will be great! Do I need a tie?" he asked.

"You'll be fine without a tie," I told him.

Haltingly he said, "It seems strange to go to shul without a tie."

"That's the great thing about the Jewish religion," I said. "You can pray anywhere, and wear anything you want. God doesn't mind if you pray in your pajamas."

"I say my best prayers in my pajamas." he replied with a smile.

"Me too, Dad," I said.

A gentleman greeted us and pointed to two open seats among the congregation. The rabbi acknowledged our presence with a smile. Dad seemed quite at ease as we opened our siddur. As I looked at the bimah (altar), I noticed the royal blue velvet cover adorning the table that held the opened Torah. The cover was embroidered, "*In Memory of Melvin Mermelstein,*" a high school friend and fraternity brother of my father's. I held my breath, hoping my father didn't notice the inscription, not wanting anything to upset his day.

Almost immediately he saw the table cover. Looking anxious, he said, "I didn't know Mel died."

I explained, "Mel had been sick for awhile, and now he isn't suffering anymore. Now he is at peace with God."

Dad seemed to relax and we continued to follow the service. Some of the tunes were a little different from those sung in the synagogue that he went to for over fifty years. Dad seemed to keep up with the congregation and remembered most of the prayers. His face was animated, and he didn't seem to mind as I moved my finger across each page to help him stay on track. It was amazing how he remembered the songs and prayers. It confirmed what I was told about Alzheimer's disease, "The first things in are the last things out."

As the Torah procession moved through the congregation, the Rabbi stopped and asked me, "How are things going?"

I whispered, "He knew Mel."

Rabbi Scheinerman didn't hesitate and walked over to Dad. She took his hand in hers and said, "I'm sorry for your loss," as if Mel had only recently passed away.

Dad responded, "Sometimes you hear bad news in good places." Astonished, I was thinking that Dad sounds just like Rabbi Kushner who wrote the book *When Bad Things Happen to Good People.*

Towards the end of the service, the president of the synagogue approached me and asked, "Would you and your father like to open the ark together for the closing song, *An'im Z'mirot?*"

I turned to Dad and asked him, "What do you think?"

Without hesitation, he answered, "Why not!" I couldn't believe his response, since at home he stopped going to synagogue out of fear someone might ask him to recite something that he no longer remembered.

While standing next to each other in front of the open

ark, I could hardly contain my emotions. My legs felt like rubber bands and my eyes were so filled with tears I could barely see the words in the prayer book. I glanced at my father as he passionately sang every word, and my heart filled with joy.

Leaving the synagogue still filled with emotion, I saw Beth Shalom's cemetery at the rear of the building. I pointed it out to Dad. Jokingly he quipped, "I'm not interested!"

Dear Dad,

I was so glad we went to Rabbi Amy's shul.

It was like having *Susie and Me Day* in synagogue.

I really enjoyed the service and being with you.

Love,
Susie

THIRTY

I decided to turn right on Liberty Road off of Route 32, instead of the usual left turn I made when I took Dad out for a ride. I really wanted him to see the forest of trees surrounding Liberty Reservoir while they still retained their vibrant fall colors. Dad had seemed a bit sluggish earlier, but he was eager to go for a ride.

As we proceeded down Liberty Road and over the first bridge south of Eldersburg, Dad started talking about how beautiful the trees looked. He said, "I didn't know it was fall already. What month is it anyway?" When I told him it was almost the end of October, he was amazed. Bewildered, he said, "October already."

I started to answer, "Don't you... and caught myself before I said "remember when we..." *I tried hard not to use the word "remember" in my conversations with him because lately he wasn't able to recall things that happened a few weeks ago or even yesterday. As hard as I tried, sometimes the word just slipped out.*

I redeemed myself by saying, "I hope the guy behind us isn't in a hurry, so I can drive slowly and we both can enjoy this magnificent beauty." I was surprised the colors on the trees were so vivid. It was evident by the ground erosion around the shoreline of the reservoir that we hadn't had much rain that summer.

Dad and I talked a little about Liberty Reservoir, and he asked me, "Where's the dam?"

Surprised by his question, I hesitated and said, "Not far from here." Mulling over the idea of taking him to Liberty Dam, I told him, "I don't think you can still see the dam anymore. The last time I went was a very long time ago when Scott was in elementary school. You could drive up those winding roads, but you had to park your car, and then hike the rest of the way to where the dam is located. I don't think I feel like hiking today, Dad."

Laughing, he said, "Me, neither."

I continued to drive south for a few more miles, then turned around and drove back up Liberty Road. I looked over at Dad as we approached the first bridge. His head was forward, and he was sound asleep. A few miles later I pulled into the Dairy Queen parking lot, parked, and turned off the ignition. Dad woke up startled and asked where we were. I asked him if he wanted some ice cream and he responded, "Now, you're talking." I ordered him an orange creamsicle. *I needed to remind him to lick the bar slowly. I watched him carefully, since ice cream turns to a thin liquid quickly and I didn't want him to aspirate. We didn't do this very often and I could tell by his expression it was a real treat for him.*

All of us were trying to take Dad out more before the weather turned too cold, and he would be limited to being indoors. Early in October, I drove Dad out to Beth Shalom synagogue to see their *sukkah,* a temporary hut or booth built during the holiday of Sukkot. It was reminiscent of those built by the Israelites during the forty years they wandered in the desert after their exodus from Egypt.

What a great day that was! I brought a kosher picnic lunch and two aluminum folding chairs. We ate, we laughed, and we talked about the sukkah we had when I was a child and we lived above my great-grandparents. We talked about another sukkah we erected from pipes and canvas when Dad's grandsons were younger. I told Dad how much we had appreciated him bringing the branches for the top of the sukkah in his truck every year. Those were fun times—decorating the sukkah, having our friends and family over almost every day or night for the seven-day holiday, and eating more sweets than we could get away with the rest of the year.

Another time I went with Dad and other assisted-living residents on a trip to Baugher's Farm. The farm was filled with everything related to fall—gourds, cornstalks, bails of hay, colorful mums, more varieties of apples than I have ever seen, and pumpkins, pumpkins, and more pumpkins. As the group walked around, Chris, the activities leader, asked targeted questions, giving people a chance to talk about what they were seeing.

Beatrice started crying. She was upset that she had not brought any money with her to buy something in the shop that sold knickknacks, homemade apple butter, jams, honey, and pies. Chris consoled her by saying, "Don't worry, we'll come back and you can bring money the next time. Everyone will get some cider and take a pumpkin back with them." Beatrice was relieved and the residents were happy. *The entire time we were at Baugher's, I kept thinking about how ironic this experience was. Here I was with my eighty-six year-old father helping him find the pumpkin he wanted. Thirty-five years ago I was doing the same thing with the kindergarteners in my class, only we picked the pumpkins from a field. Again, I had come full circle.*

As the days grew shorter and the temperature dropped, the activities department planned more exercise, physical involvement, and indoor walking programs for the residents to keep up their physical vitality and prevent any boredom or depression that might arise from constantly being indoors. Residents walked the "Appalachian Trail," stretched, tossed beach balls, played volleyball, and shot mini-basketballs into hoops. The staff really encouraged the residents to participate, and Dad was usually an enthusiastic participant.

Resident involvement was the key goal of the activities department. At the international fashion show held in the Garden Room, some of the staff and a few family members paraded down the runway, modeling the traditional dress from various countries. The residents loved seeing the bright costumes from Jamaica and Haiti, the sari from

India, and the emerald green outfit of Ireland. The United States was well represented with several styles worn by twin sister resident assistants, Karen and Sharon. It was fun for the residents to see the people who cared for them wearing something other than their everyday uniforms. Florence, a somewhat shy and introverted resident, gladly modeled a festive Korean wedding gown with a red and yellow silk bodice and an elaborate hand-sewn trim adorning a blue satin full skirt. Flo wowed her audience and bowed slightly to the oohs and ahhs of the residents. Dad and Shirley were very surprised to see me wearing a scarlet, satin embroidered Chinese robe that my grandmother had brought back from a trip to the Orient decades ago. "Excellento! Excellento!" Dad shouted as I passed by. *Where did he come up with that one? He sounded more Italian than American.*

Many activities centered on the upcoming holidays, and involved a multi-disciplinary approach incorporating a variety of art, music, literature, cooking, intellectual, and sensory incentives. They highlighted Thanksgiving, Hanukkah, Christmas, and Kwanzaa. The residents were engaged, stimulated, and seemed excited to see and hear many of the sights and sounds they remembered from their pasts.

The residents truly enjoyed the visits from elementary school students and the Brownie troop. The children helped the residents with many activities and with trimming the trees. Residents bonded with students from the local high school who volunteered after school or on weekends as part of their service-learning hours.

It was fascinating to see how well both generations connected. Age differences disappeared.

Residents and their families enjoyed a traditional Thanksgiving dinner, as well as Copper Ridge's annual holiday party. That year the theme of the holiday party was, "Jazz Up Your Holidays." During the party, Dad helped me lead the Hanukkah songs, and boisterously sang familiar Christmas carols with the group. However, when everyone was singing *O Tannenbaum, O Tannenbaum,* Dad sang *Maryland, My Maryland,* the official state song of Maryland set to the same tune.

At Hanukkah, families came together to light the menorah, eat potato latkes (pancakes) and donuts, and sing songs. Our family went to all the events at Copper Ridge. Dad appreciated having us with him, and exuberantly sang just about every song.

Dad was just as jubilant at our own family Hanukkah party later in December at Copper Ridge. He led the blessing and lit the candles with a little help and a lot of coaxing. I made sure there was a gift for Dad to give Shirley and some Hanukkah *gelt* (money) to give to all his grandchildren. I brought old pictures of Dad lighting the menorah with Dave and me when we were just children. There were other Hanukkah pictures of his grandsons when they were much younger. We all had a good laugh when Dad commented on how much hair he had in those pictures. Shirley brought an electric menorah to keep in his room, and she lit it with him every night before she left for home. Even though Dad was at Copper Ridge, we knew how important it was to celebrate this tradition with him like we always did every year.

On Super Bowl Sunday, Dave called me on his cell phone from Dad's room. I could hear the excitement in his voice as he told me he brought O'Doul's beer and some snacks to have a Super Bowl Party with Dad. *How cool was that, a private father and son Super Bowl party.* After we talked a bit, Dave put Dad on the phone to talk to me.

"Dad, its Susie. I hear you and Dave are having a Super Bowl party."

"You should see all the goodies Dave has here," he replied.

"Sounds like that's right up your alley, Dad," I said. "I think it's great that you and Dave are having your own party. I know you are going to have fun." Before I could catch myself, I said, "Who's playing, Dad?" *That was really dumb, Susan.* Dad cleverly answered, "Two teams."

To cover for my inappropriateness, I changed the subject and we started talking about the 1958 National Football League World Championship Game between the Baltimore Colts and the New York Giants. That really got Dad started. "Unitas to Berry, Unitas to Berry," he repeated. "Touchdown! Go, you Colts!" His voice was filled with enthusiasm as we recalled the game-winning field goal kicked by Steve Myhra with seven seconds left to tie up the game, sending it into the first ever overtime. "And old Alan Ameche scored the winning touchdown," I told Dad.

Dad exuberantly boasted, "THE COLTS WERE THE CHAMPIONS!"

I could almost hear the screams that erupted in our living room after that game in 1958. We all hugged. We jumped up and down in jubilant disbelief. We even had an impromptu party to celebrate the Colts' victory in our kitchen on Springdale Avenue. Dave and I made decorations to put on the wall. We relived the game details over and over again during dinner. It was an event no one from Baltimore will ever forget. Best of all, Dad didn't either.

The next day Dave called to tell me what a great time he had with Dad. At halftime, when the Rolling Stones began to perform, he told me Dad got up, turned the TV off, and said, "Great game!"

Dear Dad,

I was running around doing a bunch of errands yesterday.

I was stopped at a light and must have been daydreaming. Thoughts of you came to mind. And, of course, a smile came to my face.

All my love,
Susie

THIRTY-ONE

Chuck and I were in Florida when Shirley called. I could hear the anxiety in her voice. She was talking so fast that I could barely understand everything she was saying. Evidently she had just walked in the door from visiting Dad earlier, when she received a phone call from Copper Ridge. The nurse told her that Dad's temperature had spiked to 103 degrees not long after she left, and they were sending him to the nearest hospital by ambulance. They thought he may have pneumonia.

"I don't even know where the hospital is out there," she said.

I told her to take a few deep breaths and call Copper Ridge to ask them how to get to the hospital. I asked her to call me after she saw Dad, and I would call Dave to let him know what happened. After I talked to my brother,

I called my sons. Everyone said they were heading out to the hospital.

It seemed like the phone rang every ten minutes after making those initial calls. Thank goodness I had a full charge on my cell phone. My head was spinning, but I had the presence of mind to get a note pad to keep by my phone.

I called the Annapolis House Nurses' Station at Copper Ridge to see if I could find out more from them about Dad's health prior to being sent to the hospital. I spoke to Kim, the nurse on duty that night. Evidently Dad had taken a fall shortly after Shirley left, and he was found on the floor leaning against the wall near the heat vent. Because of his dementia, he couldn't explain what happened to the staff. He wasn't able to walk without assistance. He told Kim that he wasn't in any pain, but an examination revealed he had a tear on his elbow, which they subsequently treated. When Dad's vitals were taken, he had a temperature of 102.6. The doctor was called and they were monitoring him closely. After their initial assessment, Dad had shortness of breath, was coughing up thick yellow mucous, and his temperature rose to 103.3. He was also lethargic and hallucinating, so they called for an ambulance.

Kim informed me that there was a note from Dr. Onyike earlier in the week stating that Shirley had noticed more of a cognitive decline recently and increasing distrustfulness. Dad was also failing to recognize her more frequently, which was painful for her.

Everyone who called me from the hospital had a different take on Dad's condition. Dave thought Dad was disoriented, although Dad seemed to recognize his family. He was thrashing around, agitated, and somewhat combative since he didn't understand what the nurses were doing to him. As a last resort, Dad had to be restrained so the staff could do their job.

Shirley told me she thought there was no need for me to fly from Sarasota to Baltimore yet. Dave, Scott, and Craig thought Dad looked terrible. Craig gave me a reality check about returning to Baltimore by saying, "Zaid's eighty-six years old and may have pneumonia, Mom. Who knows what's going to happen."

Trying to get a last-minute flight from Sarasota to Baltimore on President's Day weekend was frustrating, but I was able to get a flight leaving out of Tampa at six o'clock in the morning the next day. Chuck set our alarm for 3:00 a.m., so we could get to Tampa by five. The phone calls continued with updates until about eleven that night. I didn't get upset until I received the text message from Dave when I woke up. He texted me that Dad had a mild heart attack. The last line of his message was, "It doesn't look good."

I tried to read while I was on the plane but I couldn't concentrate. I knew this was going to be a long day, so I struggled to nap without success. I tried to relax by meditating and thinking positive thoughts, but that was futile also. I kept thinking how quickly things had changed.

It was only five days ago that I had arranged for flowers

to be delivered to Pam, the family liaison at Copper Ridge, so she could give them to Dad as a surprise for Shirley on Valentine's Day. Pam called and told me that Dad was so excited about having flowers to give to Shirley that he was pacing the hallways waiting for her. However, he forgot about the flowers when she arrived. Pam told me she took Dad aside and showed him again where the flowers were. "The joy on their faces as your dad and Shirley hugged and exchanged Valentine's gifts was priceless. I loved being a part of it."

My sons must have gotten their wires crossed because they both came to the airport to pick me up. It was a really good feeling to see them both there as I came down the escalator to go to the Southwest baggage claim area. Scott was with his girlfriend, Bridget, and Craig had Shirley with him so he could drive her out to the hospital from the airport. They both took me aside to tell me that their grandfather looked the worst they had ever seen him.

After getting my own car, I headed out to the hospital. Although it wasn't the right time to visit ICU, the nurse let me go in to see Dad. When I peeked in his room, he was sleeping. I stood silently by his bed for a few minutes gathering my thoughts. He was pale but looked like he was resting comfortably and was in no distress.

I wiped away the tears before I went to the nurses' station to find out which nurse was taking care of my father. I asked what kind of night Dad had had, and what the cardiologist said. To my surprise and disappointment, his nurse told me that the hospital didn't have a cardiologist on staff. She had called one early that morning, but he hadn't arrived yet. Living in Baltimore all my life and being accustomed to having some of the best teaching hospitals in the country, I was dumbfounded to find out there wasn't a cardiologist on staff. I asked the nurse to please have the cardiologist speak with our family after he saw Dad.

Dad was awake when I returned to his room. Shirley and Dave told me that Dad had not been aware of my absence, and that he never asked about me while I was in Florida. That was a lucky thing for me because he wasn't upset that I hadn't come to visit. However, it made me sad to think that he may not be able to recall that he still had a daughter.

Any hesitancy about Dad not recognizing me evaporated when he acknowledged my presence, but he did not call me by *Susie* when I leaned over to give him a kiss. Although he was glad to see me, I could tell he was upset.

"I need to pee," he told me. I knew he had a catheter, so I told him to just go. "I need to use the bathroom now," he said.

"Daddy, the doctors and nurses don't want you to get out of bed to use the bathroom. They have a tube inside you so you can just go to the bathroom while you're still in bed. This bag catches your urine. Just relax and try to void."

Agitated, he told me, "I'm going to mess up the bed."

"You won't, Daddy," I said as I showed him the bag again, "because the tube and the bag won't leak."

He started crying. "I really have to go," he repeated again.

We went round robin about the catheter over and over again, only by this time Dave was there trying to explain the catheter. He didn't have success either. Just when we thought we'd made some headway, Dad said, "But I have to pee." His face became contorted, and he tried to get up. He flopped back down on the bed and desperately asked, "Will somebody just please let me pee?"

I got the charge nurse, who skillfully explained and showed Dad the catheter, telling him where it was placed and how it worked. "You just relax, Mr. Miller, and just go normally and the bag will catch your urine just like the toilet does at home. This is the way we do it in the hospital when the doctor doesn't want the patient to get out of bed." Dad nodded his head, as if he comprehended what the nurse had just said. As soon as the nurse left he repeated, "Will somebody just please let me pee?" Again Dave showed Dad the catheter bag, and we saw that it was filling up. *I don't know who was more relieved, Dad or Dave and me.* The ICU nurses had been lenient about letting one of us stay with Dad, since he seemed less stressed when someone was with him.

After a few hours, a cardiologist talked to our family about Dad's condition, telling us that he had had a mild heart attack. He asked us what we wanted to do next. *Wasn't it his job to inform the family about the options available or suitable for a man Dad's age? What about the possible pneumonia?* I was waiting for the doctor to give us more information or more direction, but nothing was forthcoming. Exasperated, I finally asked him to tell us what our options were. The doctor told us he would know more after Dad had an ultrasound. I was already thinking about calling Chuck's cardiologist at St. Joseph's Medical Center in Baltimore to get another opinion but decided to wait until I had more information after Dad's ultrasound. The doctor deferred us to the house doctor for our questions concerning Dad's pneumonia. None of us had seen the house doctor yet.

The hours passed, and still no sign of the house doctor. We alternated our visits with Dad, so each of us could make phone calls or get something to eat. Although Dad was sleeping, we wanted to make sure someone was with him so we didn't miss any doctors.

I was in the ICU waiting room and noticed a woman rolling the portable ultrasound machine down the hallway towards ICU. I glanced at my watch. It was already three o'clock in the afternoon. Maybe, *finally*, we'd get some answers.

About an hour and a half passed. I was talking on the phone with Chuck when I saw the ultrasound tech pass the waiting room again in the opposite direction. I told Chuck I'd call him back, and I ran out to try to catch up with her. "I know you can't give me any information, but did you do an ultrasound on my father in room six?"

She asked me my father's name and looked at her orders. "I don't have Leslie Miller on this requisition sheet." *That's just great. Now what?* I thanked her and headed back to ICU. I tried to get someone's attention. *I felt like banging on the door so they would let me in. Maybe then I could talk with someone about not scheduling Dad's ultrasound.*

Another nurse used her badge to enter the ICU, and I quickly followed her in before she asked any questions. The charge nurse checked her computer and told me there wasn't an ultrasound ordered for Leslie Miller. Trying to stay calm, I asked if his doctor was still in the hospital so he could be paged. I was informed that he had left, so I asked for the number of his office. I wanted to try to catch him before he left for the day. After explaining my dilemma to the office receptionist, I asked her if she would please have the doctor call the ICU nurses' station ASAP and order an ultrasound for my father. She graciously said she would give him the message. I tried to stress how important this was and thanked her for her time. Before I hung up, I told her our family would like the doctor to call me on my cell with the results.

Tired and really agitated, I tried to regain my composure before relaying what I knew to Dave and Shirley. It was now 4:30 p.m. and I knew we wouldn't have any answers before Chuck's cardiologist's office closed. Since things were out of my control, I tried to nap while sitting in the waiting room. My rest was short-lived, since my cell phone kept vibrating every time I closed my eyes. Wide awake, I decided to rehash the day in my mind and jot down some notes so I would have a log of what transpired that day. With the inefficiency in this hospital, I had a gut feeling I would need to refer to this information sometime in the future.

A few more hours dragged by. I checked with the ICU

nurse once again to make sure the cardiologist called in and ordered Dad's ultrasound. Her answer was yes, but no one had any idea of when the technician would be back in ICU. *Was this any way to run an airline?*

There were only a couple of people besides Shirley and Dave in the waiting room when I returned from ICU. Furious, frustrated and exhausted, I said, "This place sure isn't St. Joe's." We all looked at each other, realizing that each one of us was thinking the same thing. I broke the silence and said, "I think if we are going to get a more comprehensive diagnosis to help us make more informed decisions, Dad needs to be moved to a cardiac hospital." After finding out if it was all right for Dad to travel, and weighing the pros and cons of such a move, we unanimously decided to have Dad transferred to St. Joseph's Medical Center in Baltimore.

While nibbling on what seemed to be my staple diet of peanut butter crackers and regular Pepsi (I needed the caffeine to stay awake), the charge nurse from ICU told us that the arrangements had been made to have Dad transferred. His heart catherization was scheduled for nine o'clock the next morning. I looked across at Shirley, whose expression showed her displeasure and concern. She didn't comment, but like me, I knew she could hardly believe what this nurse had just told us. I swallowed hard. I felt tightness in my chest trying to digest both the last bit of cracker and what this nurse had just said without screaming.

Swallowing hard again and trying to remain composed, I asked her, "Who made the decision about scheduling a catherization for tomorrow? Our family asked for my father to be transferred to St. Joe's for further evaluation, not catherization."

The nurse's response did not convince any of us that she was not at fault. Knowing that losing my cool would be completely counterproductive, I calmly asked her to please call whoever at St. Joe's and clarify why Dad was being transferred. I also suggested that she call their cath lab and make sure Dad's name was removed from the schedule for the next morning.

She said she wouldn't have any problem giving me the names of the people she spoke to after she made the new arrangements. I thanked her for helping us with this matter, but I figured it was useless to ask her when we would get the results of his ultrasound at that late hour.

We stayed with Dad until the shift change to be sure his new nurse understood the arrangements and everyone was on the same page. Dad drifted in and out of sleep and wasn't always aware that he was in the hospital. To me his color seemed a little better, but I didn't know if this was really true or just wishful thinking on my part. The staff continued to monitor his vitals, and the new charge nurse introduced herself and explained in detail when and how Dad was going to be transferred. He would remain at the hospital through the night, and be transferred by ambulance to St. Joe's tomorrow morning. She told us that no family members could accompany him in the ambulance, and she assured us that she would contact one of us as soon as the ambulance left. We would have plenty of time to get to St. Joe's before Dad arrived.

All of us felt much more confident that things would be handled better with this nurse.

After being up for almost twenty-one hours, I thought I would fall asleep as soon as my head hit the pillow. But the stress of the day and the anxiety of tomorrow kept me awake. I put on my magnifying glasses and began reading the book on my nightstand.

The shrill ringing next to my ear startled me, as did the bright light that I must have left on all night. Squinting, I grabbed the phone, as my glasses and book tumbled to the floor. Half awake and in a fog, I heard the ICU nurse tell me Dad would be leaving their hospital in about an hour.

THIRTY-TWO

The elevator door opened while Shirley, Dave, and I were waiting in the second floor solarium at St. Joseph's Medical Center. Seeing Dad on a stretcher being wheeled out by the ambulance transfer team eased our anxiety. We simultaneously rushed over towards him.

To my surprise, Dad was awake and appeared to be relatively alert, which was a great relief for all of us. The ambulance team stopped so we could say a few words to Dad before they took him to the nurses' station. He acknowledged us with a smile. Shirley grabbed his hand and said, "I'm here, darling." She continued to walk closely alongside the stretcher. The attendants didn't stop her. Dave and I heard them say, "Mr. Miller had an uneventful trip over here. He slept most of the way." *Thank God. Due to his age and frail condition, I was extremely worried about the impact of transferring Dad such a long distance.*

Before I went up to the second floor, I stopped by the office of Dr. Stephen Pollock, my husband's cardiologist. Stephanie, Dr. Pollock's secretary, recognized me from being there so often for Chuck's appointments and procedures. I gave her a brief synopsis of what had occurred and asked her if it would be possible for Dr. Pollock to see Dad sometime that day. She told me Dr. Pollock, who was also director of the Heart Institute, was seeing patients in his office. She assured me that she would have someone from the practice see Dad later. I was so grateful.

When Shirley returned, she told Dave and me that a nurse had taken Dad's vitals. They were also monitoring his heart and blood pressure and giving him medication intravenously. The nurse had asked Shirley to give her about fifteen minutes to finish the admitting process. I could tell Shirley had been crying.

Dave was next to go see Dad. The staff welcomed having his family nearby, but asked that only one person be with him at a time, since there was another patient in the room. This was the perfect opportunity for me to call Copper Ridge back. Fran, the assisted-living nurse coordinator, and Pam, the family liaison, had called me on my cell phone to find out how Dad was doing. They also wanted to know if they could be of any help.

It wasn't long before Dave returned. He told us that the admitting doctor would talk to our family after he finished evaluating Dad.

Standing by the window in the solarium where I

could get a better signal on my cell phone, I saw a doctor approach Dave and Shirley. I quickly stopped dialing and walked over to them. The doctor told us that Dad knew he was in a hospital, but he had no recollection of his transfer or memory of what had occurred prior to coming to St. Joe's. He had a cough, nasal congestion, and a low grade fever. His pulse was irregular.

Before the doctor finished, I saw Dr. Pollock come off the elevator and ask to speak to the admitting doctor privately. I was stunned to see Dr. Pollock. After a brief conversation with the other doctor, Dr. Pollock started heading down the hallway. He waved at us and said he'd be back to talk to us shortly.

We thanked the admitting doctor for his time and effort, and waited in anticipatory silence for Dr. Pollock to return. When he returned, he sat down with us in the solarium. I introduced Dr. Pollock to Shirley and Dave and thanked him for taking the time to evaluate Dad. Dr. Pollock began by saying, "We probably could have taken care of this with a phone call."

I can't tell you how badly I felt at that moment. It was as if someone just punched me in the gut. Even though Dr. Pollock fully understood our dilemma with the other hospital and acknowledged this, I still felt terribly guilty for not following my instinct and making the call yesterday. If I had connected with Dr. Pollock earlier, he might have guided me differently and maybe Dad's transfer would not have been necessary. I knew I needed to let this thought go in order to hear what Dr. Pollock needed to tell us. I felt my eyes well up with tears. I took a deep breath and tried to stay focused.

"Your husband and father has a history of heart disease and has been quite fortunate not to have had any severe complications since his bypass surgery in 1983," Dr. Pollock said. "He has had a mild heart attack and has possibly contracted pneumonia, although that is not definite yet. There are two major factors that come into play here. The first is that he is almost eighty-seven years old and the second being that he has vascular dementia and Alzheimer's disease. I need to be brutally honest here. In my experience, if we can help a patient his age medically, there is usually a further and oftentimes a significant decline in their dementia. I've seen it time and time again. I really don't think that it's in Mr. Miller's best interest or yours to proceed with any aggressive coronary treatment at this time.

I was listening intently. I could feel my heart racing. My palms became sweaty. I glanced over at Dave and Shirley. It was obvious they were agonizing also. I had many questions. I rested my elbow on the armrest of my chair and placed my fingers over my lips to keep me from interrupting before Dr. Pollock had finished. I knew I tended to do that at times.

After a brief pause, allowing all of us time to digest what he had just said, Dr. Pollock continued by saying, "I had a relative who was at Copper Ridge, so I am very familiar with the quality of care there. They are experts at what they do. In my opinion, I would take your dad back to Copper Ridge. They will know how to take care of him. The thing that I want you to know—if it was my loved one, that's exactly what I would do."

There was dead silence as the three of us tried to absorb what we had just heard. Dave commented first. "You are the most candid doctor I have ever met, and I appreciate you being so honest with us." Both Shirley and I also thanked Dr. Pollock for his frankness. We unanimously decided to follow Dr. Pollock's recommendation and have Dad transferred back to Copper Ridge. Dr. Pollock said he would have the admitting doctor make the arrangements.

I was sitting by Dad's bed watching him sleep, silently wondering what affect the long trip back to Copper Ridge would have on him. *Dr. Pollock's statement, "This could have been handled with a phone call," kept resonating in my head. This was just another one of those "if only" moments in my life to add to my list of regrets. I knew I had to let those thoughts go, but seeing Dad so vulnerable and frail caused me much pain. I had to believe that if God had wanted it any other way, He would have guided me differently.*

Dad suddenly woke up with a bewildered look. I leaned in closer to his bed so he could see me. "It's Susie, Daddy." He grabbed my hand, holding it tightly. "I'm here with you, Daddy. You're at St Joseph's Hospital." Before I could say anything else, he told me in a desperate, frantic voice, "Susie, something is terribly wrong!"

"Daddy, I think it's the fever that's making you feel this way. Sometimes it goes up. The doctors are giving you some medication to make you better." He appeared to be looking straight through me. It was eerie and made me a bit uncomfortable. I nonchalantly pressed the call button for the nurse. When the nurse responded, I asked her if she would please come to Dad's room. Dad didn't have any idea that I was talking to the nurse through the intercom. He looked straight up at the ceiling. I'd never seen this look on his face before. I was scared.

The nurse asked Dad, "Are you in any discomfort or pain, Mr. Miller?" Dad looked at me. It appeared his brief trance episode had subsided. He was very cooperative while the nurse took his blood pressure, pulse, and temperature. She questioned Dad again, and he replied, "I'm OK." *I decided not to tell Dad he was going back to Copper Ridge at this time. I knew how long it could take to order a wheelchair van and have it arrive at the hospital. I thought it was best not to give him too much information that might upset or confuse him. The less said the better.*

Because the traffic was heavy, the ride back to Copper Ridge seemed to take forever. Dad slept most of the way, only stirring when we hit a pothole or heard a loud siren. For me, the trip was reminiscent of Dad's first van trip to Copper Ridge almost a year ago, only without as much anxiety. So much had transpired since that fateful day in March. Unlike then, I was confident that Dad would get the best care possible on his return to Copper Ridge.

While Dad slept, I also closed my eyes. I became conscious of my breath, trying to bring myself into a more relaxed state. Dr. Pollock's words, "This could have been handled with a phone call," still haunted me. My mind wouldn't release me from this unnerving guilt. Could this long trip to St. Joe's been avoided? To ease this uncomfortable feeling, I tried to recall a wonderful passage from Reeve Lindbergh's book, *No More Words,* (2001) about her mother, Anne Morrow Lindbergh. I hoped it would bring me some solace and relief. On page 24, Lindbergh writes:

> In a situation like mine, there is memory, and there is frustration, and there is grief, and there is guilt. In fact, there is more guilt than anything else. No matter how good the care provided, no matter how much attention or how much money is spent to address their needs, no matter how extensive the medical treatment lavished upon our beloved elders, there is always guilt, and it is always the same.
>
> We feel guilty because our parents are living at home and are not doing well. We feel guilty because they have been removed from their homes, by our arrangement and are not happy about it. We feel guilty because we live far away from them and do not see them often enough. We feel guilty because we live close by and still don't see them often enough. We feel guilty because we live with them and see them every day, but our presence does not seem to help them.
>
> I think we feel guilty about our aging parents, regardless of their circumstances, not because we have *not* done our best for

them but because we *have*. Our efforts only emphasize the truth that we and they must live with every day. Whatever we have done, whatever we continue to do, it isn't enough. It won't change the fact that we cannot keep them alive, not forever. We cannot keep them healthy and happy, we cannot keep them with us much longer. They are exactly where they are, close to the end of life. There is nothing we can do about it.

Dad didn't have much color but was all smiles as Shirley wheeled him back to his room in the Annapolis House. The staff was very welcoming and Dad reacted by saying, "It's good to be home." What a relief those words were for all of us. *I always believed that Dad considered Copper Ridge his home. I just never knew, on any given day, if he even remembered any of the previous places he had lived. It didn't really matter if he did or he didn't. He was at peace and happy there.*

Dad greeted Dr. Onyike enthusiastically when he came to examine him that afternoon. Dr. Onyike questioned Dad and Shirley and I decided to step out to give them some privacy. Dr. Onyike told us afterwards that Dad didn't recall being in the hospital at all, and Dad seemed unaware of the recent decline in his health. He believed Dad's judgment had become more impaired.

A few minutes later, a tray of light food was brought to Dad's room. He didn't seem too interested in eating.

He did take a few sips of his thickened juice which made him cough, most likely causing some of the liquid to enter his lungs. I knew this was not a good thing at all. Shirley tried to get Dad to eat a mouthful of oatmeal without success. The aide put Dad's tray aside.

Various staff members came in to check on him. He was cooperative but tired. I thought Dad just wanted everyone to leave him alone and let him rest. Eventually that did happen, and Dad easily drifted off to sleep. We left so Dad could get some well-deserved rest.

Bonnie, Copper Ridge's social worker, stopped us in the hallway to talk to us about palliative care. She explained that the goal of palliative care was to support the best possible quality of life for patients living with serious illness and their families. It was designed to customize Dad's treatment to meet his individual needs, whether they were physical, mental, spiritual, or social.

"We try to relieve the pain, symptoms, and stress of a serious illness no matter what the diagnosis or prognosis is. Right now, Mr. Miller meets the criteria for palliative care."

Bonnie told us that the staff wanted to do everything they could to make Dad comfortable and help him handle his illness better, particularly since he didn't understand everything that was happening to him. "If he only wants ice cream for all his meals, and that's the only thing he will eat, then we will give him ice cream." *I was thinking Dad would love that.*

Bonnie told me there was a form that she would like to go over with me so I could sign it as his power of attorney. Seeing how exhausted I must have looked, she told me that she would bring me the form tomorrow. She suggested we go home and get some rest, and encouraged us to call the nurses' station later for a report.

I called Chuck in Florida while sitting in my car in front of Copper Ridge. I really needed to hear his voice, even though I'd talked to him several times that day. He always knew the right words to say to lift my spirits and keep me focused and grounded. He asked me if I wanted him to fly up, and I told him that I was OK. Now that Dad was back at Copper Ridge, I was confident about his care. We talked for over a half an hour and Chuck urged me to get something to eat before I headed home. I promised him I would and also told him I would call when I got home.

I stopped at Zi Pani just to get some soup or something, realizing only then that I hadn't eaten lunch. The place was empty and one employee was stacking chairs on tables, while another swept. They were nice enough to let me in, and told me they were getting an early jump on closing since they weren't busy. No soup, but a delicious, gooey sticky bun and Diet Coke really hit the spot.

I usually would turn left to head south down Liberty Road towards Deer Park Road to get to 795. Instead I continued straight across on Route 32. Something in my head was telling me to go back to Copper Ridge. Since I was on a sugar high, I was energized.

I walked down the hall towards Dad's room. As I rounded the corner to Dad's hallway, I was shocked to see him walking slowly with Beth, his physical therapist.

Beth saw me, but Dad was looking down at his feet. I heard Beth say, "Just a little bit more, Mr. Miller. You're doing great." I quickly backed away before Dad saw me, so I didn't interrupt and break his concentration.

I sat down in a high back chair in the television room. A few residents were wandering around, but most were in their rooms. It was very quiet. *I was thankful for the silence. I needed to gather my thoughts. What a roller coaster day this had been. Seeing Dad up and walking was encouraging. Was palliative care necessary? Bonnie and Fran had both told me he met the criteria. I was not a professional, just his anxious daughter wanting the best for him. I did trust their judgment, like I always had.*

Beth interrupted my thoughts. She told me she stayed late to evaluate Dad, and she would be working with him every day to help build up his strength. "He's very frail and understandably tired, so I didn't want to do too much right now. I'll reevaluate him in the morning." I thanked her and gave Beth a hug before I went to see Dad.

Dad was asleep, so I just stood by his bed for a few moments. I kissed him on the forehead and said a silent prayer before I left.

THIRTY-THREE

Bonnie went over each item on the palliative care form with me to be sure I understood what was involved for every item before I checked "yes" or "no". Her patience, clarity, and support helped me get through this arduous responsibility as Dad's power of attorney. Even though I was familiar with the content of Dad's medical directive and knew his wishes, this was still a difficult experience.

"Thank goodness your dad has an advance directive," Bonnie told me. "It takes the burden of making those critical decisions off your shoulders." I appreciated her thoughts, but my stomach still felt tied in knots.

As I attempted to press the door code to the Annapolis House on the way to see Dad, I noticed one of the flight-risk residents standing on the other side of the door. I didn't want to have a confrontation with this person, so I turned around and decided to enter through the Carroll County House door. Fran, who was standing in the hallway talking to a nurse by her office door, signaled for me to wait just a minute until she was finished.

I sat down in her office. "Susan, your dad has no appetite and has stopped eating. I didn't say anything to Shirley last night when she was trying to get him to eat some oatmeal. I know how difficult this is for her because we've all been conditioned to believe that if you just get the patient to eat, they'll get better. Your dad isn't taking in food, and liquids are extremely difficult because of his aspiration."

Fran looked directly at me. Her concerned face told me things weren't good. Fran said, "Many times, loss of appetite is one of the first signs that the patient is dying." I leaned over and rested my head on my hands.

The tears trickled down my face uncontrollably. Fran hugged me and just let me cry. I didn't think I could get any words out if I tried. There was total silence except for my sniffling. Fran handed me some Kleenex. I don't know how long we sat there. When I did get my composure, I looked up at Fran and said, "I was so hopeful. Beth had him up last night walking. I certainly didn't expect this."

Fran let me ramble. "Does Shirley know?" I asked.

"She knows he's not eating, but I'm going to talk to her. I have a consultant from Carroll Hospice coming in later this afternoon to assess another resident. With your permission, I would like her to see your dad."

"Hospice," I muttered. "I just completed the palliative

care checklist with Bonnie, and now we're talking about *hospice*."

Fran said, "I know just the word *hospice* frightens many people, but for now this is just an evaluation." *Intellectually, I was OK with the assessment because I knew Fran was also a hospice nurse and had been for many years. Emotionally, my heart was breaking. I was a mess.*

I saw Beth coming around the corner as I left Fran's office. "Are you on the way to see my dad?" I asked. Her answer was yes. Fran shook her head. Beth was surprised and put her arms around me, and said, "I'm so sorry."

Before I went back, I called Dave. "Are you at work?"

"No, I'm in the parking lot at Copper Ridge. I'll be inside in a minute,"

"We need to talk."

Shirley was coming out of Dad's room when Dave and I came down the hallway. Fran was right behind her. Shirley saw us and we all hugged. No words were spoken between us.

Shirley said, "I need to call Bob. He's waiting for my call."

I asked her if she wanted me to call him, and she said, "I'll do it after I get myself together."

Dave and I went into Dad's room. Dad was asleep and still sounded congested, although he was receiving an antibiotic and nasal spray. Dave sat down on the window bench by Dad's bed. He watched Dad intently. He leaned over and crossed his arms against the bed railing to rest his head. In the silence, I heard him break down.

I didn't go over to console him. I was lost in my own thoughts sitting in Dad's La-Z-Boy chair. I had a flashback of me sitting on Dad's lap in our old living room when I was about three. I was facing Dad and I had one of his pipes in my mouth. I was trying to imitate what he was doing. Dad and I were laughing. How I loved to play with his pipe collection housed in the circular humidor next to his overstuffed chair. At his best height, Dad was five foot eight, not exactly a giant of a man. Now he looked so small and frail in that bed. Yet, in my heart he was still that giant to me.

I had an urgent need to talk to Chuck. I left Dad's room without saying anything to Dave. I was walking towards the lobby, when I saw Fran talking to a slim, relatively young woman with long brown hair. I knew immediately that she must be the hospice consultant. After a few introductions, Robin and I walked to a more private area where she began telling me about what she did as a certified hospice and palliative care nurse. Following our conversation, Robin told me to please go get something to eat in the coffee shop, and she would find me after she evaluated Dad.

The items on the hospice form weren't very different from the ones on the palliative care sheet I signed earlier, only now I didn't need as much explanation for each entry. The task was still difficult. There would be no CPR (cardiopulmonary resuscitation). That was a unanimous family decision we had made almost a year ago. Since the medical team agreed that Dad was in the end stage of cardiomyopathy, he was not to be sent to the hospital for IV hydration, antibiotics, or for any other medical treatment not related to his current condition. I checked "yes" for in-house pain management, comfort measures, bowel care, and oral hygiene. I checked "yes" for pleasure foods and hydration, even though I had finally come to grips with the idea that Dad had no appetite and there were valid reasons for this. I also checked "no" for tube feedings per Dad's wishes.

Robin said she would be leaving recommendations in Dad's chart for pain and comfort meds. Either Lorrie, the physician's assistant, or one of the doctors would approve the hospice plan and write the prescriptions. She also told me that one of their staff would be coming to Copper Ridge to check on Dad tomorrow and then every couple of days thereafter.

She comforted me by saying, "The sooner a resident receives hospice care, the sooner the benefits of hospice care can begin. This includes pain and symptom management, specialized medical and nursing attention, along with emotional support for your Dad and his family. I know it's hard, but you did the right thing." *I couldn't help feeling that if I had done the right thing, how come I wished it wasn't my signature on that form.*

I was still curious about what the differences were between palliative and hospice care. I found out that palliative care was unlimited, where hospice was usually recommended for people who were terminal—those having six months or less to live.

Dave and Shirley were standing in the hallway outside Dad's room when I returned. Lorrie, the physician's assistant, was in the room with Dad. I didn't hear any conversation between the two of them, and I just assumed Dad was still asleep. When Lorrie came out, I told her I just signed the hospice care forms. The sadness on our faces was apparent, and she reminded us that this was what Dad had specifically asked for. "I'm going to the nurses' station to check and update his chart. Please let me know if you need anything."

It wasn't long before we saw Doris from dining services pushing a cart towards the sitting area not far from Dad's room. The cart had small cans of soda, water bottles, and a variety of fruit, cookies, and snacks, along with plates, napkins, ice, and cups. Doris told us Fran ordered the hospitality tray for our family and we were to help ourselves. She left her extension and told us to call her if there was anything else we needed.

Bob and Jan, Shirley's children, were coming down the hall. Bob was just what Shirley needed. She hugged him, clinging to him as tears streamed down her face. I heard Bob tell her that he had cleared his calendar for the rest of the week so he could be with her and all of us. Jan hugged Dave and me, and told us her daughter, Jenny, would be flying in from California tomorrow to see her Grandpa.

That's when I lost it. Through my sobs I heard Shirley tell Bob and Jan, "He's been resting comfortably and the nurses and aides have been in and out of his room constantly." Then the three of them walked into Dad's room together.

I needed a break. I walked towards the lobby to

call Chuck and to notify our synagogue so that the
congregation would say prayers for Dad each day. *Dad
always had a list of people who were ill and wanted him
to say prayers for them for a speedy recovery from illness
or for upcoming surgery. A person's religion, race, or age
didn't matter to Dad. Everyone was important to him. His
grandson Drew once called Dad to ask him to say prayers for
Superman, when Christopher Reeves fell off his horse and
suffered paralysis. Dad took this responsibility seriously and
earnestly tried his best to say prayers daily, even when it was a
struggle because his memory was declining. Now it was Dad
who needed others to return the favor and pray for him.*

Before I reached the lobby, Nancy, the director of
nursing, stopped to ask how I was doing. We talked for a
few minutes before she said, "We know that most families
cannot be here 24/7, so we often suggest that there be
a trained companion with their loved one around the
clock to be with them when the end comes."

*The reality that "the end" may be soon was starting to
sink in, even though I hated hearing those words. How
naive I was about Dad's illness when Shirley first called me
in Florida. I just figured that he would get better.*

Nancy reassured me that their staff would be monitoring
Dad continuously, but they couldn't remain at his bedside
because of their responsibilities to the other residents.
Nancy gave me a business card from *Being There Senior
Care*, a company Copper Ridge recommended, and one
that many families had used and had been pleased with.
My call to Chuck and our synagogue would have to
wait.

THIRTY-FOUR

Dad was declining quickly. Word of Dad's condition spread rapidly throughout Copper Ridge. Our family was overwhelmed by everyone's concern and support. There was a steady parade of staff coming into Dad's room to offer words of comfort. Reverend Larson was just a gem during this very difficult time. He came in periodically during the day to talk with us, to let us cry on his shoulder, and to say psalms and prayers with us at Dad's bedside.

Alice, a resident across the hall from Dad, was standing in the hallway by Dad's room while Reverend Larson was reciting a psalm. When I approached her, she asked me what was going on. I told her Dad hadn't been feeling very well that morning, and the nurses were giving him medicine so he'd get better. She responded, "He doesn't look well. I guess I'll just let him get some rest for now." I thanked her for her concern and walked with her up the hall to the TV living room.

Dad's condition had really deteriorated in the last forty-eight hours. He was lethargic and almost nonverbal, barely responding when someone called his name.

Brenda, our synagogue's secretary and "jack of all trades," called and assured me that prayers were being said for Dad. She asked if we needed anything or wanted to get in touch with Rabbi Adler. I had already spoken to Rabbi Adler and had his cell phone number if needed.

When Dad had his will and medical directive drawn up, we discussed what his wishes would be for his funeral. "I want a plain wooden box and an aluminum shovel," he told me. (The shovel was in case he went down instead of up to heaven. He used to joke about not wanting a heavy shovel because it would be too hard for him to use with his arthritis. I would get so exasperated every time he would bring up the subject of the shovel, but I ended up just laughing with him.)

Our family practically camped out in the small sitting area near Dad's room. Bob and Jenny did work on their laptops, Dave was working from his BlackBerry, and I was making all sorts of lists in preparation before I forgot them. The other residents didn't seem to mind us being there since they were used to our family being around and we knew how to approach and make conversation with most of them.

The hospitality carts continued to appear several times a day. Scott came from work one night and brought pizzas for all of us. Alice and Ned, Dad's hallmates, each had a slice along with us, after we got permission from the nurses. Alice and Ned were glad to have the company. A resident's daughter brought us a tray of bagels with assorted cream cheeses one morning. Our Copper Ridge family was truly extraordinary and we were appreciative for everything they were doing to make things easier.

We took turns visiting Dad. His geriatric nursing assistants, Jerry and Teewon from Being There Senior Care, always respected our need for privacy when any one of us was by Dad's bedside. We were told that although many body functions would gradually be shutting down, Dad could still hear us, and it would be good to talk to him and reassure him even if he couldn't respond. Each of us had our own one-sided conversations with Dad, most being spontaneous private thoughts, whatever we each felt needed to be said. At times it was hard to talk without tears. There were things none of us wanted to leave unsaid, although most things had already been said many times throughout his life. He knew he was loved and how important he was in our lives. We considered ourselves fortunate to have had him almost eighty-seven years. Dad's legacy to us was clear. He had already given Dave and me the greatest gift a father can give his children—unconditional love. What more could we ask for? Although we hated having to say goodbye and let go, we each told Dad that when he was ready, it was OK for him to pass on.

I was thankful for this time to say my goodbyes, and I thought about how awful it must be for those who don't get that opportunity when a loved one dies suddenly. I was so grateful, too, that he and our family were spared the agony of the end stages of Alzheimer's disease.

I often rambled on and on by Dad's bedside, reminiscing about our times together when I was a little girl, a teenager, a teacher, and a mother. Those short, spontaneous vignettes seemed to surface at the oddest times. They occurred in no sequential order, and with unusual clarity, as if they happened just yesterday. I relived many of the milestones Dad had shared with both Dave and me and his grandchildren. I was heartbroken knowing that he wasn't going to be here to share any future milestones with us.

As I rambled, I often wondered if Dad was really hearing me, or was this banter just an exercise to make me feel better and help me have closure. Hospice explained that oftentimes people who are dying are silently working through unresolved issues from their own lives so they can have closure.

Each time I drove out to Copper Ridge, I wondered if this would be Dad's last day. It was an unsettling feeling. I tried very hard to keep that thought out of my mind while driving. I knew I was already sleep deprived, and I really needed to stay alert and concentrate on what I was doing.

I don't know why I didn't just get out of bed last night and review Dad's medical directive to confirm his wishes, instead of lying awake with such frightening thoughts about "starving him to death." Those ghastly thoughts interrupted my sleep and clouded my rational thinking. It was only this morning that I remembered Fran telling me, "People do not die because they stop eating, they stop eating because they are dying."

In my mind, time seemed to be standing still, yet somehow the days were passing. It was now Friday, five days since Shirley first called me and this final nightmare began. Reverend Larson called to let me know that Rabbi Scheinerman was back in town. He told me she wanted me to call her on her cell phone.

Rabbi Scheinerman sincerely wanted to know how each of us was holding up, and she lent a sympathetic ear through my rambling and my tears. I was really surprised and touched when she told me that she wanted to see Dad that evening after services were over at her synagogue. I knew it would be quite late before she could come. She reminded me to let the staff know of her plans so someone would let her in after normal hours.

Although I was dressed in a jogging suit and warm boots, not exactly the most appropriate clothing for synagogue, I attended services at Beth Shalom of Carroll County. It was located about seven miles north of Copper Ridge. Before Shabbat services began, Rabbi Scheinerman asked me for Dad's Hebrew name, and a special *mishaberach* prayer for the sick was said for him. I had a difficult time holding it together and concentrating during the service, but I did find some comforting passages while thumbing through the siddur.

After services, Rabbi Scheinerman followed me over to Copper Ridge. It was almost ten o'clock when we arrived. It was eerie walking into Copper Ridge that late at night. Some of the hallway lights were dimmed, the dining room doors were closed, and the silence was unsettling.

As we rounded the corner to Dad's hallway, I was

shocked to see my sons, Craig and Scott, waiting outside Dad's room. They told me they came together so they could have some uninterrupted private time with their Zaid. How proud I was of them at that moment! I hugged them both through my tears and introduced them to Rabbi Scheinerman.

Dad's door was closed. Scott said, "The nurses have been in with Zaid for the past ten minutes." No one left, including Rabbi Scheinerman. She talked with us and acted like she had nothing else to do that night besides being there. *What a remarkable woman and human being she is.*

We continued to wait, and finally Carol and Teewon told us we could go in. Rabbi Scheinerman went in first and closed Dad's door. When she returned she told us she recited the *Viddui,* (deathbed confessional) for Dad, since he was unable to say it for himself. We couldn't thank her enough for coming to Copper Ridge and for her words of genuine comfort and support. "I'll keep in touch with you and Reverend Larson," she said as she was leaving. "Give Shirley my best. Shabbat Shalom."

Throughout this ordeal, I had been e-mailing family and friends, keeping everyone updated on Dad's status. It was so much easier on me to use the Internet to keep everyone informed, rather than making a bunch of phone calls late at night when I was exhausted. I appreciated the phone messages of concern and support that I received, but I had already notified people that I was too tired to reply to all their calls. Everyone understood and several people offered to make calls to those people that did not use a computer.

The weekend brought more family out to Copper Ridge to see Dad, probably for the last time. Dad's grandchildren, Chad and Drew, flew in from Phoenix, and Ryan and Annie flew in from Kentucky. Chuck came in from Florida after taking care and organizing all the things that needed to be done there.

How wonderful it was to feel his arms around me and sense his strength. Intellectually, I knew all was not well and the worse was yet to come, but having him by my side was a blessing and made everything easier.

Dad's great-nephew and niece visited with their newborn daughter. My cousin hugged me and said, "I just had to come. Uncle Bim is so special in my life. I will always remember him leading the Miller Seder."

As I looked at the tiny baby, I was overwhelmed with emotion. This was truly the circle of life, one person was born and another would pass away.

My oldest cousin called to see if we needed anything and to tell us she would be coming to Copper Ridge on Tuesday. When there was silence on my end of the phone, she said, "I'll be out in a few hours." No one stayed long, but all of them being there was a great comfort to us. I assumed it brought some closure for them.

I knew some people felt uncomfortable coming and others wanted to remember Dad in life not in death. I believe that visiting someone who is dying is a personal choice that each person needs to make for themselves. For me, there is no right or wrong way, and I didn't think any less of those who chose not to come.

THIRTY-FIVE

It was a gloomy, grey morning, quite appropriate considering my solemn mood. Dad was resting comfortably with a cool washcloth on his forehead. I saw my unopened letter setting on his nightstand. Soothing music was playing by his bedside. He looked very pale. I leaned over the bed rail and gave him a kiss. There was no response to my voice. I began to sing *Ma Tovu*, a prayer recited on entering the synagogue, hoping to spark some type of reaction. I sang softly in Hebrew, *How goodly are your tents, O Jacob, your dwelling places, O Israel.* Dad taught me this song. Out of the corner of my eye I saw Dad's aide, Jerry, leave the room. I was grateful for the privacy but saddened by Dad's lack of response. My heart sank. I pulled a chair over to Dad's bed and took his hand. I continued to sing other prayers and read some psalms and selections from the book I brought. I swallowed hard, conscious of the lump in my throat. Surprisingly there were no tears. I was at peace with those words. I hoped Dad was also.

I sensed someone behind me and turned to see Fran respectfully standing in the doorway. She apologized for interrupting, but needed to check on Dad and give him his Ativan. Fran hugged me before I left Dad's room and said, "That was beautiful." I was not even out the doorway, when I felt my phone vibrating again. I didn't answer it. I didn't even look to see who was calling. Whoever it was would have to wait. I was trying not to allow any anxious thoughts to interfere with my peacefulness as I walked over and sat alone by the window at the end of the hallway.

The day passed slowly. Keeping a vigil by Dad's bedside was draining, yet no one was going home. It was good we were all together, lending support to one another while reminiscing about the past. There were tears, there were smiles and laughter, and often there were feelings of helplessness. At times, there was silence except for the occasional vibrations from someone's cell phone. The medical team continued to monitor Dad judiciously and didn't seem to mind our large family presence.

As darkness fell, Dad had even more visitors: his brother and sister-in-law, and his niece. I was so glad they came and only wished that Dad knew they were there. Maybe in his own way he did know. None of us would ever know if that was true. Having them there with Dad and all of us together was the important thing.

It was very late. Everyone was saying their goodbyes

and heading home. I took Chuck aside to tell him that I wanted to stay with Dad that night. "I'm not discussing this with anyone else, because I don't want anyone to feel guilty that they aren't staying. This is something I want to do." Initially Chuck seemed reluctant about me staying, but didn't question me. He asked if I wanted him to stay with me. "I'm OK," I told him. "I just have this premonition that I need to be here. I have a tote with a change of clothes and some toiletries in my car."

Chuck waited for the others to leave before getting my tote. "I can see the tiredness in your eyes, Sugar. Please try to get some rest." Hugging me, he whispered, "I love you."

I returned to Dad's room and pulled his La-Z-Boy chair away from the wall, so I could open it fully. Teewon brought me a pillow and a blanket. We talked for a bit, and then I tried to read my book. I started to doze, although I was somewhat conscious of the staff moving about in Dad's room. Teewon and Carol, the night nurse, persuaded me to go rest in the hospitality room in the Baltimore House, where there was a comfortable bed. They both promised they would come get me if there was any significant change in Dad's status.

I fell asleep the minute my head hit the pillow. I woke up suddenly, startled from a sound sleep. The bed felt strange and I realized I was fully dressed. I tried to get my bearings to figure out where I was. I glanced at my watch. It was two-thirty in the morning. I had been asleep for about three hours. I ran my fingers through my hair and quickly put on my shoes. I decided not to straighten out the sheets since I was anxious to get back to Dad's room. I planned to come back later.

I was amazed to see so many residents walking the halls at this hour. I saw Jim, Dad's neighbor, walking up the hallway with his coat and hat on. I said hello and Jim told me he was going to visit his mother. I smiled and told him to have a nice visit, and I went into Dad's room. To me, Dad looked so much worse. Instinctively I took his tallis out of his drawer and gently placed it around him. "Daddy, this is God's blanket. Whenever you are ready, it's OK to let go and be with Him."

Teewon lowered the side railing so I could sit on his bed close to him. I leaned over and put my arms around him, laying my head on his chest. He felt so thin. What I wouldn't have done to have him hug me back, but I knew that was not possible now. I sat on his bed for a long time, holding his hand and stroking his face. Occasionally I heard him moan, even though he was routinely getting Ativan and morphine now. At times, he appeared to be frowning, but since my vision was blurred with tears, I wasn't seeing with the best clarity.

Carol came in to tell me that Shirley called to let them know she was driving out to Copper Ridge and needed someone to let her in. "I tried to talk her into waiting until morning, but she insisted," Carol said. "She probably hasn't slept much either."

I wasn't happy about Shirley driving such a long distance at night, much less at 3:30 in the morning, especially when she was alone, upset and hadn't had much rest. I did understand her need to be here, so I was hoping she would get here safely.

Shirley was very surprised to see me in Dad's room at this hour, but I was glad she didn't have any problems getting here. "I've had my turn," I told her. "Now you take the time you need. I'll be down the hall reading if you need me." She noticed Dad's tallis lying across his chest and said, "I hope his tallis brings him comfort and peace. Please leave it on him," she told Carol.

As I was leaving Dad's room, I saw the door to Jim's room open. Out came Jim wearing a different coat and hat from the ones I saw earlier. He told me again he was going to visit his mother. I said, "I'll see you a little later, Jim."

I read that as we age, many people have changes in their sleep patterns. However, in people with Alzheimer's disease, sleep disturbances tend to occur more frequently and are more severe. These changes may be a result from them waking up more often during the night, taking frequent daytime naps, an inability to lie still, or in some cases a complete reversal of their usual day and nighttime sleep patterns. Oftentimes during these sleep interruptions, people will wander or call out. When this happens at home, it can often disturb the sleep of their caregiver, so everyone becomes sleep deprived.

Our local television station WBAL once did a report on the number of assisted-living and nursing homes in the Maryland area that don't maintain *awake* staff at night. I was appalled to find out this information, but I knew the Copper Ridge staff had an excellent awake staff. It was reassuring for me to be there in the middle of the night to experience first-hand what happened after scheduled visiting hours. The night staff was not only *awake* but they were the unsung heroes that most families didn't see. They were continuously engaging residents, calming fears, and redirecting resident's behaviors towards a more positive outcome. Having a registered nurse on duty at night was also necessary and provided a valuable bonus for the residents at Copper Ridge.

As the sun rose, daylight fell on Dad's face. He still looked like Dad, but his cheeks were sunken in and his color looked a bit gray. His mouth was open, but he always had slept with his mouth open and wondered why his mouth was always dry. Carol showed Shirley and me the skin on Dad's legs. It had become warm and mottled, indicating blood vessel changes under the skin, which gave his legs a blotchy appearance. Carol asked us, "Do you have a Rabbi?"

Simultaneously, we both answered, "Yes."

"I think you should call him," she told us.

I felt myself trembling inside. I turned to Shirley and told her, "I'll make the call."

First, I called Dave, who said he was already nearing Liberty Road. He would be here in ten minutes. I gave him an update and then dialed Rabbi Adler's cell phone. It was six-thirty in the morning. I told Rabbi Adler the latest on Dad. He said, "Let me make a few changes in my morning schedule, and I'll be out there as soon as I can." I then called Craig, Scott, Bob, and Jan.

I returned to Dad's room and by then, a new day was beginning for the other residents. I heard the familiar voices of some of the staff as they started the daily routine of dressing, toileting, and directing residents to the dining room for breakfast. It was another normal day for everyone else, but a very abnormal, sad, and sobering day for our family.

Rabbi Adler's prayers and gentle words were comforting and reassuring. By this time, all the immediate family were there near Dad. It was very quiet. There was very little talking and what little conversation there was, was whispered. *It was so different from the boisterous and often overwhelming chatter that usually happened when our family got together. At that moment, I thought each of us was engrossed in their own private, silent prayer.*

The hours dragged by slowly. Nurses and doctors filed in and out of Dad's room monitoring him, taking his vitals, administering medications, making him more comfortable, and supporting us. It seemed like Fran came in about every twenty minutes to check on Dad and our family. She was unbelievably special. Everyone was so respectful of Dad's tallis, always placing it back over him when they had completed their particular task. We were very grateful that they were honoring our family's wishes.

I was surviving on hot tea and crackers, which was about the only food that didn't upset my stomach. No one was pushing me to eat more, although Chuck asked me often if I wanted him to get me something from the coffee shop or pick something up. By the time darkness fell, I was ravenous, but still refused Chuck's offer to take me out for dinner. I was too anxious that things might change if I left. I nibbled on some fruit from the hospitality cart and ate a bagel that Bob had brought earlier.

It was almost ten o'clock. We knew we all couldn't stay. Shirley, Chuck, and Craig decided to sleep in the three empty resident rooms that Copper Ridge offered to us. Everyone else left for home. I decided to rest in Dad's La-Z-Boy. I watched the covers gently rise and fall as my comatose father breathed in and out. Dad's breathing was labored. Every now and then, there was a pause. I realized that each breath could be his last. Sleep eluded me.

At midnight, Carol came in to suction the mucous from Dad's throat, to give him morphine, and to reposition him. I refused her offer to sleep in the hospitality room. At two o'clock in the morning, I had this sudden urge to go outside for some fresh air. The coolness felt absolutely wonderful, and it quickly dried the wet streaks on my face. I hadn't thought about grabbing my coat. I inhaled a few deep breaths and headed back in. The early morning air was frigid.

Teewon was with Dad, so I waited quietly in the hall. When she was finished, I told her that it was OK for her to take a break. I was alone with Dad, standing next to his bed. His breathing seemed more labored. I stood there watching him for a few minutes. Suddenly he gasped and stopped breathing. Instinctively I put my hand on his heart. There was no heartbeat. I knew this was the end. Vivid flashbacks of my childhood came rushing back, as I held his hand and gazed at his pallid face. Everything seemed to be spinning, yet I was still in control. I knew I needed to get the nurse, to wake the others, but I wanted to hold on to this last private moment with my Dad. My throat felt tight, as I leaned over to kiss him for the last time.

In seconds, Carol returned and validated my suspicions. She told me she would wake the others. Teewon hugged me and cried with me until Chuck took over. While Shirley had her private time, I called Dave, Bob, and Scott. Everyone was on their way.

Carol asked me if I wanted her to make the call to Sol Levinson's Funeral Home. I said I'd make the call. The night supervisor at Levinson's calmly told me their procedure and asked me if the family wanted the funeral the next day or on Friday. I never even gave that aspect any thought. I told him, "Dad has an older sister in Florida now, so I doubt if it can be tomorrow. I'll check with the rest of my family and get back to you." *It was amazing how nice and professional that man was at four-thirty in the morning.*

A great emptiness filled Dad's room. We all held hands as we stood around Dad's bed in silent reflection. For me, the reality set in when Carol told us that two gentlemen from Sol Levinson's were already there. I threw Dad a kiss and we all waited in the hallway. When Dad's door reopened, I could see that Dad had been placed on a gurney in a navy blue body bag. It was so difficult seeing him like this, but we all walked silently with him through the hallways to the waiting hearse. We passed a couple of staff who were diverting the attention of several roaming residents away from us, so they wouldn't become upset.

As the back door to the hearse closed, we again said our goodbyes as dawn was breaking.

Everyone left. Chuck and I walked back to Dad's room to get a few of his more personal items. Fran assured me earlier that their staff would pack up Dad's things and store them for us until after the week of *shiva* (mourning period). The moment I reached Dad's room, I froze, suddenly paralyzed with emotion. There was his tallis, lying across his empty bed.

EPILOGUE

Six months later...

Silent Understanding

The sun wanes low in the sky.
Darkness soon will blanket the earth.
Congregants gather in synagogues around the globe
As greetings of *L'Shana Tovah,* Happy New Year, are heard.

The cantor begins, chanting the centuries old melody
Of *Kol Nidre,* the opening prayer of *Yom Kippur,*
the Day of Atonement.
I glance across the aisle at my father,
His white *yarmulke* rests atop his thick, black hair
His *tallis*, prayer shawl, draped around his strong shoulders.
I know he will be looking at me
As those ancient words penetrate our hearts.
We smile together, in silent understanding—
our private ritual, repeated year after year,
acknowledging our love, our connection to our faith
on this, the holiest of days.

The sun wanes low in the sky.
Darkness soon will blanket the earth.
Congregants gather in synagogues around the globe
As greetings of *L'Shana Tovah,* Happy New Year, are heard.

The cantor begins, chanting the centuries old melody
Of *Kol Nidre,* the opening prayer of *Yom Kippur,*
the Day of Atonement.
I glance across the aisle at my father,
His white *yarmulke* rests atop his thinning white hair
His *tallis,* prayer shawl, draped around his arthritic shoulders.
I know he will be looking at me
As those ancient words penetrate our hearts.
We smile together, in silent understanding—
our private ritual, repeated year after year,
acknowledging our love, our connection to our faith
on this, the holiest of days.

The sun wanes low in the sky.
Darkness soon will blanket the earth.
Congregants gather in synagogues around the globe
As greetings of *L'Shana Tovah,* Happy New Year, are heard.

The cantor begins, chanting the centuries old melody
Of *Kol Nidre,* the opening prayer of *Yom Kippur,*
the Day of Atonement.
I glance up towards the *Ner Tamid,* the everlasting light,
then towards the heavens,
picturing my father in
his white *yarmulke* and his striped *tallis.*

I hope he will be looking at me
As those ancient words penetrate my heart.
I smile, as tears stream down my cheeks—
physically, our private ritual has ended
but our love, our connection to our faith,
is eternal, on this the holiest of days.

At Copper Ridge's Memorial Service...

Dear Dad...

How often during the day
do I close my eyes
and just for a fleeting moment
wish you were still here with me...
so I could see your smile
hear your voice
feel your love
once again.

How often during the day
do I close my eyes
and just for a fleeting moment
wonder what it's like...
where you are
if you can see me
and still feel my love
once again.

How often during the day
do I close my eyes
and just for a fleeting moment
sense you in my heart...
celebrating all that we shared
the eternal bond
linking father and daughter,
uniting us once again.

All my love always,
Susie

One year later at the unveiling of Dad's tombstone...

With Time

As day after day passes
and month after month slips by—
the stormy clouds of loss, emptiness
gradually begin to lift—
replaced by rays of sunshine
from the glow of your memory
and the warmth of your love.

As day after day passes
and month after month slips by—
raindrops of sadness
occasionally still surface
often at the most unexpected times
vivid reminders of what we once shared,
a lifetime of treasured milestones and memories.

As month after month passes
and this year has flown by—
the bright light of your life
shines deep within me
giving me strength and courage,
bringing smiles, joy to my heart—
your everlasting legacy
to a grateful daughter.

In sifting through a box of family pictures and memorabilia, I found this note from my Dad written after his surprise 80th birthday party.

My dear Susie,

How do I thank you for the wonderful surprise party that you and David gave me? For that matter, how do I thank you for all the years that you have been the finest daughter anyone could ever have. From infancy to the present you have always been a great joy to me. In addition you have given me two wonderful grandsons who I love as I do you. I shall always treasure the beautiful poem that you wrote, as I shall always treasure the hundreds of dear things you have done for me. Whenever I feel old and tired the warmth of your love revives me. Thank you my darling daughter.

leslie c. miller

all my love,
Your
Dad

APPENDIX

TEN REQUESTS FROM THE PERSON WITH ALZHEIMER'S

We, as caregivers, family, and professionals need to remember that people suffering with Alzheimer's disease, dementia, or other memory-impaired illnesses are human beings, with the same feelings and needs as everyone else. The following piece is reprinted with the permission of the *Alzheimer's Association-Northeast Tennessee Chapter*.

Please...

- Be patient with me—remember I am the helpless victim of an organic brain disease which is out of my control.

- Talk to me—even though I cannot always answer you. I can hear your voice and sometimes I can comprehend your words.

- Be kind to me—for each day of my life is a long and desperate struggle. Your kindness may be the most special and important event of my day.

- Consider my feelings—for they are still very much alive within me.

- Treat me with human dignity and respect—as I would have gladly treated you if you had been the victim lying in this bed.

- Remember my past—for I was once a healthy, vibrant person, full of life, love, and laughter, with abilities and intelligence.

- Remember my present—I am a fearful person, a loving husband, wife, father, mother, grandfather, grandmother, aunt, uncle, or dear friend who misses my family and home very much.

- Remember my future—though it may seem bleak to you, I am always filled with the hope of tomorrow.

- Pray for me—for I am a person who lingers in the mists that drift between time and eternity. Your presence may do more for me than any other outreach of compassion you could extend to me.

- Love me—and the gift of love you give will be a blessing which will fill both our lives with light forever.

TIPS FOR CAREGIVERS

Being the caregiver for a person with dementia or Alzheimer's disease is a tough, challenging job. Your loved one's ability to function or cope may change from day to day, even hour to hour, as the disease progresses. Try to remember that people with dementia are doing the best that they can, and whatever is happening to them is hidden inside their brain.

- Learn to appreciate all you do as a caregiver.

- Make staying healthy and taking care of yourself a priority. Try to get enough rest and eat a well-balanced diet. Try to exercise or walk as often as you can. Do not neglect your own doctor appointments while caring for your loved one.

- Maintain your identity and your social contacts. Stay connected with friends and family. Share your concerns with others. Make time for the things you like to do.

- Take a proactive role with your caregiving by staying informed. The more you know about Alzheimer's and other dementias, the better prepared you will be to handle problems as they arise. Knowledge is power.

- Plan ahead when taking the person to a doctor. Try to schedule appointments based on what you have found to be his/her "best times" whether it be morning or afternoon, or when the office is less crowded and there are fewer distractions. Since it is often difficult to speak candidly to the doctor in front of your loved one, consider faxing a list of symptoms and when they began, a brief summary of changes you have noticed since your last appointment, or any new information you feel the doctor should know prior to your scheduled visit. This may avoid any unnecessary embarrassment for, or confrontation with, your loved one. Remember, a doctor's office may be an unfamiliar environment, so bring a snack and something to keep the person occupied in case you have to wait longer than expected. If you don't think you can handle things by yourself, bring someone with you.

- Prepare a list of questions for your doctor prior to each appointment. Bring a current list of all medications, including herbal and dietary supplements, taken by your loved one. These two lists will help you stay focused and insure your visit goes as planned. Be sure to ask the doctor to clarify terms you don't understand. Familiarize yourself with the side effects of any new medications. Ask for copies of lab work and test results and procedures, and keep an ongoing file. This can be quite helpful if you consult with another physician or specialist.

- Keep a medication log on all the meds currently being taken. Include name of medication (generic name), date started, doctor's name, pharmacy, and phone number, color, shape, and dosage. Keep track of any side effects you notice and if the medication was stopped. Periodically update the log.

- Create a safe environment by removing any clutter or obstacles that may cause the person to trip or fall. Make sure there is sufficient lighting in bedrooms, hallways, and bathrooms, particularly at night. Be sure dangerous items are out of reach or locked away. It may be necessary to unplug small appliances, remove stove knobs, install grab bars in tubs or showers and install hand rails where needed. Minimize electronic distractions and noise so the person can remain focused on what you or he/she is saying or doing.

- Pace yourself and define your priorities. Don't try to accomplish too much at one time. Acceptance, tolerance, patience, and praise are so important when helping a person who has dementia. Take one step and one day at a time.

- Notice which part of the day (morning, afternoon, or evening) the person is more alert or focused. Try to plan more challenging tasks or physically demanding activities during this time. Playing his or her favorite music can be calming and relaxing and make the task easier for everyone.

- Plan ahead and establish routines to help make the day more predictable and less confusing. Get everything that is needed for a particular task ready ahead of time (bathing, dressing, etc.), to avoid having to leave your loved one unattended by interrupting the task at hand. Limiting his/her choices or options will make things easier for you both. (Choose between two cereals rather than all those in the pantry or two outfits rather than the entire closet). Organization and adaptability are crucial.

- Use a calm, gentle, and reassuring voice. Choose simple words and short sentences, without patronizing the person. Make things simple by providing clear, step by step instructions if a person needs prompting. Remember, as the disease progresses, you may need to give visual, verbal, and/or tactile clues in order for the person to complete the simplest of tasks successfully. Allow them to do as much as they can by themselves, without being judgmental. Expect that tasks are going to take longer for someone with dementia, and allow for that extra time. Practice patience. Avoid correcting and arguing.

- Try not to take hurtful or upsetting comments personally. Remember, the disease is causing the behavior. The person may not be able to control his/her outbursts, aggression, or comments.

- Use your creativity, imagination, and flexibility. If something can't be done one way, try another.

- If possible, limit daytime napping. Encourage exercise during the day. Try to keep the person engaged in an activity he/she enjoys.

- Understand the family dynamics with which you are dealing. Have ongoing family conferences in person, by phone, or email to keep other family members informed and involved with the status of the person and what difficulties you may be having as their caregiver. Brainstorm with each other to come up with new solutions or alternatives to recurring problems.

- Ask for help. Don't try to go it alone, and don't be ashamed to share your true feelings. No one is going to think you are inadequate or incapable if you need extra help. Caregiving is stressful and mentally and physically draining. Recognize what you can and cannot do, and make a clear list of what assistance you need from family, friends, and neighbors. Be specific and keep that list near the phone so you won't be caught off guard when someone calls and asks what they can do to help. If someone is not comfortable being alone with a person with dementia, ask him/her to do a few errands for you while they are out.

- Use humor to get through the difficult times. Laughter is a great stress reliever. Surround yourself with positive images and people.

- Use the community resources in your area. Consider joining a support group to share experiences with other caregivers that are going through similar situations.

- Consider consulting a good elder law attorney who is knowledgeable with health care issues and benefits in your state, and can advise you on matters concerning long–term care insurance, Medicare, Medicaid, Veterans Administration benefits, estate planning, and guardianship. Creating a *durable power of attorney* verifies and gives you the authority to make sound financial decisions for the person when he/she becomes legally incapacitated. Address health-care issues by preparing a *living will* or an *advance medical directive*, which usually names a health-care agent who can make decisions for the person if they are not capable. It also describes the end of life wishes of the person making the living will. Be sure that you give a copy to your physician or other health care providers, as well as family members or designated individuals of your choice. Having legal and financial issues in place early on will allow you to focus on the daily care issues, giving both you and the person with dementia peace of mind.

- Have a contingency plan prepared if the person becomes aggressive or violent and you are unable to handle him/her. Know who to call for help and what steps you might have to take to protect yourself.

- Plan for the "what if" scenarios that may arise. What if I get sick? What if I'm no longer able to care for my loved one? It is so important to plan ahead to know what to do if an emergency arises. All pertinent information concerning the person should constantly be updated and readily accessible for anyone called upon to take over your responsibilities as caregiver.

- Keep a journal. Make entries as frequently as you can. Writing down your thoughts and experiences is not only therapeutic; it can also be helpful in tracking the course of the disease. With each entry, include two or three things that you are thankful for. Try to end your thoughts in a positive light.

Consider preparing a laminated business type card to keep in your wallet or purse with the following statement, reprinted with the permission of the *Alzheimer's Association, Florida Gulf Coast Chapter*:

> **My companion has memory loss,** which makes it difficult for them to find the right words and understand what has been said. **Thank you for your patience.**

Use this card when you are at a restaurant, bank, library, store, etc. to let others know about your situation without embarrassing your loved one.

- When all else fails and you are at your wits end— smile and sing. How can anything be upsetting when someone is singing!

FACILITY CHECKLIST

Facility: **Date of Visit:**
Address: **Follow-up Visit:**
Contact Person:
Contact Number:
Fax Number:

LOCATION

- Near a quiet street?
- Near a busy street with traffic?

PHYSICAL ENVIRONMENT

- Is the facility noisy?
- Is the facility clean and odor-free?
- Is the memory-care unit separate from rest of facility?
- Is the unit on one level?
- Is the unit home-like?
- Is it a locked unit?
- Does the unit provide safeguards for residents who wander?
- Is the unit bright and cheerful?
- Is there an area where residents can interact with each other?
- Are hallways free of furniture or obstacles?
- Are there secure handrails throughout all indoor walking areas?

- Are there visual clues to help residents orient themselves?

- Are there easily accessible, secure outdoor areas with walking paths?

- Is there a private area for a family to have a meal or celebration with a resident?

MISSION OR PHILOSOPHY

- Is there a written description of the facility's or the unit's mission?

- Can the contact person tell you about the different levels of care being offered?

- Will a person need to be transferred to another facility if there is a decline in their dementia?

- Is the unit able to accommodate late-stage dementia patients? Hospice?

- Is the unit able to treat debilitating illness that may occur?

- Does the unit recognize ethnic, cultural, and religious beliefs of the person?

- Are accommodations made for these differences?

- Does the facility review and honor advanced health care directives?

- How does the staff handle disruptive or difficult behavior?

- Does the unit use chemical or physical restraints? Under what conditions?
  For what length of time?

- Does the unit keep the family informed?
  How often?

STAFF

- What is the staff-to-resident ratio for each shift?

- What is their staffing? RN? LPN? GMA (geriatric medical assistant)?   Number of each?

- What is the staff turnover?

- How often is a doctor called in to evaluate residents?

- Is there a doctor or physician's assistant at the facility?

- Is dementia-specific training required for all staff members?

- Is there continuing education and training required for staff members?

- Are the same staff members assigned to the same residents?

- Is there a dietician on staff? Can that person meet the dietary requirements if food needs to be pureed? Are thickened liquids provided if needed?

- Is there an onsite physical therapist? Occupational therapist?

- Is there an activities coordinator?

- Is there a social worker at the facility?

- Is there a dentist?   Podiatrist?   Speech therapist?

CARE PLAN

- Does the unit develop and customize care plans for each resident?

- Does the staff work as a team to develop the care plan? Who draws it up?

- Does the staff meet regularly to update the plan and make changes?

- Will I be notified when changes are made in the care plan?

ACTIVITIES AND PROGRAMS

- Does the unit offer varied activities everyday? Weekends?

- Does the unit have an established routine on a daily basis?

- Are individual interests and hobbies encouraged?

- Is there art therapy?   Music therapy? Exercise therapy?

- Where do activities take place?

- Are there activities for residents who have difficulty sleeping?

TOUR OBSERVATIONS

- Are the majority of the residents wearing soiled clothing?

- Are most residents involved in an activity?

- Are most residents in their rooms?

- Is there uncollected garbage visible?

- Is there dirty bed linen in the hallways?
- Are the bathrooms clean?
- Is there a separate dining room for residents?
- Are there clues strategically placed to help the resident find his/her room?
- Is the staff neat and clean?
- Does the staff seem stressed?
- Is the staff courteous?

PERSONAL QUESTIONS

- Are residents encouraged to remain continent?
- Does the staff assist residents in the bathroom if needed?
- Do they accept medications from the Veterans Administration?
- Can residents bring their own things?   Furniture? Pictures?   Clothing?
- Are residents able to leave the facility for events and outings with family?
- Can I review the contract?
- Can I have a menu?
- Do they have a support group for families?
- What is the cost of the facility? What services are included? Which are extra?
- What safeguards insure the protection of the resident's private financial, medical, and personal information?
- What are their pharmacy arrangements?

NOTES:

ADVICE FOR VISITING PEOPLE
WITH DEMENTIA

Visiting a person who has any severe memory impairment, whether in their home or at an assisted-living or nursing home, may not always be an easy or pleasant experience. However, it can be a most rewarding one if you plan ahead and remember that it's the personal connection that is most important. The person may not always remember you or anything about your visit, but they will realize that you cared enough to share some time with them. It's the warm feeling you leave them with that brings the person real pleasure and makes the visit worthwhile.

- Check with the family or the facility to find out the best time to visit and how long a visit they think the person can handle.

- Be prepared. Realize that the person you are visiting may have changed physically, regressed intellectually and emotionally. Understand that cognitive impairment may cause them to repeat things or ask you the same questions over and over. Likewise, the person may say things that you know are incorrect. Try to let it pass. Remember, you are there to create a feeling, not to correct them. Be kind instead of right.

- Let the person you are visiting set the pace. He/she may not be ready for a visit the minute you arrive, may already be involved in an activity, or may be having a bad day. Be adaptable to their wants and needs. Be patient.

- Learn to be an engager and initiator. Frequently people

suffering with dementia cannot start a conversation, task, or activity, but, once engaged, can respond to you or to your cues if you begin first and guide them.

- Speak with a calm reassuring voice. Preserve the person's dignity and avoid talking to them as if he or she is a child. Avoid confrontation by redirecting their attention or conversation to something else if they seem agitated or become upset.

- Call the person by name to get their attention and try to establish eye contact with them. Look them in the face. Speak directly to them. Let them see your smile.

- Don't be upset if the person doesn't recognize you, or if they seem confused about who you are initially, or anytime during your visit. Make light of it and just introduce yourself by your first name. Although this may be disconcerting for you, even painful, it's not critical that they remember your name or their relationship to you. What is important to the person is your presence; that you cared enough to spend some time with them, and the comforting feelings they feel by you being there.

- Remember that you are the architect of this visit, so plan ahead. As the disease progresses, people remember less and less about recent events, but remember much of what happened many years ago. Bring props: a family photograph album, a favorite book or poem to read aloud, large picture books or magazines, an item related to their job, or something from home, something from a hobby, or maybe a small gift or their favorite food or snack. Anything really, that you can use as "starter" topics for conversation or to engage them. Be creative, but realize with all your good intentions and planning, the person may not be interested in anything that you brought or do on that particular day. Take your cues from them and try not to get discouraged.

- Be prepared for the possibility of other residents wanting to join in your conversation or activity when you are visiting someone in an assisted-living facility or nursing home. You may or may not feel comfortable with this, but including others may make your visit more pleasant and rewarding.

- Be a patient and attentive listener even if what is being said by the person is unintelligible. A smile, a nod, or a "yes" lets the person know you are hearing what they are trying to get across and that what they are saying is important to you.

- Recognize that sometimes all that is needed is your presence, that it's OK to say nothing, rather than trying to force a conversation. Sometimes a smile, a gentle touch, or thoughtful silence is the best communication. A simple, quiet walk requiring no verbal communication can be a positive and rewarding experience for both of you.

- Limit the number of family members or friends visiting at the same time, unless it's a special occasion or holiday. Too many people all at once may be too overwhelming or confusing for the person. Staggering their visits may be more appropriate and more beneficial.

- Remember, your visit can truly make a difference. Make it a positive one.

RESOURCES

Alzheimer's Association-National Office
225 North Michigan Avenue
Chicago, IL 60601-7633
800-272-3900
alz.org

The Alzheimer's Association provides health information, care consultations, referrals to medical resources, advocacy, publications, support, and funds for research. They operate a twenty-four hour nationwide contact hotline. Easily locate your local chapter through the web or by phone.

Alzheimer's Disease and Education Referral Center (ADEAR)
P O Box 8250
Silver Spring, MD 20907-8250
800- 438-4380
nia.nih.gov/Alzheimers

The ADEAR Center operates as a service of the **National Institute on Aging** (NIA). The NIA conducts and supports research about health issues for older people, providing information on Alzheimer's disease for professionals, people who suffer from the disease and their families, as well as the general public. They are the primary Federal agency for Alzheimer's disease research.

Center for Drug Evaluation and Research
Food and Drug Administration
800-463-6332
fda.gov/cder

Centers for Medicare and Medicaid
7500 Security Blvd.
Baltimore, MD 21244-1850
877-267-2323 or 410-786-3000
cms.gov

Copper Ridge
710 Obrecht Road
Sykesville, MD 21784
800-531-6539 or 410-795-8808
copperridge.org

Copper Ridge is a nationally recognized accredited facility dedicated exclusively to the care of persons with Alzheimer's disease and other memory-impairing illnesses. Their partnership with the Johns Hopkins Neuropsychiatry and Memory Group assures that all programs at Copper Ridge, both outpatient or residential, are expertly designed and rendered by staff trained in the latest and best techniques for specialized care.

The Copper Ridge Institute
710 Obrecht Road
Sykesville, MD 21784
800-531-6539 or 410-795-8808
crinstitute.org

The Copper Ridge Institute is affiliated with the Johns Hopkins School of Medicine. Developing evidence-based care methods, advancing research in the treatment of Alzheimer's disease, and teaching this new knowledge is the work of The Copper Ridge Institute. Its mission is to improve the quality of life for patients and families with Alzheimer's disease and other memory impairing disorders.

Eden Alternative
100 Melody Way
Suite D
Wimberley, TX 78676
512-847-6061
edenalt.com

The Eden Alternative is a not-for-profit organization dedicated to remaking the experience of aging and disability across America and around the world. They provide education and resources for improving quality of life for the elderly and for recapturing a more meaningful life for their caregivers.

Eldercare Locator
Public service of the U.S. Administration on Aging
800-677-1116
eldercare.gov

The Eldercare Locator provides connections and resources that enable older persons to live independently in any U.S. community. The service links those who need assistance with state and local area agencies on aging and community-based organizations that serve older adults and their caregivers.

Family Care Alliance
180 Montgomery St., Suite 1100
San Francisco, CA 94104
800-445-8106
caregiver.org

Family Care Alliance is a public voice for caregivers. It provides information, education, services, research and advocacy to support and sustain families nationwide that care for loved ones with chronic, disabling health conditions.

Johns Hopkins Hospital-Division of Geriatric Psychiatry and Neuropsychiatry
Department of Psychiatry and Behavioral Sciences
Meyer 4-113, Chairman's Office
600 North Wolfe Street
Baltimore, Maryland 21287-7413
410-955-6736

This Division provides inpatient, day-hospital, and outpatient care for psychiatric disorders experienced by the elderly and for disorders of mood, thought, and behavior that occur in patients with neurological disease. It trains health professionals and conducts extensive multidisciplinary research to find causes and improve treatment. The division publishes *The Johns Hopkins Memory Bulletin,* a quarterly in-depth report on the latest scientific breakthroughs, research findings, and medical discoveries for safeguarding your brain against aging and memory loss.

The Leeza Gibbons Memory Foundation
3050 Biscayne Boulevard, Suite 605
Miami, Florida 33137
888-655-3399
leezasplace.org

Leeza's Place, a program of her Memory Foundation, was established to provide education, empowerment, and energy to caregivers and those diagnosed with any memory impairment. Its goal is to provide safe and intimate settings throughout the country where caregivers can gather to prepare themselves for the challenging journey ahead.

National Council on Aging
300 D Street, SW, Suite 801
Washington, DC 20024
202-479-1200
ncoa.org

This association for professionals, organizations, volunteers, and individuals provides services and care to older adults and their families. It offers referrals to appropriate organizations and services in your area.

National Family Caregivers Association
10400 Connecticut Avenue, Suite 500
Kensington, MD 20895
800-896-3650
thefamilycaregiver.org

This association is dedicated to improving the lives of family caregivers through education, outreach, research, and support.

National Institute on Aging
Building 31, Room 5C27
31 Center Drive, MSC 2292
Bethesda, MD 20892
800-222-4225   301-496-1752
nia.nih.gov

National Institute on Aging leads a broad scientific effort to understand the nature of aging and to extend the healthy, active years of life. NIA provides leadership in aging research, training, health information dissemination, and other programs relevant to aging and older people.

U.S. Department of Veterans Affairs (VA)
Veterans Affairs Central Office
810 Vermont Avenue NW
Washington, D.C. 20420
800-827-1000   Health Care Benefits: 877-222-8387
va.gov

ADDITIONAL RESOURCES AND LINKS

alzcast.org
An educational resource of the Copper Ridge Institute, this website helps caregivers, doctors, nurses, and other healthcare professionals successfully cope with the impact of Alzheimer's disease on patients and family members. Download informative podcasts from this site and watch the informative webcast *Caring for a Loved One with Alzheimer's Disease* in either English or Spanish. A DVD is also available.

alzstore.com   800-752-3238
The Alzheimer's Store provides the best and most dependable products serving the needs of people with memory impairments and those who care for them.

caregiver.com
Today's Caregiver, the first national magazine dedicated to caregivers, provides information, support, and guidance for family and professional caregivers.

caringtoday.com
Caring Today, a magazine providing practical advice and knowledge for family caregivers.

clinicaltrials.gov
This informative and searchable database provides patients, family members and the public with information about current ongoing clinical research studies.

cognicity.com
Geriatric psychiatrist, Dr. Miquel Rivera, provides insight into cognition and health in the 21st century, and the impact medications and diet have on cognitive decline. This is a resource for cognition, mental wellness, Alzheimer's and other forms of dementia affecting the aging population.

enhancedmoments.com
Author and educational speaker, Jolene Brackey, provides powerful, practical tools that create positive outcomes for those caring for someone with memory impairment. *Enhanced Moments* helps guide people through the Alzheimer's journey.

fullcirclecare.org
This site provides support, education, information, and assistance needed to support caregivers in their efforts to keep their older family members living at home in a secure and loving environment for as long as possible.

healthpropress.com
An excellent resource of books and DVDs for professionals, caregivers, and families interested in wellness and aging, long-term care, eldercare, Alzheimer's disease, and health care management.

JohnsHopkinsHealthAlerts.com

Johns Hopkins Health Alerts provides cutting-edge information on healthy living after 50 in an easy-to-read format, completely free of charge. Visitors to the website can read special reports on different health topics including *memory* and related articles, written by many of the top physicians in their field.

nia.nih.gov/Alzheimers/ResearchInformation/Newsletter

Connections, a free newsletter developed by the National Institute of Aging, is designed to deliver important information and to provide a resource for people working across the Alzheimer's disease and dementia spectrum.

timeslips.org

TimeSlips opens storytelling to people with cognitive challenges by replacing the pressure to remember with the encouragement to imagine. They offer products and printable sample images to start you on your way toward creative engagement.

teepasnow.com

Occupational therapist, Teepa Snow, is a nationally recognized dementia care specialist and trainer. She is an expert on how dementia affects a person and has developed positive hands-on approaches, teaching healthcare professionals and caregivers ways to handle the situations that may arise when dealing with someone who has a memory impairment. Teepa's understanding of these challenges can be seen on her free video segments on You Tube. Check her website for other resources, videos, and DVDs.

SUGGESTED READING

For Adults:

Atkins, Charles, M.D. *The Alzheimer's Answer Book.* Naperville, IL: Sourcebooks, Inc., 2008.

Berman, Claire. *Caring for Yourself While Caring for Your Aging Parents: How to Help, How to Survive.* New York: Henry Holt and Company, 2005.

Bell, Virginia, and David Troxell. *The Best Friends Approach to Alzheimer's Care.* Baltimore: Health Profession Press, 1997.

Brackey, Jolene. *Creating Moments of Joy for the Person with Alzheimer's or Dementia, Fourth Edition.* West Lafayette, Indiana: Purdue University Press, 2008.

Broyles, Frank. *Coach Broyles' Playbook for Alzheimer's Caregivers, a Practical Tips Guide.* 2006. Download the playbook for free at www.alzheimersplaybook.com

Callone, Patricia, et al. *A Caregiver's Guide to Alzheimer's Disease: 300 Tips for Making Life Easier.* New York: Demos Medical Publishing, 2006.

Doka, Kenneth J. *Living with Grief—Alzheimer's Disease.* Washington, DC: Hospice Foundation of America. 2004.

FitzRay, B.J. *Alzheimer's Activities: Hundreds of Activities for Men and Women with Alzheimer's Disease and Related Disorders.* Ray Productions, Inc. 2001.

Genova, Lisa. *Still Alice.* New York: Pocket Books, a division of Simon and Schuster, Inc. 2007.

Gibbons, Leeza, et al. *Take Your Oxygen First: Protecting Your Health and Happiness While Caring for a Loved One with Memory Loss.* New York: Lachance Publishing, 2009.

Glenner, Joy, et al. *When Your Loved One Has Dementia*. Baltimore: The Johns Hopkins University Press, 2005.

Glenner, Cynthia, and Joan Beloff. *Through the Seasons: An Activity Book for Memory-Challenged Adults and Caregivers*. Baltimore: The Johns Hopkins University Press, 2008.

Lokvig, Jytte. *Alzheimer's A to Z: Secrets to Successful Caregiving*. Santa Fe: Endless Circle Press, 2002.

Mace, Nancy L. and Peter V. Rabins, M.D. *The 36-Hour Day: A Family Guide to Caring for Person's with Alzheimer's Disease, Related Dementing Illnesses, and Memory Loss in Later Life. 4th Edition*. Baltimore: Johns Hopkins University Press, 2006.

Nelson, James Lindemann, and Hilda Lindemann Nelson. *Alzheimer's, Answers to Hard Questions for Families*. New York: Doubleday, 1996.

Petersen, Ronald, M.D. *Mayo Clinic Guide to Alzheimer's Disease*. Rochester, MN: Mayo Clinic Health Information, 2006.

Roche, Lyn. *Coping with Caring: When Someone You Love has Alzheimer's or a Related Condition*. Journey Publications, 2006.

Roche, Lyn. *Coping With Caring: Daily Reflection for Alzheimer's Caregivers*. Elder Books, 1996.

Sheehy, Gail. *Passages for Caregiving: Turning Chaos into Confidence*. New York: William Morrow, 2010.

Strauss, Claudia A. *Talking to Alzheimer's*. Oakland, CA: New Harbinger Publications, Inc. 2001.

Taylor, Richard. *Alzheimer's from the Inside Out*. Baltimore: Health Professions Press, 2006.

Westbrook, JoAnn. *Do You Know Where your Parents Are? An Insider's Guide to Choices and Options in Senior Health Care*. Bloomington, IN: AuthorHouse, 2004.

Zeisel, John, Ph.D. *I'm Still Here: A New Philosophy of Alzheimer's Care.* New York: Penguin Group, 2010.

For Children:

Acheson, Allison. *Grandpa's Music: A Story About Alzheimer's.* Morton Grove, IL: Albert Whitman and Company, 2008. (Ages 8-10)

Bahr, Mary and David Cunningham. *The Memory Box.* Morton Grove, IL: Albert Whitman and Company, 1995. (Grades 1-3)

Ballman, Swanee. *The Stranger I Call Grandma: A Story about Alzheimer's Disease.* Newnan, GA: Jawbone Publishing Corporation, 2002.

Gosselin, Kim and Tom Dineen. *Allie Learns About Alzheimer's Disease: A Family Story About Love, Patience, & Acceptance.* Jay Jo Books, 2001.

McIntyre, Connie. *Flowers for Grandpa Dan: A Gentle Story to Help Children Understand Alzheimer's Disease.* St. Louis: Thumbprint Press, 2005. (Reading level 9-12)

Scacco, Linda, Ph.D. *Always My Grandpa: A Story for Children About Alzheimer's Disease.* Magination Press, 2005. (Ages 6-10)

Simard, Joyce. *The Magic Tape Recorder.* Joyce Simard Publishing, 2007.

Schnurbush, Barabara. *Striped Shirts and Flowered Pants: A Story about Alzheimer's Disease for Young Children.* Magination Press, 2006. (Ages 4-8)

Shriver, Maria. *What's Happening to Grandpa?* New York: Little, Brown Books for Young Readers, 2004. (K-Grade 3)

About the Author

A native of Baltimore, Maryland, and a retired kindergarten teacher, Susan Garbett developed a better understanding of dementia/Alzheimer's disease after witnessing her father's cognitive decline. She began to seek practical solutions to help her dad.

Enthusiastic about working with aging adults, Susan developed activities and programs for her father and the other residents at Copper Ridge, an assisted-living facility for all types of memory impairments in Sykesville, Maryland.

Susan is the mother of two sons, and currently resides in Sarasota, Florida, with her husband. She is a volunteer support group facilitator for the Alzheimer's Association, Florida Gulf Coast Chapter.

Susan plans to donate a portion of the profits from this book to an Alzheimer's charity.

Visit: **susieandmedays.com**